The Fielders

Jim Kaplan

A
BOOK

The Fielders

A spectacular fielding play does more than turn a hit into an out. It stuns the opposition, and can turn the inning—if not the game—completely around. For the team in the field it's an unexpected gift, a wave of enthusiasm on which to ride. Third baseman Graig Nettles was a master of the art.

Mr. Impossible

t's all guts and instincts and reflexes. Highlight films prove it: there are more bang-bang plays at the hot corner than anywhere else. That's because a third baseman rarely has time to position himself before fielding a batted ball. On one play he's diving to his left to prevent a base hit in the hole. On the next he's sprawling to his right to stop a smash down the line from going into the corner. Then he's racing forward to barehand a bunt, switching from a five-fingered to a three-fingered grip, and firing the ball to first while falling down.

This workplace of wonders was never so pivotal as it was in the 1970 World Series, when Baltimore's Brooks Robinson gave the most celebrated fielding exhibition in baseball history. His nine hits and two home runs would have been enough, but it was Robinson's dazzling, rally-killing play in the field that cemented each of the Orioles' four wins and earned him the Series' Most Valuable Player award. Reds manager Sparky Anderson summed it up: "Robinson beat us." And thanks to Robinson, fielding outshone pitching and hitting that October and became an honored art.

Fielding a baseball is the rare sporting act that requires a special ambidexterity—catching with one hand, throwing with the other. And Brooks Robinson, a left-hander in everything he does but baseball, was ideally suited to the role. A hulking 190-pounder, the 33-year-old Robinson had already won ten straight Gold Gloves for fielding excellence with his lightning reflexes, his sure arm, and most of all his sparkling glove. He wasn't known as

In the 1970 World Series, Brooks Robinson (opposite) raised the art of fielding to new heights. Robinson opened his Series by spearing a liner to end the Reds' first inning in Game 1, and closed it by throwing out Pat Corrales for the last out in Game 5.

Reds catcher Johnny Bench couldn't get anything past Robinson in the 1970 World Series. The photos above show just one of three line drives that Robinson stole off Bench's bat. "I hope we can come back and play the Orioles next year," Bench said. "I also hope Brooks Robinson has retired by then."

"the Human Vacuum Cleaner" for nothing, and in the 1970 Series he earned his other nickname, "Mr. Impossible."

Robinson had a feeling he'd be in for a lot of work. "We were playing the Reds, and they had righthanded pull hitters like Johnny Bench, Lee May, and Tony Perez," he recalls. "We had Dave McNally and Mike Cuellar, who were lefthanded pitchers, and Jim Palmer, who threw a lot of slow curves. So I expected that [shortstop] Mark Belanger and I would get plenty of business."

Game 1 gave Robinson all the opportunity he needed. By the fifth inning, both teams had three runs on the scoreboard, and it was anybody's ballgame. In the bottom of the sixth, Cincinnati first baseman Lee May smashed a one hopper down the third-base line that hooked behind the bag and well into foul territory. Robinson lunged for the ball, made a backhanded, behind-the-body stop, and recovered to bounce a long throw to first ahead of the runner. "He was going toward the bullpen when he threw to first," said Reds reliever Clay Carroll. "His arm went one way, his body another, and his shoes a third." The play was Robinson's third fielding gem of the day, and it saved at least one run, because the next two Cincinnati batters, Bernie Carbo and Tommy Helms, walked and singled in that order before the side was retired. Not content to dazzle 'em with his glove, Robinson came up in the top of the seventh and homered to give the Orioles a 4–3 win.

In Game 2 Robinson's diving stops turned one shot by Bobby Tolan into a critical force out and another by Lee May into a double play. The Orioles won, 6–5, to take a 2–0 lead in the Series. Anderson knew just what was happening. "Without Robinson," he said, "it would be 2–0 the other way."

In the first inning of Game 3, with two on and none out, Robinson leaped to snare a Tony Perez hopper, stepped on third for a force, and threw to first

Birds of Prey

Since 1960 the Baltimore Orioles have been baseball's most successful team. Through 1988 they finished below .500 just five times in 29 years, and in that span won 55.7 percent of their games, seven division titles, six American League pennants and three world championships. One constant in the Orioles' success has been superior team fielding. The chart shows the Orioles' year by year American League ranking in fewest errors, most double plays, fielding percentage, and league/division standings.

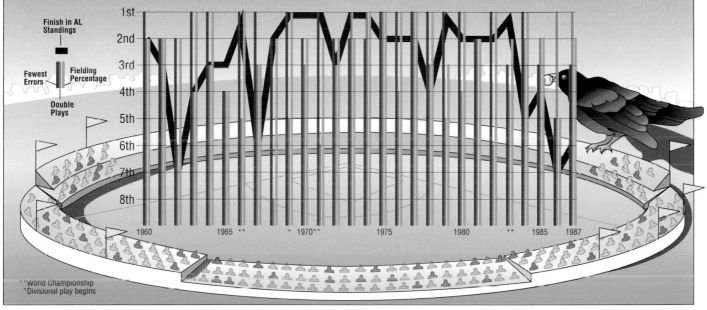

to complete a rally-squelching double play. In the second he barehanded Tommy Helms' swinging bunt and threw to first for the out. And in the sixth Robinson dived to his left to stab a liner from Johnny Bench. "I will become a lefthanded hitter to keep the ball away from that guy," moaned Bench. Oh, yes: Robinson knocked in the game's first two runs with a double, and the Orioles went on to win, 9–3.

By Game 4, many fans weren't paying attention to the score anymore. Their only interest was in the next Robinson miracle. With two Reds runners on base and none out, a fan yelled, "Get three, Brooks"—a plea for a triple play. Brooks didn't come through; all he could manage was four hits, one of them a homer, but the Reds won, 6–5, avoiding a Series sweep.

In the final game, Robinson backhanded another screaming liner from Johnny Bench, helping the Orioles win, 9–3, and take the Series. Sparky Anderson, for one, was tired of being generous toward him. "That guy," he said, "somebody ought to shoot him."

Robinson had been aiming toward this World Series triumph almost since birth. He grew up across the street from a minor league stadium in Little Rock, Arkansas, and as a boy he spent countless hours catching golf balls rifled off his doorstep. Little Rock Central High School did not have a baseball team, but he sharpened his skills by playing American Legion ball and was signed by the Orioles in 1955, right after graduation. It was clear that he could hit and field; the question was where to put him. After working young Robinson around the infield for minor league teams and bringing him up to the Orioles at the end of the season, Paul Richards, Baltimore's legendary executive and manager, settled him at third.

*Of all the spectacular plays Robinson
made in the Series, his lunging stab and
amazing throw to get Lee May in the sixth
inning of Game 1 (above, and opposite)
was probably the biggest. It kept the game
tied, 3–3, and took some steam out of the
Big Red Machine. With no opportunity to
stop his momentum away from first or set
himself, Robinson wheeled 180 degrees and
threw May out from behind the third-base
coaches' box. "When you play with
Brooks," said first baseman Boog Powell,
"you just go to the bag and hold the glove
out. He'll get the ball there, you always
know that."*

Robinson was tough enough to handle the hot corner. Chasing a foul fly
into the dugout in one minor league game, he impaled his right arm on a hook
and severed a nerve. Robinson's reaction was not to turn gun-shy but to be
grateful he wasn't hurt worse. He once broke five teeth on a ledge while
chasing another foul ball, stayed in the game, and drove in the winning run.

With the Orioles, Robinson was both a gloveman and the biggest glove-
hound in baseball. "I'm always searching for the right one," he once said. "I
wander around the locker room testing the feel of extra gloves that players
have in their bins. I've traded with lots of players over the years—both
leagues—and it usually costs me two for one." Finding a glove he liked, Robinson would relace and repad it, creating a mosaic of a mitt to suit his needs.

Baltimore kids in the 1960s and 1970s grew up imitating Robinson's
mannerisms afield—slipping the glove off while smoothing the dirt with his
foot, or holding position for an extra second after throwing to first. And by the
end of the 1970 World Series, he was considered the greatest fielding third
baseman ever—not just by kids, but by all of baseball.

When I look back on that Series, I see two plays," says Robinson. "I
see myself taking May's grounder in foul ground, wheeling, and
throwing without stopping to brace myself. That's unusual. And I
see myself diving to the left and catching Bench's liner, which was hooking
back toward me something awful. A play like that is all instinct."

With the benefit of hindsight, Robinson also sees the 1970 Series as a
watershed—for himself, his position, his art. "I don't think there's any doubt
that the Series helped establish me as a fielder and was a springboard for getting me into the Hall of Fame." Robinson also helped himself by lasting 23

seasons in the majors, by winning a position-record 16 Gold Gloves, and by retiring in 1977 with a .971 fielding percentage, the highest ever for a third baseman.

Never before a glamour position—for many players it was little more than a way station between an early career in the outfield and a late career at first—third was suddenly all the rage. The position reached new heights in the 1970s and 1980s with stars like Sal Bando, Buddy Bell, Carney Lansford, Bill Madlock, Ron Cey, Paul Molitor, Mike Schmidt and George Brett. Brooks Robinson, however, remained the standard with which others were compared. When Graig Nettles made four sparkling plays in a 1978 Series game, his performance was deemed "Robinsonian," and when Doug De-Cinces turned a diving stop into a double play during the 1979 playoffs, he was "positively Brooksian."

But Robinson's performance reverberated beyond his position. "I think the Series gave writers more awareness of fielding in general," he said, "and helped some other good fielders like Luis Aparicio and Pee Wee Reese make the Hall."

Just how great a case did the 1970 Series make for fielding? Well, consider Robinson's hitting. He batted .429, drove in the game-winning run twice, tied five batting marks, and set a five-game Series record with 17 total bases. These feats were so obscured by his fielding that *The New York Times* felt compelled to run a story headlined: "Brooks Robinson's Bat Had a Good Series, Too." ◗

The Hot Corner

Graig Nettles

Playing 30 yards from home plate, a third baseman has about four-tenths of a second to react to a line drive. In 1948 Detroit's George Kell had his jaw shattered by a line drive off the bat of Joe DiMaggio. Kell managed to pick up the ball and crawl to third for a force out. Then he fainted.

Because the ball gets to him so quickly, a third baseman can turn a game around with his glove. With runners on base, his reflexes can turn a hard-hit ball that could blow a game wide open into a rally-killing double play. Third basemen need quick feet, quick hands and guts. It's a reactive position, and one for which the old baseball truism "keep the ball in front of you" applies in spades. If a third baseman can knock down a hard smash and keep the ball within reach, he'll probably have time to recover and get an out. Pepper Martin of the Cardinals' famed Gashouse Gang earned a reputation for playing third with his chest, and without a protective cup. He played 429 games at third without a serious mishap, prompting Leo Durocher to say, "God watches over drunks and third basemen."

Until the 1970s, however, third basemen got little glory for putting their bodies on the line.

Fewer third basemen have been elected to the Hall of Fame than players from any other position. But Brooks Robinson led a parade of outstanding all-around third basemen into the 1970s and 1980s.

And while it's only recently that third base has become a high-profile position, it's long been acknowledged as the site of some of the game's most acrobatic defensive plays. The position's nickname—the hot corner—dates back to an 1889 game in which Cincinnati third baseman Hick Carpenter snared seven line drives "that almost tore him apart," according to sportswriter Ren Mulford. "The Brooklyns had Old Hick on the hot corner all afternoon and it's a miracle he wasn't murdered." Carpenter was probably the finest third baseman of his era. Around the turn of the century Jimmy Collins was the game's pre-eminent defensive third baseman, and in 1900 his 252 putouts for Boston set an NL record that still stands.

Until Babe Ruth and the lively ball turned baseball into a slugfest in the 1920s, third basemen were judged largely on their ability to field the bunt. Quick response, as opposed to speed, was and is a primary asset of a good third baseman. Buck Weaver of the White Sox was so quick that even the

Following in the cleat marks of Brooks Robinson was no picnic, but Doug DeCinces soon won the respect of Oriole fans with his glove. DeCinces led the league three times in double plays and total chances and twice in assists.

When Terry Pendleton (above) joined shortstop Ozzie Smith in 1984, the left side of the Cardinal infield became almost impenetrable. Pendleton led the NL in putouts, assists and double plays in 1986.

great Ty Cobb wouldn't bunt on him. The 1920s were also the heyday of two of the hot corner's finest—Pie Traynor and Willie Kamm. Traynor was particularly good at going to his right and turning potential doubles down the left-field line into outs, while Kamm led the AL in fielding percentage eight times in his 12 full seasons, six straight from 1924 to 1929.

In the 1930s managers wanted more than just a good glove; they also wanted a high batting average. The talent pool responded with such underrated hot-corner heroes as Harlond Clift of the St. Louis Browns.

Clift labored in obscurity for mediocre to awful Browns' teams in the 1930s and early 1940s but was an all-around star. From 1934 to 1941 Clift averaged .281, 20 home runs, 108 runs scored, 86 RBI and 103 walks. But Clift's best work was done with glove in hand, especially in 1937, when he set major league records with 405 assists and 50 double plays, and an AL record with 637 total chances. In 1971 Cleveland's Graig Nettles came along and set new records for assists and double plays, but Clift's record for total chances is still on the books.

George Kell proved that playing third can be hazardous to your health. In 1948 his jaw was broken by a Joe DiMaggio line drive, and in 1952 he suffered a groin injury chasing a foul pop (above).

This line drive eluded Detroit's Tom Brookens (left), but in the 1987 AL Championship Series against Minnesota, he was perfect, handling 18 chances without an error. The Dodgers' Ron Cey (below) was also solid in the clutch, committing just one error in four World Series covering 23 games and 56 chances.

The AL's parade of fine-fielding third basemen continued with the likes of Cleveland's Ken Keltner, who made himself famous by almost single-handedly ending Joe DiMaggio's hitting streak at 56 games on July 17, 1941, with two outstanding plays on hot shots down the third-base line. On Keltner's heels came George Kell, whose ability at the plate often overshadowed a fine glove. Kell led the AL in fielding percentage six times and assists four times from 1945 to 1956, finished his career with Baltimore in 1957, then in 1983 was inducted into the Hall of Fame on the same day as the man who replaced him at third with the Orioles—Brooks Robinson. Kell's stranglehold on the AL fielding percentage title was broken in 1947 by Hank Majeski of the Philadelphia Athletics. Majeski committed just five errors the entire season for a major league record .988, a record that stood until Milwaukee's Don Money turned in a .989 season in 1974.

The NL had its share of good gloves at third between the World Wars. Perhaps the best of the era was Arthur "Pinky" Whitney, who played for the Phillies and the Braves from 1928 to 1939, never played in a World Series, but led NL third basemen four times in assists and double plays, and three times in putouts and fielding percentage. Merrill "Pinky" May succeeded Pinky Whitney as the Phillies' third baseman in 1939 and led the NL in fielding percentage three times in a career that lasted just five years.

The AL's entry in the "third basemen named Pinky" sweepstakes was Mike "Pinky" Higgins, who played 1,768 mostly solid defensive games for the Athletics, the Red Sox and the Tigers from 1930 to 1946. On May 2, 1938, he tied an AL mark with four errors in a game, but in the 1940 Tigers-Reds World Series, he set a major league record for assists by a third baseman with 30 in seven games.

The NL can lay claim to the two best-fielding third basemen of the 1950s—Willie "Puddin' Head" Jones of the Phillies and Billy Cox of the Dodgers. Jones simply dominated the decade, using his great range and sure hands to lead NL third basemen seven times in putouts and five times in fielding percentage, including a stretch from 1953 to 1956 during which he won both titles each year. In *The Boys of Summer,* Roger Kahn called Cox "the best third baseman since the dawn of baseball."

Billy Cox' play for Brooklyn in the 1952 and 1953 World Series prompted Yankee manager Casey Stengel to say, "That ain't a third baseman. That's an acrobat."

St. Louis' Pepper Martin (left) used to discourage batters from bunting by aiming his throws at them on their way to first, while Clete Boyer (below) took better aim, leading the AL three times in assists.

Cox, like a lot of third basemen of his time, was small and slight at 5′ 10″ and 150 pounds. By the 1960s power was the name of the game, and third basemen got bigger. This created a dilemma for managers like Dodger Walter Alston: "Maybe that's why the position is so tough for some clubs to fill. In looking for a power hitter, they're looking for a man whose size may restrict the physical agility that third base demands defensively." The hot corner has had burly sluggers like Harmon Killebrew and Jim Ray Hart, but a great glove could still earn a spot in the lineup every day. The Yankees' Clete Boyer hit .242 lifetime with average power, but his glove ensured his place on five straight Yankee pennant-winners from 1960 through 1964. Brooks Robinson said Boyer was the best third baseman he had ever played against. The field was Boyer's stage, and he played it like a true ham. "Even when we took infield practice, I knew people were watching me . . . I loved it. No distraction bothered me. A third baseman has got to be like that, loaded with confidence."

Boyer's brother Ken was a power-hitting third baseman who was also an excellent fielder, as was the Cubs' Ron Santo, who led NL third basemen in putouts and assists from 1962 to 1967. The 1970s and 1980s saw all-around headline-grabbing stars the caliber of Kansas City's George Brett and Philadelphia's Mike Schmidt. Brett is a two-time batting champion who flirted with a .400 season in 1980, and he has worked hard to improve his fielding. In 1985 he won his first Gold Glove Award, breaking the six-year reign of Texas' Buddy Bell, another good-hitting, good-fielding third baseman.

Mike Schmidt is in a class by himself. Although his 509 homers are the most ever by a third baseman, he has also earned ten Gold Gloves for his stellar work in the field, leaving a challenge for a new generation of third basemen like Minnesota's Gary Gaetti and Montreal's Tim Wallach. Schmidt added raw speed to the usual arsenal of a great third baseman, allowing him to play deeper and farther off the line. "I'll tell you this about his range," said sportswriter Allen Lewis. "I once saw Schmidt go to his left and cut off a ball in the hole. As he was moving and throwing to second for a force, he saw that his throw would be off-line. It tipped the second baseman's glove, and Schmidt never stopped moving. He ran down his own throw in right field."

In Defense of Fielding

othing in any other sport compares to fielding in baseball. Absent is the familiar and ritualistic tugging over turf that we find in most ball-and-goal games. In baseball, unlike most of our other sports, the defending team is given the ball and initiates the action. In fact, the interplay between hitting and fielding teams is so fluid that the term "defense" doesn't really apply. It wasn't even used in baseball until recent years, when some writer, probably bleary-eyed from watching football on television, mistakenly attached it to the diamond sport.

And it's beautiful to watch. An infielder taking a relay and firing it home, a first baseman leaning forward to catch a throw on a close play, an outfielder in pursuit of a long fly ball—a fine fielding play is the essence of athletic finesse.

For those who have mastered it, the fun is in fielding. Everyone enjoys it, even players known for other skills. When Ted Williams chased after fly balls in the minors, he would slap his rump and cry out, "Hi-ho, Silver!" Williams later got as much of a kick out of mastering Fenway Park's "Green Monster" wall as in mastering pitchers. In 1975 Boston's Fred Lynn was elected Most Valuable Player and Rookie of the Year, but winning his first Gold Glove made the season particularly memorable for him. "I don't get excited over too many things," he said, "but this means a lot, more than anything, maybe."

Billy Sample wasn't much of a second baseman—he led the Class AA Texas League with 23 errors in 1977. Two years later, as a left fielder for the Texas Rangers, (opposite) he played the entire season—103 games and 180 chances—without an error.

Shortstop Garry Templeton led NL short-stops in errors from 1978 to 1980, but his errors didn't bother Cardinal manager Vern Rapp. "Garry makes so many plays other people don't make that I'm not worried about his slip-ups." In 1982 Templeton (above) was traded to San Diego for another pretty good shortstop—Ozzie Smith.

Baseball was invented as a fielding game. The pitcher lobbed the ball underhand where the batter asked for it, and the purpose was to put the ball in play and let the game unfold in the field and on the base-paths. "The best player in a nine is he who makes the most good plays in a match," Henry Chadwick, baseball's first great commentator, wrote in the 19th century.

Later events conspired to take the emphasis away from fielding. Pitching benefited from high mounds and tricky deliveries. Slugging was born of close-in fences and lively balls. Despite these changes, fielding has never lost its importance, along with hitting and pitching, as one of the key elements of the game. A team can't win without excelling in at least two of the three.

While some say pitching is 75 percent of the game, the 1987 Minnesota Twins proved they could do without it as long as they had big bats and gloves. The Twins had a miserable 4.63 team ERA, but they did have seven players with ten or more home runs and committed 98 regular-season errors. In 12 postseason games they committed just six errors on their way to a stunning world championship.

In fact, nothing short of stellar hitting and pitching performance can overcome poor fielding: the 1985 Dodgers' 166 errors was the highest total in the majors that year, but their 2.96 ERA was the lowest and their division-leading 129 home runs gave them 95 wins and the NL West title.

In 1982 St. Louis manager Whitey Herzog traded for shortstop Ozzie Smith, moved Ken Oberkfell from second to third, and inserted Tommy Herr at second—the first baseman was Keith Hernandez. With the greatest infield of recent years in place, the Cardinals won a world championship. Herzog is a stickler for fielding. So is Detroit's Sparky Anderson, the most successful

St. Louis second baseman Red Schoendienst (left) was just getting loose when he eluded Milwaukee's Bill Queen on his way to a spring training double play in 1951. Schoendienst was a double-play wizard that season, turning 137 to tie the NL single-season record set by Jackie Robinson in 1951.

manager of the 1970s and 1980s. "I want defense," he says, using the right idea if the wrong term. "I'll take the offense second."

What makes fielding so important? It gets back to the notion of putting the ball in play and letting the game unfold on the field. No major league pitcher averages a dozen strikeouts per regulation 27-out game—Nolan Ryan's season average of 11.48 strikeouts a game in 1987 is the best on record. The pitcher, therefore, must rely on his fielders to supply most of the outs. Good fielders make the pitcher's job simple: as they say in baseball, "let 'em hit," and with runners on base, "a pitcher's best friend is the double play." In 1987 Dodger pitcher Orel Hershiser was 16–16. In 1988 he was 23–8. Better technique? "No," said Los Angeles pitching coach Ron Perranoski, "but in '87 we didn't have people like shortstop Alfredo Griffin to catch the ball."

Lesser pitchers benefit just as much from good fielders. Instead of painfully working the corners of the strike zone, they can confidently throw the ball over the plate and let their fielders take over. That's the secret of success for the many Tiger sinkerballers who have had shortstop Alan Trammell and second baseman Lou Whitaker behind them. And a key for high-ball pitchers, too. As Hall of Famer Lefty Gomez once said of his career with the Yankees, "I owe my success to clean living and a fast outfield."

Unfortunately, fielding is the least appreciated art in baseball. Part of the problem is that—Henry Chadwick and later generations of baseball analysts notwithstanding—there is no good way to measure fielding skill. There are no flashy fielding stats to compete with 20 wins or a 3.00 earned run average for pitchers, a .300 average, 30 homers, or 100 runs batted in for

Detroit shortstop Alan Trammell (above, leaping over Chicago's Rudy Law) and second baseman Lou Whitaker have been one of baseball's best double-play combinations since they were rookies in 1978. And they can hit, too. In 1983 they became the first shortstop-second-base combo to each hit over .300 since Luke Appling and Cass Michaels did it for the 1949 White Sox.

6' 1½" 190 lbs.   b 6/6/1871
BR TR   d 7/23/1950

BILL LANGE

Bill Lange might be entirely forgotten if not for one legendary play, a game-saving catch that culminated in Lange crashing through an outfield fence. The play is probably mythical, but Lange deserves to be remembered.

Lange played center field for the NL Chicago Colts from 1893 to 1899. He ran swiftly on slender legs and had a strutting manner on the field. In his seven-year career, Lange batted .330 and stole 399 bases, with a league-leading 73 steals in 1897. Several writers of the time placed Lange ahead of Ty Cobb in their all-time all-star out-fields. Lange pioneered many of the reckless, cut-throat baserunning tactics that Cobb made famous.

Lange's slightly scandalous reputation as one of the Colts' "Dawn Patrol Boys" endeared him to fans and infuriated strait-laced manager Cap Anson. At 28, after a sixth-straight .300 season, Lange quit professional baseball to marry a San Francisco socialite, moved to California, and entered the real estate business.

As for the spectacular catch of August 31, 1896, Arthur Ahrens gave the most likely explanation in the Society for American Baseball Research's 1980 *Baseball Research Journal.* To rush an injured player to the hospital, Washington's Kip Selbach had knocked down part of the outfield fence with a ladder. A couple of outs later, Lange made his running catch at the broken fence, and a legend was born.

Howard Johnson (above) is a third baseman by trade, but replaces light-hitting short-stops occasionally when the Mets need more punch in the lineup. In 1986 Johnson had trouble all over, with a .903 fielding percentage at each position.

batters. The most commonly cited fielding numbers seem to accent the negative: how many points under a perfect 1.000 fielding percentage; or how many errors, not how many good plays.

Without catchy numbers, fielding performance is difficult to evaluate and constantly deprived of acclaim. In 1987 Ozzie Smith finished second behind Cub outfielder Andre Dawson in balloting for the National League's Most Valuable Player award. Dawson had glitzy power-batting stats. Smith fielded superbly at short while almost surreptitiously producing more runs than Dawson. The Cardinals couldn't have finished first without Smith. The Cubs finished last with Dawson. The lesson: hitting counts more than winning.

Worse, some executives in baseball front offices believe fielding just isn't entertaining. "The purist in me knows that games are won by pitching and defense," Milwaukee general manager Harry Dalton commented, "but the executive in me knows something else. Offense is what puts bodies in the seats." So baseball owners are as reluctant to pay fielders as sportswriters are to elect them MVPs. Of course, clubs aren't afraid to criticize poor fielders at contract time.

This practice can directly affect a team's won-lost record. "Too many players are guarding their statistics," says broadcaster and former Yankee shortstop Tony Kubek. "You have pivotmen who aren't trying to get double plays. They get that one out at second but refuse to go for two because they might make an overthrow and be charged with an error."

Errors stand out more these days because there are relatively few of them; fielding percentages have improved dramatically over the years. In 1908 the American and National League percentages were .958 and .961, respectively. In 1948 they were .977 and .974; and in 1988, .981 and .979.

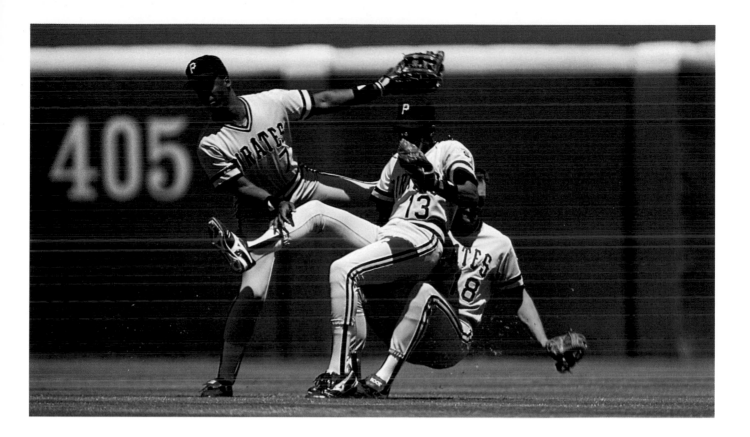

In 1914 Rabbit Maranville made 65 errors as shortstop for the world champion Boston Braves; in 1984 Alan Trammell made ten as shortstop for the world champion Detroit Tigers.

Some teams have such low regard for fielding that they'll put players at unfamiliar positions just to get their bats in the lineup. In 1987 rookie outfielder Kenny Williams showed the White Sox he could hit, hit with power, and run the bases. Trouble was, the Sox were overloaded with outfielders. In 1988 they switched Williams to third, a position he'd never played. Williams was so rattled by his problems in the new position that he fielded abysmally and couldn't hit his weight, committing 17 errors in only 73 games. Demoted to the minors in midseason, he cursed his bosses and threw a chair across the clubhouse. The White Sox deservedly had a poor season.

Better clubs are equally guilty of misusing their glovemen. The 1988 Mets, favored to win their second world title in three years, eventually foundered on fielding. In the NL Championship Series against Los Angeles, Mets manager Davey Johnson replaced light-hitting, good-fielding rookie shortstop Kevin Elster with power-hitting Howard Johnson, a natural third baseman. "My offensive lineup," said manager Johnson. Offensive indeed. Player Johnson failed to take charge on a fly to short left center, allowing the Dodgers to score first and go on to win Game 2. After five games Johnson had fielded poorly, had one hit for 17 at-bats, and had earned a seat on the bench. Johnson the manager also insisted on keeping inexperienced rookie Gregg Jefferies at third. One of his bobbles set up a big inning for Los Angeles in Game 7, and that set up the Mets' loss of the pennant. In his Series obituary, *New York Times* columnist George Vecsey referred to the left side of the Mets' infield as "the Bermuda Triangle."

Even the best fielders get banged around sometimes. This Pirate collision involved outfielders Jeff King (7), Andy Van Slyke (18)—a 1988 Gold Glove winner—and second baseman Jose Lind (13), second to Chicago's Ryne Sandberg in assists and total chances in 1988.

Richie Ashburn

Richie Ashburn could hit, run, and field with the best of them. As a center fielder with the Philadelphia Phillies, he won NL batting titles in 1955 and 1958, and led the league in singles a record-tying four times, in walks four times, and in hits three times. He hit an average of .308 over his 15-year career and topped .300 nine times. Defensively, Ashburn led the league in outfield putouts and in total chances nine times. Bill James, baseball historian, writes, "Richie Ashburn has the best defensive statistics of any outfielder ever to play major league baseball."

Although Ashburn was praised for his hitting, fielding and running, he's perhaps best remembered for a throw he made from center field in 1950. Ashburn's Phillies led Brooklyn by one game as the two teams met for the final game of the season. It was the bottom of the ninth and the score was tied at 1–1, but Brooklyn had men on first and second with no outs. Duke Snider stepped up to the plate and lashed out a single to center field. Ashburn charged the ball, scooped it into his glove and rifled it home, in time for catcher Stan Lopata to put the tag on Cal Abrams, trying to score from second. Ashburn's perfect strike from the outfield saved the game—and the pennant. In the top of the tenth inning Dick Sisler homered and the "Whiz Kids" were in the World Series.

Even though Ashburn could do it all, he never received as much recognition as Willie Mays, Mickey Mantle or Duke Snider. His lack of home-run power may have been the reason; in 8,365 trips to the plate he hit only 29 homers. But his peers certainly knew how valuable he was. In the spring of 1951 Stan Musial looked at the three-year veteran and predicted, "Ashburn's going to surprise everyone. He's learned how to hit . . . Take my word for it he'll be up among the leaders." Musial was right. Ashburn chased him for the batting crown and finished the year at .344.

Ashburn was known as an intelligent and patient hitter. "The way I figure it, a walk is as good as a single," said Ashburn. "If I can't work a pitcher for a good pitch to hit, I'm going to try to work him for a walk."

Ashburn also earned a reputation as a fervent foul-ball hitter. An enterprising statistician once estimated that Ashburn cost the National League more than $4,000 in foul balls each season; figuring he fouled off three balls that cost two dollars a piece at each of his at-bats. When Giants president Horace Stoneham watched him foul off 13 consecutive pitches in one at-bat in 1955, he remarked, "Look at that little devil taking money right out of my pocket." Ashburn was quick to explain the method in his madness: "By fouling off pitches, you keep the pitcher in the hole. Either he's going to miss the strike zone eventually and walk you, or he's going to come in with a fat pitch on which you can level off."

One of the game's most durable players, Ashburn played in 730 consecutive games from June 7, 1950 to September 26, 1954 — the 12th longest streak in the majors. He missed only 22 games from 1949 to 1958. Richie Ashburn played his last game as a member of the infamous 1962 New York Mets, one of the losingest teams in baseball history. True to form, Ashburn went out in style, hitting .306 for the year; one of only ten players in history to hit over .300 in his final season.

RICHIE ASHBURN

Center Field
Philadelphia Phillies 1948–1959
Chicago Cubs 1960–1961
New York Mets 1962

GAMES	**2,189**
FIELDING PERCENTAGE	
Career	.983
Season High	.990
PUTOUTS	
Career *(5th all time)*	**6,089**
Season High *(2nd all time)*	**538**
PUTOUTS PER GAME	
Career *(2nd all time)*	**2.89**
Season High *(3rd all time)*	**3.49**
ASSISTS	
Career	178
Season High	23
ASSISTS PER GAME	
Career	.08
Season High	.15
CHANCES	
Career *(5th all time)*	**6,377**
Season High *(2nd all time)*	**560**
CHANCES PER GAME	
Career *(2nd all time)*	**3.04**
Season High *(5th all time)*	**3.64**
ERRORS PER GAME	
Career	.05
Season Low	.03
DOUBLE PLAYS	
Career	43
Season High	7
WORLD SERIES	**1950**

6' 175 lbs.
BR TR
b 11/14/1929

JIMMY PIERSALL
Outfield

Jimmy Piersall got off to a rough start in the majors. He suffered a nervous breakdown as a rookie in 1952 but recovered to play 17 seasons with a .272 batting average, becoming one of the game's finest outfielders and most outrageous characters.

Even though Boston center fielder Dom DiMaggio called Piersall the best center fielder in the AL, the Red Sox converted the rookie to shortstop, a position he'd never played before. The move may have hastened Piersall's breakdown, for which he was hospitalized.

The next year, Piersall was back, a full-time outfielder—and entertainer. He baited umpires and, following his frequent ejections, littered the field with objects not securely fastened to the dugout. He did sit-ups in the outfield to distract batters. He cursed on-field photographers. A right-handed hitter, he once batted left-handed; he struck out, then drop-kicked his helmet into the dugout. To celebrate his 100th career homer, he ran backwards around the bases.

Such antics partially obscured Piersall's fielding skills, first honed by his father, a semipro catcher who drove his son to succeed. Piersall won Gold Gloves in 1958 and 1961, recklessly challenging fences throughout his five-team career. He led AL outfielders in putouts twice, chances per game twice, and fielding percentage three times—adding an errorless season as a 34-year-old part-timer in 1964.

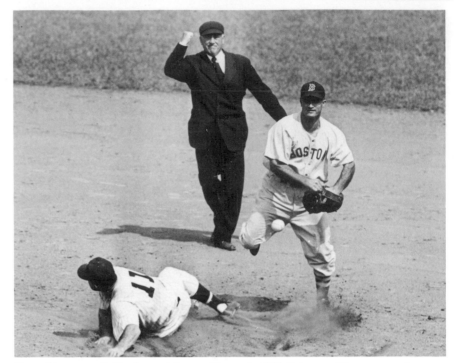

Second baseman Bobby Doerr (above, with umpire Bill Grieve and Senators catcher Newt Grasso) helped bring the Red Sox a pennant in 1946, then hit .409 and handled 49 chances without an error in Boston's World Series loss to St. Louis.

Almost any time a team surprises the experts by contending, you can be certain that fielding was a factor. Consider the main reason why the California Angels and the Baltimore Orioles led their AL divisions at the 1989 All-Star break. In 1988 Joe Orsulak, an old-timer compared to most of the team, was considered the fastest outfielder on the Orioles; by 1989 he was rated fifth fastest. Meanwhile, Craig Worthington was playing the best third base at Memorial Stadium since Doug DeCinces in 1981, and the Orioles' infield, fraternally anchored by shortstop Cal and second baseman Billy Ripken, made no errors from April 30 to May 20. Out in Anaheim, the Angel outfield committed 48 errors in 1988. At the midway point in 1989, Angel outfielders were almost perfect, having committed a mere five errors. Why? Because sure-handed Claudell Washington had come over from the New York Yankees and Devon White had developed into possibly the league's best outfielder.

These are tough times for fielders. The twin evils of the age—artificial turf and the designated hitter—conspire against glovemen. Those not-so-magic carpets were introduced to the majors in 1966 and are now used in ten of the 26 major league parks. On plastic grass, true bounce is more predictable, reducing the likelihood of errors from bad hops, but artificial turf is so springy that routine grounders become high-bounding base hits, and sharp line drives skip up the gaps for extra bases. Without the traction of natural grass, fielders don't get the jump on balls that aren't hit right at them. Pivoting on turf, in the words of broadcaster and ex-catcher Tim McCarver, is like "trying to stop on your driveway on roller skates."

Since 1973 American League teams have used a permanent pinch hitter to bat in place of the pitcher. This hitter never fields; he need not even own a

Perfect Play

Good outfielders average just a handful of errors each season, but once in a while an outfielder turns in a completely error-free season—about two dozen outfielders have turned the trick in the game's history. Usually it happens to great defensive outfielders but every once in a while a dark horse like Rocky Colavito goes errorless for a whole season. Below are the outfielders who played errorless ball for an entire season—in at least 100 games—ranked in order of the most chances accepted.

Position	Player	Team	Year	Total Chances	Assists	Career Fielding %
CF	Curt Flood	Cardinals	1966	396	5	.987
CF	Terry Puhl	Astros	1979	359	7	.993
LF	Brian Downing	Angels	1982	330	9	.995
CF	Mickey Stanley	Tigers	1970	320	3	.991
LF	Danny Litwhiler	Phillies	1942	317	9	.982
LF	Roy White	Yankees	1971	314	8	.988
CF	Mickey Stanley	Tigers	1968	304	7	.991
LC	Carl Yastrzemski	Red Sox	1977	303	16	.981
CF	Ken Berry	Angels	1972	285	13	.989
LF	Brian Downing	Angels	1984	277	5	.995
CF	Tony Gonzalez	Phillies	1962	276	8	.987
RF	Rocky Colavito	Indians	1965	274	9	.979

glove! But that's not the only way the DH insults AL fielders. Back when pitchers still batted, managers had to decide whether to use pinch hitters for them. Even when pitchers weren't due to bat, there was a tendency to lift them in close games. When pitchers were removed, managers could often make a double switch, bringing in both a relief pitcher and a new fielder, flip-flopping them in the batting order to get the fielder up in the next at-bat. Therefore, a whole cottage industry existed for utility fielders. Now AL pitchers stay in games longer because they aren't pinch-hit for, and AL utility players languish on the bench.

But in other respects things are looking up for fielders. The Cardinals' Ozzie Smith, baseball's number one gloveman, is at least paid like the star he is. The Hall of Fame now has a permanent exhibit honoring the Gold Glove—the annual award given top fielders. Five players recently elected to Cooperstown—Brooks Robinson, Pee Wee Reese, Luis Aparicio, Bobby Doerr and Arky Vaughan—were as celebrated for their fielding as for their hitting. Another promising sign was the 1988 election of the excellent Oakland shortstop Walter Weiss as AL Rookie of the Year over lesser fielders with glitzier batting or pitching stats.

Harry Dalton's assessment aside, good fielding puts bodies galore in the seats. The most entertaining, enlightening, and even amusing moments come in the field. World Series have been made memorable by plays like Bill Wambsganss' in 1920 against the Brooklyn Dodgers, turning an unassisted triple play in Game 5 to help Cleveland win its first World Series. And Sam Rice, back in 1925, falling into the bleachers after Earl Smith's long fly and coming up out of the crowd with the ball in his glove, a smile on his face, and nary a word to anyone. Or an incredible throw like Cardinal

Perhaps the toughest play for a left fielder is a fly ball down the foul line. Often the ball is tailing away from him, and he may have to avoid walls, bullpen mounds, even security guards. St. Louis' John Morris (above, right)—a typically speedy 1980s Cardinal outfielder—had to fight a fan to make his catch.

Taking out the pivot man on the double play becomes especially challenging when the target is an acrobat like Ozzie Smith (opposite, middle). The Dodgers' Jay Johnstone used his arms to take down the high-flying Smith during the shortstop's tenure in San Diego. Padre second baseman Tim Flannery went airborne to get a better look.

Enos Slaughter's in 1942, from right field to third ahead of startled Yankee Tuck Stainback.

Even bad fielding plays can be worth the price of admission. According to baseball folklore, 1930s outfielder Babe Herman was once hit on the head by a fly ball. "He did not always catch balls on top of his head," wrote John Lardner, "but he could do it in a pinch." After chunky pitcher Dave "Snacks" LaPoint dropped a throw covering first in the 1982 Series, his teammate Keith Hernandez quipped, "If it had been a cheeseburger, he would have caught it."

It's the universe of possibilities that sets fielding apart. Once a ball is hit in fair territory, anything can—and probably will—happen. On September 3, 1986, Giants pitcher Terry Mulholland fielded a grounder by the Mets' Keith Hernandez, but the ball stuck in the webbing of his glove. He ran toward first, yanking at the ball in panic, then threw the whole thing—ball and glove—to first baseman Bob Brenly for the out.

On July 27, 1988, Yankee pitcher Tommy John committed three errors on one play, tying a mark set by the Giants' Cy Seymour in 1898. The play started when John fumbled a grounder by Milwaukee's Jeffrey Leonard, allowing him to reach first and letting baserunner Jim Gantner take second. John then threw the ball into right field, giving Gantner and Leonard a green light. Gantner scored, and as Leonard reached third, John took a relay throw from the right fielder and fired it into the Milwaukee dugout. Leonard trotted home. "When I fielded the ball one-handed, I threw it like I was putting the shot," John said. "I should have eaten it. But with a thunderstorm coming through, there were a lot of negative ions in the air and, wearing a metal cup, it just glitched my mind." ◗

Tris Speaker

Captain Outfield

Center field is baseball's sexiest position. Marilyn Monroe wouldn't have given the time of day to a big-nosed shortstop named Joe DiMaggio, but let him glide and dive across the lush green power alleys of Yankee Stadium, and she ups and marries the guy.

Philip Roth wrote an elegy to it, John Fogerty made it the only position with its own anthem. The one fielding play that has its own nickname—"The Catch"—was made in center field by one of its most celebrated residents, Willie Mays.

What makes center field so special and its occupants such stars? Is it the position itself or is it the players who've played there? A little of both. Center fielders see more acreage than any other fielders, and are expected to cover more as well. The more ground a center fielder can cover, the closer toward the lines his fellow outfielders can play. Center fielders are responsible for any balls they can get to.

The players bring a medley of skills to the position. Speed is probably the most important requirement, but it's not nearly enough. A center fielder must also have a "nose" for the baseball, quick reflexes, acrobatic ability, daring, a strong

and accurate arm, the intelligence to know in an instant which base to throw to, and confidence that borders on arrogance. A good center fielder has to want the ball to be hit to him. And the record books demonstrate that: the ten players with the highest single-season totals for chances accepted by an outfielder are all center fielders.

Because center fielders have responsibility for such vast territory, they have to work harder than other fielders at positioning. The better a center fielder is at going back on fly balls, the shallower he can play, thereby turning potential line-drive and bloop singles into outs. They have to know their own teams' pitchers and the opposing hitters in order to get an edge before the ball is hit. Joe DiMaggio, one of the best ever, never stopped working. "Getting a good jump on a fly ball is instinctive to many center fielders, but timing and concentration are the most important techniques," DiMaggio said. "And that requires constant practice and dedication to the game."

One catch fans still talk about is a play DiMaggio made off Detroit slugger Hank Greenberg in 1939. Greenberg hit a high drive that was headed for Yankee Stadium's center field wall,

The Giants' Willie Mays let nothing—not even Wrigley Field's ivy-covered brick wall (left)—stop his pursuit of fly balls. His 7,095 putouts are an all-time high.

Whether on the road at Wrigley Field (above) or at home at St. Louis' Busch Stadium, center fielder Willie McGee covers a lot of ground. In 1982 he tied a World Series record with 24 putouts.

461 feet from home plate. DiMaggio, playing shallow as usual, put his head down and ran a 50-yard dash to the wall, turned, leaped, and caught the ball just as he crashed into concrete. "I didn't even know if I had caught the ball," he said. "Sometimes you have to be lucky, too."

The man who was first to combine enough speed, guts and brains to play center field shallow is also the man considered by many to be the greatest center fielder ever—Tris Speaker. Speaker reasoned that since most balls he couldn't catch fell in front of him rather than going over his head, playing shallow was merely going with the percentages. In April 1918 Speaker made an unheard-of two unassisted double plays—he was playing so close behind second base that when he caught a line drive, he was able to beat the baserunner back to the bag. Speaker also had a great arm, and still holds the major league record for career assists—448 runners thrown out—and the AL record for assists in a season with 35 in 1912. But it was his uncanny ability to catch balls hit over his head that made the rest of Speaker's magic possible. Smoky Joe Wood, Speaker's teammate with the Red Sox, said, "Nobody else was even in the same league with him."

Playing in Speaker's shadow was Pittsburgh's Max Carey, who caught 6,363 fly balls and line drives in his 20-year career, more than anyone else except Speaker and Willie Mays. Carey was a speedster, and led the NL nine times in putouts and ten times in stolen bases. The Cardinals' Taylor Douthit is rarely mentioned in the same breath as other great center fielders, but in 1928 his 547 putouts set a major league record that still stands. Like a lot of great center fielders, Douthit went after everything in sight, and as a result piled up a misleading number of errors on balls that ordinary outfielders wouldn't have gotten to. Douthit led the NL in errors in 1926 and 1927, Speaker still holds the AL record for most errors in a season with 25, and Mays once committed four errors in a single game—statistics that don't reflect inability; they just mean these fielders were taking a lot of risks.

In the 1930s DiMaggio came to dominate the position, but another, less heralded center fielder may have been his equal, at least in the field. Terry Moore played with the Cardinals from 1935 to 1948, and in addition to having great overall fielding and throwing ability, he fashioned several of the era's most memorable plays. In Game 3 of the 1942

They called Pittsburgh's Max Carey "Scoops" with good reason. He led NL outfielders nine times in putouts and four times in assists.

Nicknamed "the Little Professor" for his bookish appearance, Dom DiMaggio wasn't as heralded as his brother Joe but was every bit as good an outfielder. In 1948 he set an AL record for center fielders with 503 putouts, a record that stood until Chet Lemon broke it in 1977.

World Series, Moore made DiMaggio his victim. With two outs in the sixth, a runner on first, and the Cardinals holding to a precarious 1–0 lead, DiMaggio jolted a shot to the deepest part of Yankee Stadium, but Moore chased it down and saved the game for St. Louis. "It seemed like to me I ran a full minute before I caught up with the ball," Moore said. But more famous was a sliding, bare-handed catch Moore had made six years earlier off another Hall of Famer, Giants slugger Mel Ott. And the fastest man ever to play baseball, Cool Papa Bell, played center field in the Negro leagues in the 1930s and 1940s. Bell, who once circled the bases in 12 seconds, just plain outran fly balls, and made up for a mediocre arm with a fast release.

Perhaps center field greatness is genetic. Rosalie DiMaggio gave birth to three great glovemen who roamed center field in the majors from 1936 to 1953. Joe is the most famous, but Dom was the first AL player to top 500 putouts in a season, and Vince led the NL twice in putouts, averaging 2.6 a game in his career, 14th best on the all-time list.

If there was a golden age for center fielders, it has to have been the 1950s, and its capital was New York City. Arguments still rage over who was the best—the Giants' Willie Mays, the Yankees' Mickey Mantle, or the Dodgers' Duke Snider. Each was a gifted athlete who excelled at all five of baseball's requisites: hit for average, hit for power, run, field and throw. Between them they hit 1,603 career home runs. Mantle and Mays played center field recklessly, with the sprinter's speed necessary to cover the huge areas in Yankee Stadium and the Polo Grounds. "It's doubtful that there ever has been a more enthusiastic thrower than Willie Mays, who acts as if the possession of a baseball were a crime punishable by imprisonment," wrote Tommy Holmes in the *Brooklyn Eagle*. Mantle was one of the fastest players in baseball, but his career was plagued by injuries, the most serious coming in the 1951 World Series when he tripped over a loose drainage cap while chasing a fly ball hit, ironically enough, by Willie Mays. Brooklyn pitcher Carl Erskine said Duke Snider had "a grace and carriage which, like Joe DiMaggio, set him apart." What also set him apart was a shotgun for an arm. One story tells of Snider standing at home plate before a game and throwing a baseball over the right field wall, 38 feet high and more than 300 feet away.

Winner of eight Gold Gloves from 1980 to 1988, the Cubs' Andre Dawson (right) led NL outfielders in total chances from 1981 to 1983, playing for Montreal.

Despite recurring leg injuries, Mickey Mantle was a wall-to-wall wonder in Yankee Stadium's spacious center field. His 20 assists in 1954 led the majors.

Snider once climbed the wall in Philadelphia's Shibe Park going after a fly ball, caught his spikes in a groove in the wall, and managed not only to catch the ball but hold onto it after crashing to the ground.

The three New York masters and their records were challenged by several great center fielders in the sixties, such as Curt Flood of the Cardinals, Jim Landis and Ken Berry of the White Sox, Mickey Stanley of the Tigers, and Paul Blair of the Orioles. In 1966 Flood handled 396 chances without an error, still an NL record, while Landis and Berry are tied for seventh on the all-time list with a career fielding percentage of .989. Blair is a point behind at .988, and played one of the game's shallowest center fields en route to six World Series appearances, while Stanley had errorless seasons in 1968 *and* 1970.

Speed became even more important when artificial turf became popular in the 1970s and 1980s; center fielders had to race to prevent line drives from skittering into the outfield gaps. The best of the breed include the acrobatic Fred Lynn, who made managers cringe with his tendency to ignore the perils of immovable objects like fences and the ground; Detroit's Chet Lemon, whose 512

putouts in 1977 rank fourth best of all time, just ahead of Dwayne Murphy, who caught 507 balls for Oakland in 1980; Gary Pettis, a three-time Gold Glove winner; Dale Murphy, Atlanta's "Mr. Everything," who has five Gold Gloves to go along with his two home run titles; Garry Maddox, eight times a Gold Glove winner; and Minnesota's diminutive Kirby Puckett, who has made an art form of snatching potential home runs back into the ballpark.

Center fielders have always been—and will probably always be—on baseball's center stage, its most glamorous and envied stars. As Philip Roth wrote: "Oh, to be a center fielder, a center fielder—and nothing more!"

STYLE IS EVERYTHING

Bare Hands to Sure Hands

n June 19, 1846, the Knickerbocker Base Ball Club and the New York Nine played a game of baseball at Hoboken, New Jersey's Elysian Fields. The new game had been played within athletic clubs as a diversion from the more complicated sport of cricket, but this was the first time on record that two clubs played baseball competitively under the rules set forth by the Knickerbockers the previous year. What made the contest interesting wasn't hitting or pitching as much as fielding.

Rulesmaker Alexander Cartwright inaugurated many customs we find familiar today: the four-sided infield, foul lines, 90 feet between bases, three strikes to an out, three outs to an inning, and baserunners retired by a throw to a base or by a tag instead of by being struck with a thrown ball.

But in this seminal game there were some rules that have since vanished. Standing 45 feet from home, the "bowler" threw a parchment-and-catgut ball to the "striker" with the gentlest of underhand tosses. There were no called strikes, and batters swung at balls they liked much as they do on the cricket pitch, the object simply being to put the ball in play. Fielders, or "scouts," played barehanded, and a ball caught on one bounce was an out. The real challenge lay in how many fine fielding plays were made, because the first team to score 21 runs won.

Adding two extra runs for good measure in their half of the fourth inning, New York beat the Knickerbockers, 23–1. The Knickerbockers probably

The White Sox have a history of great middle infielders, and in 1951 shortstop Chico Carrasquel (opposite, right) and second baseman Nellie Fox combined for 926 assists, more than any other shortstop and second baseman that year.

Barehanded fielding—as practiced by players like Jim Patterson of the Columbia City, Indiana, team in the 1880s (right)—may have been manly, but it wasn't very effective. For example, in Game 7 of the 1885 Championship Series, Chicago of the National League committed 17 errors on its way to a 13–4 loss to St. Louis of the American Association.

Besides being the first to write down many of the basics of the game of baseball— including the configuration of the diamond, three strikes to an out, and three outs to an inning—Alexander Cartwright also handed out baseball's first fine. As umpire in an 1846 game between the Knickerbockers—the team for which he starred—and the New York Nine, Cartwright fined one of his own players for swearing.

would have scored more, but their star, Alexander Cartwright—ever the gentleman—was umpiring. Cartwright told his pitcher before the Hoboken game, "Let him hit it—you've got fielders behind you."

Despite many rule changes since 1845, this was the way the game was played for some 40 years. While most players fielded barehanded until late in the century, they weren't playing "hardball" as we know it. Baseballs varied widely in size and weight; some teams used red ones, others white. Home teams chose the ball, and a single ball was often used for an entire game. Just as softball is sometimes played barehanded today, except for the catcher and first baseman, it was normal in those early years to catch the ball barehanded. And catch they did, admittedly making plenty of errors.

Among baseball's artifacts are the diaries of "Father of Baseball" Henry Chadwick, the early sportswriter who edited *Beadle's Dime Base Ball Player*. Describing the Seton Hall Alerts' 42–4 win over New York University on May 21, 1874, Chadwick recounted the game's highlights: "On the University side, Lee, on second base, made some fine running catches; Wiley, at first, played effectively, and Funkhauser did good work at catcher. . . . On the Alert side, LaMarche caught excellently; McEntee, Shanley, and Daizley would not let anything go past them; Nealon was 'just there' on first; while McFadden and Murphy moved around lively in the field. McFadden caught the best fly in the game . . ." Typically, the reader had to go to the box score—an idea that Chadwick came up with—to determine the pitchers and the winners.

Nineteenth-century newspaper accounts tended to focus on fielding almost to the exclusion of other aspects of baseball. Princeton's 8–1 win over

Germantown on June 8, 1874, was a "creditable triumph of fielding over batting skill." Princeton made three errors to Germantown's 25.

In Harvard's 10–4 win over Yale, the next day, "the Yale catcher caught no less than six foul tips, one taken after he had received a hard rap over the right eye from a tip which was too quick for him, and which required him to retire long enough to bathe his forehead." A Harvard player introduced the first catcher's mask the next season, a remedy for the dangerous practice of catching without protection, but professional players generally worked without masks until the 1890s.

Fielding could take strange turns. In an 1889 entry, Chadwick noted that "during the Athletic-Baltimore game, Aug. 6, in Philadelphia, a laughable incident occurred in the third inning when, with three men on the bases and two hands out, Bauer popped up a foul fly. Tucker made a hard try for the ball, but it fell in the seats out of reach. A spectator gave the ball to Tucker, who threw it to Kilroy, and the latter stepped thoughtlessly into the [pitcher's] box, not noticing that [the catcher] Tate, who had also tried for the catch, was not yet in position. Larkin, who was on third base, took advantage of the situation, and scored before either Kilroy or Tate could reach the home plate."

With the emphasis on spectacular fielding, spectacular fielders elbowed one another for the spotlight. The century's dominant second baseman was Cincinnati's Biddy McPhee, who played barehanded all but his last three seasons. Playing eight seasons for the Red Stockings in the American Association and ten seasons with Cincinnati's National League franchise, he was a league leader in double plays 11 times,

The 1866 Championship Series between the Brooklyn Atlantics and the Philadelphia Athletics was typical of its era. Barehanded fielders rarely strayed far from their appointed bases, and the catcher never got too close to the batter. Game 1 was called off when the crowd got out of control, and the teams split the next two games, with Brooklyn winning 27–17 at the Capitoline Grounds (above), and the Athletics winning Game 3 in Philadelphia, 31–12.

GEORGE WRIGHT cincinnati red stockings SS.   DICK McBRIDE philadelphia athletics P.

Playing barehanded, Cincinnati second baseman Bid McPhee (above) made 529 putouts in 1886, a major league record that may never be broken. Baltimore's Bobby Grich came closest with 484 in 1974. Great fielders like George Wright (above, center, while with Cincinnati) helped make the careers of great pitchers like Dick McBride (above, right, while with the Philadelphia Athletics). But Wright was concerned that improvements in gloves—of which he was a major manufacturer—would hamper hitters, and in the 1890s he called for restrictions on the use of gloves.

fielding percentage nine times, putouts eight times, assists six times, and averaged 6.7 chances per game.

Outfielder John Chapman of the Brooklyn Atlantics was known as "Death to Flying Things" for his many leaping, over-the-shoulder, one-handed catches. Chapman, who played in the 1860s and 1870s, didn't have to make all those plays so spectacular, he may just have been baseball's first "hot dog." That honor might also go to George Wright, the star shortstop for Providence and Boston, who used to warm up by catching baseballs Frisbee-style between his legs and throwing behind his back. But he knew what he was doing when the game started. With runners on first and second or the bases loaded, Wright would fail to catch easy pop-ups, then grab the ball on a short hop and double up two of the runners. His "trap-ball trick" led to adoption of the infield-fly rule in 1895, allowing the umpire to make the out automatic on any pop fly to the infield with men on first and second, or with bases loaded and one out.

Early baseball clubs used eight players per team, probably because baseball evolved in part from the eight-man British game, rounders. In 1845 the Knickerbockers' D. L. Adams inserted himself in an intraclub game as a ninth man, and managers eventually played with "picked nines."

But the shortstop didn't settle down between second and third bases. Possibly named for the cricket "short fielder," he was first used as an outfield relay man much the way a tenth man is positioned in some forms of softball. When a somewhat heavier ball came into use in the 1850s, Brooklyn Atlantics shortstop Dickey Pearce moved into the infield, but the typical shortstop still

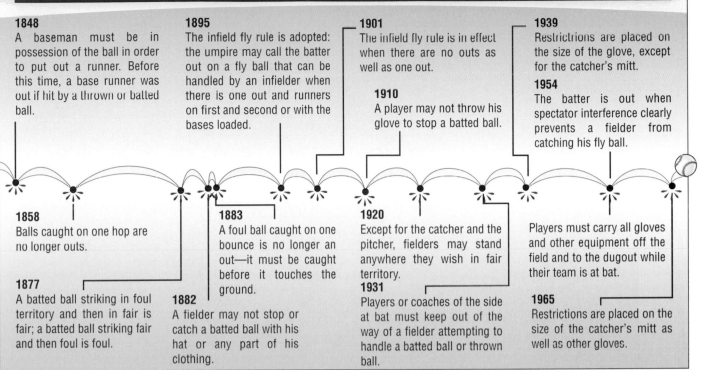

Changes in the Field

1848
A baseman must be in possession of the ball in order to put out a runner. Before this time, a base runner was out if hit by a thrown or batted ball.

1858
Balls caught on one hop are no longer outs.

1877
A batted ball striking in foul territory and then in fair is fair; a batted ball striking fair and then foul is foul.

1882
A fielder may not stop or catch a batted ball with his hat or any part of his clothing.

1883
A foul ball caught on one bounce is no longer an out—it must be caught before it touches the ground.

1895
The infield fly rule is adopted: the umpire may call the batter out on a fly ball that can be handled by an infielder when there is one out and runners on first and second or with the bases loaded.

1901
The infield fly rule is in effect when there are no outs as well as one out.

1910
A player may not throw his glove to stop a batted ball.

1920
Except for the catcher and the pitcher, fielders may stand anywhere they wish in fair territory.

1931
Players or coaches of the side at bat must keep out of the way of a fielder attempting to handle a batted ball or thrown ball.

1939
Restrictions are placed on the size of the glove, except for the catcher's mitt.

1954
The batter is out when spectator interference clearly prevents a fielder from catching his fly ball.

Players must carry all gloves and other equipment off the field and to the dugout while their team is at bat.

1965
Restrictions are placed on the size of the catcher's mitt as well as other gloves.

---

roamed freely. He'd often stand behind and to the first-base side of the pitcher, but he could locate himself from baseline to baseline. Not until the mid-1860s did the old hot dog George Wright move to the left of second base and revolutionize the game.

The first and third basemen rarely ventured far from their respective bags, and for good reason. Any fair hit caught on one bounce was an out until 1858; any foul ball caught on a bounce, until 1883. The "fair-foul" rule made a batter a baserunner if his hit struck in fair territory before curving foul. So first and third basemen had to guard against balls hit to the left and right of the bases, and as a result, second basemen and shortstops had vast reaches of fair territory to cover.

Second basemen began straying off the bags by the time the Cincinnati Red Stockings became baseball's first paid professional team in 1869. In the 1870s Cincinnati manager Harry Wright invented the strategy of his second baseman backing up fielders on hits and throwing to the farthest base to stop an advancing runner.

By 1887, when both the fair-foul-hit and the one-bounce-foul outs were eliminated, cornermen began edging timorously off their bases. Middle infielders were far more dramatic, not only ranging far and wide but fighting pitched battles with baserunners. A single umpire worked the game, and mayhem could reign behind his back: runners cut directly from first to third, and middle infielders blocked their paths like sentries at a fort.

The double-play pivot is a bruising enough affair today. A century ago Hall of Famer King Kelly, then playing in Chicago, described what runners routinely did to fielders: "The score in the last inning was four to three in favor of the Providence club. There was one man out when I snatched a hit.

Baseball fans in the 1890s could use the spring-launched pitching and batting devices of Zimmer's Base Ball Game to play with a band of all-time greats. The team in the field featured six Hall of Famers, including pitcher Amos Rusie, catcher Buck Ewing, first baseman Dan Brouthers, second baseman John Montgomery Ward, left fielder Billy Hamilton and right fielder Sam Thompson, while the team at bat featured three Hall of Famers— pitchers Cy Young and Kid Nichols and outfielder Ed Delahanty.

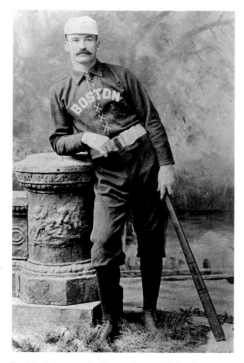

In his 16 years in the majors, Michael Joseph "King" Kelly played all nine positions, and made at least one play when he wasn't even in the lineup. Once, during a game in which he was a manager, a foul pop was hit out of the reach of his catcher. It was the era of free substitutions, so he called out, "Kelly now catching for Murphy," stepped out from his spot in the dugout, and caught the ball.

I got on first and was about to make an attempt to steal second, when Burns, who followed me, hit a hot grounder to George Wright. There was one player out, and if George ever got the ball to second it meant a double play. Instead of fielding the ball to the second baseman, he started for the bag himself. I never ran so hard in my life. I reached the bag a second before George, and then like a flash, he raised his arm to send the ball to first base, to cut off Burns. Somehow or other an accident occurred at that moment. My arm went up in the air, and it caught George on the shoulder. The result was, that when the ball left George's hand it went away over into the grandstand. I scored first, and Burns followed me a moment later. The cheers from a thousand enthusiastic spectators, proved that the Chicago club had won . . ." Evidently, runners could advance as far as they were able while fielders searched the grandstand for an errant throw. But anyone who swallows the word "accident" in Kelly's story believes in the tooth fairy.

In a 1931 interview, the versatile Kid Gleason, a peripatetic NL starting pitcher from 1888 to 1895 and a second baseman from 1896 to 1908, described what fielders routinely did to runners: "Know how I used to play second base? I'd let 'em slide into the bag, then kick them off the bag. That's the way we put 'em out. Take the pitchers. You never see a pitcher nowadays run in front of a man when he's going to second or third, do you? Well, we did it when I was pitching. Any time a man tried to steal I'd run over in front of him and slow him up. Another thing I used to do, I'd tell the catcher not to throw the ball to anyone but me when a runner was going down. I'd back off the rubber after a pitch and yell for the ball. Many a man I tagged out at second when I was pitching. But the way I liked best to put 'em out after I became a second baseman—just booted 'em in the pants and set 'em off the base."

John McGraw managed the New York Giants to ten pennants, but when he joined them in 1902, he wisely cut back on his time at third base. He had made 23 errors in 69 games for Baltimore in 1901.

Outfield play was no less inventive. Some fielders hid baseballs in the long grass, so that when a fly ball was hit well over their heads, they could retreat a few steps, grab the hidden ball, and fire it in. Until 1891 no substitutions were permitted, so, if a pitcher was hit hard or injured, he would switch with the "change pitcher," usually the right fielder, who was expected to have an especially good arm.

Most early hitters were right-handed, and few of them thought of hitting to the opposite field. But that changed in the 1890s, as batters learned to place hits and pitchers started using deceptive deliveries. Outfielders playing deep learned to back each other up and throw to the relay man, although "Big Sam" Thompson, a Hall of Fame right fielder for the Phillies in the 1880s, became the first outfielder on record to throw home without a relay.

By the 1890s virtually all managers were strategists working to outsmart each other. Bill Shettsline's roustabout Phillies stole signs and watered the infield to slow down baserunners. The Baltimore Orioles' Ned Hanlon taught his players to back up throws, take relays from the outfield, and give the hip to baserunners. In 1899 John J. McGraw succeeded Hanlon and more than earned the nickname "Little Napoleon."

Managing the New York Giants from 1902 to 1932, McGraw called pitches from the dugout and insisted that his infielders whip the ball "around the horn" in sophisticated pregame practices. While McGraw was barking at umpires and opponents and inciting beered-up fans to threaten visiting teams, his players slapped the ball out of infielders' hands, yelled at batters, and slid with sharpened spikes. McGraw could be tough on his own players, too, but until his final years they were willing to sacrifice for a winner and a

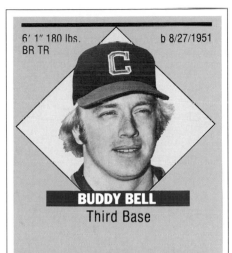

6' 1" 180 lbs.　　　　b 8/27/1951
BR TR

BUDDY BELL
Third Base

Like father, like son. Buddy Bell followed his father, outfielder Gus Bell, into the major leagues. And he played like his dad—solid, smooth and consistent. Although father and son racked up eight All-Star games between them, neither attracted much national attention.

Buddy Bell broke into the majors with Cleveland in 1972. During his rookie season he played the outfield, but when a deal sending teammate Graig Nettles to the Yankees opened up the third-base slot, Bell took over full-time the following season.

Bell played for unimpressive teams; after seven years with the Indians, he was traded to the Texas Rangers in December of 1978. It was with the Rangers, however, that Bell came into his own.

In the next seven years, Bell hit .292 for Texas and became a fielding wizard. He won the AL Gold Glove for third basemen six years in a row, from 1979 through 1984.

His former teammate, pitcher Jim Kern, explained Bell's lack of recognition. "It's partly because he's played for mediocre teams in parks that aren't great for hitters, but I think the main reason is, he's so smooth he makes everything look simple."

Bell, who retired in the summer of 1989 after playing 2,182 games at third base, never participated in even one inning of postseason play.

Busch Stadium

Busch Memorial Stadium sits at the foot of the massive arch that symbolizes St. Louis' status as "the Gateway to the West." But on its east side, the stadium is bounded by a street named Broadway. And in the tradition of the big eastern cities, St. Louis has a stadium in the heart of a bustling downtown that rocks when the Cardinals are in town.

Completed in 1966, Busch Memorial Stadium was the centerpiece of an ambitious downtown revitalization project. Looming as large as the arch over the project was August Anheuser Busch, Jr., president of Anheuser-Busch, Inc. The Cardinals became part of the Busch empire in 1953, and shortly thereafter the team's home, Sportsman's Park, was renamed Busch Stadium. In their first year in the new stadium the Cardinals drew a record 1,712,980 fans but finished sixth in the NL. The following season 2,090,145 fans crowded Busch Stadium as the Cardinals won 101 games and the pennant. With strong pitching, speed and defense, the team was tailor-made for the park, which features faraway fences and wide expanses of foul territory. Besides, the ball just doesn't seem to carry well there.

With the pitching of Bob Gibson, the speed of Lou Brock, the defense of center fielder Curt Flood, plus the double-play combination of Dal Maxvill and Julian Javier, the Cardinals won the World Series in 1967. In 1968 they came within one win of repeating as world champions and again drew over two million fans. Astroturf replaced grass at Busch Stadium in 1970, except for a dirt infield,

which was carpeted in 1974. In 1973, after posting a major-league-low 75 home runs, the Cardinals had the fences moved in ten feet at the power alleys and in dead-center field. In 1976 the team lowered its own record with just 63 homers and finished fifth in the NL East. With closer fences obviously not the answer, they were moved back in 1977.

In 1981 manager Whitey Herzog took over and went back to Busch Stadium basics—pitching, speed and defense—and created what has been the most successful team of the 1980s. Herzog's Cardinals, winners of four NL East titles, three pennants and one World Series from 1981 to 1987, bore a striking resemblance to their late 1960s counterparts. Herzog's Cards had a speedy left fielder hitting leadoff in Vince Coleman, a fine double-play combination in shortstop Ozzie Smith and second baseman Tommy Herr, a center fielder with speed and a great glove in Willie McGee, and a stellar pitching staff, led by stopper John Tudor. It's NL baseball at its finest—not many home runs, but a lot of excitement that keeps fans coming back for more. The Cardinals have drawn at least two million fans every year since 1982 and in 1987 topped the three million mark.

Baseball at Busch Stadium is more than exciting, it's the most colorful version around. "Cardinal red is the only game-day color allowed in St. Louis," wrote Bob Wood in *Dodger Dogs to Fenway Franks*. "Nowhere else in the majors do hometown folks feature such a loyal wardrobe. No other baseball color is so passionate."

Busch Stadium, built smack in the middle of downtown St. Louis, was among the first of the symmetrical, bowl-shaped, concrete-and-steel stadiums constructed in the 1960s and 1970s. Its rabid and faithful Cardinal fans give it an excitement few ballparks can match. In 1987 a massive seating-replacement effort was finished, and now every seat in Busch Stadium is Cardinal red.

Busch Stadium

300 Stadium Plaza and
7th Street
St. Louis, Missouri

Built 1966

St. Louis Cardinals, NL
1966-present

Seating Capacity
54,000

Style
Multipurpose, symmetrical
with artificial surface

Height of Outfield Fences
10 feet, 6 inches

Dugouts
Home: 1st base
Visitors: 3rd base

Bullpens
Foul Territory
Home: right field side
Visitors: left field side

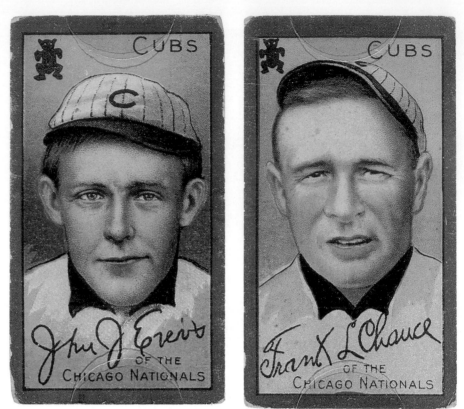

The Cubs' Tinker to Evers to Chance is baseball's most storied double play trio, but in fact they probably weren't the best of their era. Only shortstop Tinker ever led his position in double plays, and although all three were good fielders, during the eight years they were together, 1903 to 1910, the Cubs never led the NL in double plays.

genius. In the ultimate tribute to the ultimate manager, second baseman Larry Doyle marveled, "Oh, it's great to be young and a Giant."

In the 1890s Fred Pfeffer's *Scientific Ball* was a popular guide to the finer points of the game. Pfeffer advised managers to use signs, to position fielders where "percentages" dictated the batters would hit and to have players back each other up. The ultimate fielding maneuver was the double play; to ensure a maximum number of them, Pfeffer suggested using the most "scientific"—not to mention the most athletic—player at shortstop. The ideal second baseman of the period was a little fellow with nimble hands and feet, the first baseman a big clod with a long reach, the third baseman a "locomotive which is backing up and down a railroad track switching cars," the catcher a quarterback, the outfielders "scampering hares."

The analytical school of playing the field continued through the dead-ball era of hit-and-run baseball and thrived until the lively ball, swing-for-the-fences era started in 1920. The incomparable Red Sox outfield of 1910 to 1915—Duffy Lewis, Tris Speaker and Harry Hooper—was trendsetting. When the Red Sox moved to Fenway Park in 1912, Lewis was forced to climb a ten-foot incline in deep left field. He played it so well that it came to be known as Duffy's Cliff. "You had to take one look at the ball," Lewis wrote, "and go up if you had a chance to get it. You couldn't keep looking at the ball. If you did, down you went when you hit the bank."

Down went right fielder Hooper with his inventive "rump slide," a skidding catch of short flies that fielders still use today. Hooper also mastered a tough sunfield and learned positioning and throwing so well that he set an unofficial right fielders' record of 344 career assists.

They called Pittsburgh's Honus Wagner "the Flying Dutchman" for his great range and athletic ability. Wagner's career average of 2.4 putouts per game is second only among shortstops to Dave Bancroft's. Tommy Leach, a teammate of Wagner's for 13 years, called him "The greatest shortstop ever. The greatest everything ever."

But center fielder Speaker set fielding standards for all time. In his day, outfielders tended to bunch up toward the middle of the field, the right and left fielders playing deeper than the center fielder. Speaker may have played the shallowest center ever, and he turned a position-record four unassisted double plays by catching bloopers and running in to get runners off at second.

Speaker's thinking was that most hits fall in front of outfielders, so why not play shallow enough to steal some? Dead balls and high grass convinced him that balls wouldn't scoot through or over him, but his strategy continued to work when conditions changed. It's said that to make doubly sure he wouldn't allow balls to fall behind him, Speaker learned to retreat by fielding thousands of practice flies hit by pitcher Cy Young.

Almost half a century before Willie Mays' circus catch for the New York Giants in the 1954 World Series, Speaker had the back-to-the-plate technique down pat. "Speaker . . . had that terrific instinct," Boston pitcher Smoky Joe Wood recalled. "At the crack of the bat he'd be off with his back to the infield, and then he'd turn and glance over his shoulder at the last minute and catch the ball so easy it looked like there was nothing to it, nothing at all." From Speaker to later center fielders like Negro league star Cool Papa Bell and Baltimore's Paul Blair, shallow-playing center fielders have invariably been the best.

Playing outfield was tough in those days. There were no warning tracks to alert fielders that they were approaching a fence, and grassy pastures were full of bumps and ditches. Low grandstands and daytime baseball made the sun a constant headache. Yet Speaker, who retired after the 1928 season, still holds American League records for 7,244 chances and 6,794 putouts, and major league records with 450 assists and 135 double plays.

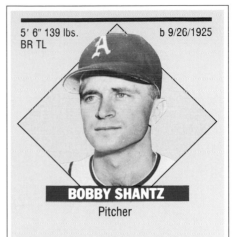

5' 6" 139 lbs.
BR TL

b 9/26/1925

BOBBY SHANTZ
Pitcher

Bobby Shantz won eight straight Gold Glove awards. He might have won more, but the award didn't exist until 1957, eight years after Shantz first flashed the agility and sure hands that made him the finest fielding pitcher of the postwar era. "I've been around this game for 50 years," Casey Stengel said, "and that boy is the best fielding pitcher I ever saw."

Shantz had to do all the little things right to coax success from limited gifts and to conserve his strength because, at 139 pounds, he was the smallest pitcher in the majors. But Shantz nearly missed his chance to debut. In April 1949 Philadelphia manager Connie Mack demoted Shantz to Buffalo, then reconsidered. As Shantz was driving to his new team, the Athletics asked the state police to send him back. Troopers spotted Shantz near Harrisburg and pursued him. Thinking he was about to receive a speeding ticket, Shantz slipped onto a back road to dodge the cops. It wasn't until reaching Buffalo that he discovered he was wanted by the Athletics.

The next day, Shantz was summoned to relieve in the fourth inning with none out. When reminded of a runner on third, the rookie brashly replied, "Let him stay there." Shantz then hurled nine hitless innings to secure the first of his career 119 wins.

In 1952 Shantz was voted the AL's MVP, winning a league-high 24 games, losing only seven, and leading the circuit with a .774 winning percentage.

With the Red Sox, Tris Speaker was the centerpiece—with Harry Hooper and Duffy Lewis—of a sterling outfield. In 1928, his last season, Speaker teamed with two other Hall of Famers—Ty Cobb and Al Simmons—for the Philadelphia Athletics.

Right field has hosted some great arms throughout baseball's history, but no 20th-century right fielder has thrown out more runners from right—322—than Harry Hooper. He had at least a dozen assists in each of his 17 major league seasons—12 of which came with the Red Sox, five with the White Sox.

nfielders faced an equally stiff challenge. Basepaths were poorly tended and the turf they played on was rough and uneven, and even the best shortstops made 50 to 70 errors a season. All infielders wore gloves after the turn of the century—pancake mitts with five unconnected fingers and no webbing. It was hard enough to get a glove on the ball, much less hold it, and one-handed stops were virtually out of the question. Yet Wagner averaged 5.8 chances a game in 1907 and 1908; Donie Bush, 6.7 in 1911; and Dave "Beauty" Bancroft, 7.1 in 1918. Plainly, fielders were making great strides in positioning and technique.

The best-known infield of all time may have been the double-play combination of the Chicago Cubs of 1903 to 1910: shortstop Joe Tinker, second baseman Johnny Evers and first baseman Frank Chance; the Cubs' third baseman for most of those years was Harry Steinfeldt. Sportswriter Hugh Fullerton called Evers "a bundle of nerves with the best brain in baseball." Evers is given credit for popularizing the cutoff on steal situations with men on first and third. Cutting behind the mound, he'd intercept the throw to second and prevent the runner on third from scoring. Tinker, Evers and Chance also invented the stratagem now used on sacrifice bunts. With the batter squaring around and a runner edging off first, Chance would rush the plate, Evers would cover first, and Tinker would head to second. The Chance-to-Tinker force on that play really made the threesome famous, even if Franklin P. Adams' famous poem lauded their double plays: "These are the saddest of possible words: 'Tinker to Evers to Chance.' "

Catchers were growing ever more sophisticated, too. In the 1880s and 1890s Connie Mack, playing for Washington and for Pittsburgh, distracted hitters by talking to them, tipping their bats, and clapping like the sound of bat

meeting ball. By 1900 all catchers crouched close behind the batter, and most were calling pitches. Nineteenth-century catchers had fought off the ball, trying to catch unpredictable pitches without killing themselves. Twentieth-century catchers, wearing masks, chest protectors and shin guards, confidently placed their mitts where they expected the pitch to arrive and moved into the infield when they had to. Ray Schalk, who caught for the White Sox from 1912 to 1928, was the first to come out of the crouch and back up first basemen on throws from other infielders.

Despite starting out his career as a catcher, the Brooklyn Dodgers' Gil Hodges became a great first baseman. He led the NL in fielding percentage five times and won the Gold Glove in each of its first three years, 1957 to 1959.

By the turn of the century, barehanded fielding was as dead as the ball itself. That slow-moving dead ball, of course, determined how the game was played—few long balls, an occasional home run, and lots of well-placed ground balls and looping flies. Hit-and-run baseball gave fielders plenty of action, and a man had to be quick on his feet and skilled with his hands to survive.

In a deliberate move to perk up the game, the major leagues experimented with a livelier cork-centered ball in 1910 and made it the regulation ball for the 1911 season. In 1920 the majors got the cushioned-cork-centered ball that has been standard ever since. A new kind of padded glove with a simple web between thumb and forefinger appeared in 1920, too. That year Babe Ruth hit 54 homers and the game's emphasis shifted, perhaps forever, from the battle between hitters and fielders to the battle between batter and pitcher. But if the ball was harder to field, the glove was easier to field it with.

In those days, before the designated hitter, a man had better be able to use that glove to stay in the lineup. In 1931 the Phillies brought up the greatest minor-league slugger in history, Buzz Arlett of the Oakland Oaks. Arlett

promptly hit .313, with 18 homers and 72 runs batted in. But the "mightiest Oak" couldn't catch a fly. Next season he was back terrorizing bush league pitchers.

In the 1930s major league fielding averages poked over .970. Glove improvements, along with a new breed of fielder, pulled averages higher still in the 1940s and 1950s. In 1947 Jackie Robinson broke the color barrier, opening up the largest untapped source of player talent in baseball history.

Major league teams began using Negro league stars, many of whom had sharpened their fielding skills on rough fields with poor or no lighting. They were naturals in well-tended big league parks. In 1950 another player pool—one particularly celebrated for fielding skills—was tapped when Venezuela's Chico Carrasquel made the White Sox roster and opened the door for flashy Hispanic shortstops. His countryman, Luis Aparicio, succeeded him in 1956 and dominated the position through the 1960s. Noting how Aparicio helped the White Sox and the Orioles win pennants, managers again turned to sharp fielding. "If you had to have one trait, it was not to carry your offensive shortcomings onto the field," says Cardinal shortstop Dal Maxvill, a .217 career hitter whose glove kept him in the majors for 14 seasons. "If we could hit, we'd be playing somewhere else."

These days fielders had better be able to hit, or they'll be playing nowhere else. With better gloves and more competitive glovemen, sure-bouncing artificial turf, and improved scouting and coaching techniques, today's fielders handle an incredible 98 out of every 100 chances without error. As a result, fielding is taken for granted. It's ironic. At the dawn of baseball, nearly 150 years ago, fielding was the game's most uneven and best-noted facet. Now it's the best practiced—and least appreciated. ◗

The Fifth Infielder

Ron Darling

Often it seems that pitchers wear gloves just so they won't look out of place on the diamond. But a pitcher who can use his glove can turn potential losses into wins. It's not that pitchers are expected to be acrobatic fielders, leaping off the mound to snare hot shots and turn them into game-ending double plays. For a pitcher, it's making routine, fundamental plays that really counts. Getting a good jump off the mound to cover first base on grounders hit to the first baseman or to pounce on sacrifice bunts, making quick, accurate throws, and backing up plays at third and home are the plays good fielding pitchers are made of.

Forgetting to cover first because you were so drained after throwing a wicked curve on a three-two count won't wash with any manager. As Baltimore's Dave Schmidt said, "As soon as you release the ball, you're a fielder." But the forward thrust required to throw a baseball 90 mph rarely allows a modern pitcher to finish his follow-through facing the hitter and in position to field a ball hit at him. "You show me a pitcher following through in good fielding position and I'll show you a pitcher who ain't following through," said St. Louis' Dizzy Dean, a pretty fair fielding pitcher.

Pitchers are often excellent athletes who can right themselves even after a violent follow-through. No one had a more violent follow-through than St. Louis' Bob Gibson, and some say there's never been a better fielding pitcher. Gibson's follow-through carried him almost completely off the mound and in the direction of the first-base line, but the former basketball and track star combined his athletic ability with matchless competitive fire to give the Cardinals a fifth infielder. In 1964 Gibson's leg was shattered by a line drive off the bat of San Francisco's Orlando Cepeda. Gibson was carried off the field and taken to the hospital, but not before he recovered the ball and threw Cepeda out.

A pitcher's bread-and-butter play is the three-one putout: a grounder to the first baseman, where the pitcher must beat the runner to the bag, catch the first baseman's throw on the run, and step on the bag for the out. Pitchers must break toward first as soon as they see the ball hit to the right side of the infield. "When a hitter beats a pitcher, nine times out of ten it's because the pitcher didn't get a jump," said Jim Kaat, winner of 16 Gold Gloves and master of the three-one play. According to Kaat, pitchers should run toward a

Covering home plate without shin guards and a chest protector is dangerous work, as San Diego pitcher Lance McCullers (left) found out when he took on the Mets' Darryl Strawberry. St. Louis' Bob Gibson (above) won nine straight Gold Gloves from 1965 to 1973.

spot 10 to 15 feet down the line from the bag, then turn and run straight up to the base so that when they catch the ball and touch the bag, they can avoid crossing into the runner's path.

Jim Coates' inability to make that basic play may have cost the Yankees the 1960 World Series. The Yankees led the Pirates, 7–5, in the eighth inning of Game 7, but Pittsburgh had runners on second and third with two outs and Roberto Clemente at bat. Coates had come in two outs earlier to replace Bobby Shantz, an outstanding fielding pitcher. Clemente hit a slow roller to first baseman Moose Skowron, but Coates was slow to cover and Clemente was safe. The next batter, Hal Smith, hit Coates for a three-run homer and the Pirates went on to win, 10–9.

The pitcher's other major fielding responsibility is on bunts. On drag bunts toward first, he is the key, for if the ball gets by him, it almost always goes for a hit. In sacrifice situations, his responsibility is to get off the mound as quickly as he can, get to the ball, listen to the catcher for advice on which base to throw to, and then make an accurate throw. It's especially important that pitchers set themselves before throwing, because they

He was known as "Fat Freddie" back in the 1930s, but Freddie Fitzsimmons was quick enough off the mound to cover baseline to baseline. With 79 double plays, he ranks third all time among pitchers.

aren't used to throwing in a hurry and can wind up making some of the worst throws on record.

While a pitcher's fielding responsibilities come mainly on fielding slow hits, his nightmares are filled with line drives back through the box. There's no way to prepare for a 150-mph shot straight at your throat. Former White Sox pitcher Bart Johnson put it this way: "We pitchers always get a kick out of third base being described as the hot corner. Hot corner? If the third baseman crept in 50 feet from home plate, people would say, 'He's nuts. He'll get a harelip.' We pitchers are 50 feet from home every time we follow through." The nightmare became reality for Cleveland fireballer Herb Score on May 7, 1957, when a line drive off the bat of New York's Gil McDougald smashed into Score's right eye, ending what might have been a brilliant career.

In baseball's early years, pitchers didn't have to worry much about the danger of line drives. They threw underhand and had lots of time to prepare before the ball was hit. And they were playing with a ball that wasn't as hard as today's ball, nor was it hit as hard before the 1920s, the era of the lively ball. The early pitchers were safer but much busier fielders. Infielders didn't come rushing to their aid on pop-ups. On the list of the top-ten single-season putout totals for pitchers, all but one came before 1900. It was Baltimore's Mike Boddicker, who had a freaky total of 49 putouts in 1984, good for fifth all time. And the major league record for most single-season assists by a pitcher was set by Ed Walsh of the White Sox in 1907.

When you look through the years for baseball's best fielding pitchers, the names are familiar because, for the most part, they're the best pitchers. They may also have chalked up a record-setting number of errors. "Sir Timothy" Keefe, an 1880s Hall of Famer with 344 career wins, holds the all-time season record with a whopping 63 errors in 1883. Fellow Hall of Famer Warren Spahn led NL pitchers in errors five times in the 1950s and 1960s, but he also led them in double plays five times.

The early 20th-century honor roll includes the great Walter Johnson, whose 103 chances without an error in 1913 is still an AL single-season record, and Grover Cleveland Alexander, who ranks eighth all time with a .985 lifetime fielding percentage. Freddie Fitzsimmons, whose physique earned him

Philadelphia Athletics manager Jimmy Dykes called 5' 6", 139-pound Bobby Shantz (opposite) "the best fielding pitcher who ever stepped out on the mound." San Francisco's Rick Reuschel (above) outweighs Shantz by almost 100 pounds, but is a two-time Gold Glove winner.

Jim Kaat (above) was an expert at covering first base. In Game 2 of the 1965 World Series, he set a Series record for pitchers with five putouts.

the nickname "Fat Freddie," was probably the best fielding pitcher around from 1925 to 1943. Fitzsimmons was a knuckleball specialist, and the knuckleball is baseball's slowest pitch, giving its practitioners time to prepare for batted balls coming their way.

Fine fielding pitchers of the 1940s and 1950s include Cleveland's Bob Lemon, who led AL pitchers eight times in total chances and six times in assists, and Bobby Shantz, who started pitching in 1949, eight years before the first Gold Gloves were awarded, and still managed to win eight of them. But the best fielding pitcher of the era may have been Claude Passeau, who pitched through all of World War II—or at least the United States' involvement in World War II—without making an error. Passeau's errorless streak began on September 21, 1941, and ended a major-league-record 273 chances later, on May 20, 1946.

Gibson and Kaat led the way in the 1960s and 1970s, and didn't let anyone else win a pitching Gold Glove from 1965 through 1973. Baltimore's Jim Palmer won four straight from 1976 to 1979, while San Diego sinkerballer Randy Jones induced hitters to beat the ball into the ground, then fielded

every one that came his way in 1976, as he set an NL single-season record with 112 chances without an error. Atlanta's Phil Niekro and the Yankees' Ron Guidry got Gold Gloves in the early 1980s, winning five each from 1978 through 1986. The 1980s produced another crop of good fielding pitchers, including the Dodgers' Fernando Valenzuela and Orel Hershiser, both Cy Young award winners as well as Gold Glovers; San Francisco's Rick Reuschel; Toronto's Dave Stieb; and Montreal's Mark Langston, who had the highest AL strikeout total three times in his first five years in the majors.

It's not likely that any pitcher will ever top Kaat's total of 16 Gold Gloves, but he's convinced his reputation as a fielder began with a ball he didn't catch. "There was a game in 1962 when I was hit in the mouth by a high-bouncing grounder," he said. "The play cost me six teeth. The next time I pitched, two ground balls were hit back to me—sharp one-hoppers—and I got them both. People took note."

Leather

"Baseball is fathers and sons playing catch, lazy and murderous, wild and controlled, the profound archaic song of birth, growth, age and death."

—Donald Hall

f all the technical changes that have affected the playing of baseball—the removal of most pitching restrictions in 1884, the cork-centered ball in 1910, the lively ball in 1920, the enclosed stadium, artificial turf, the designated hitter, adjustments to the mound and strike zone—the evolution of the glove may be the most significant. One hundred years ago, one of every two runs scored was unearned—a gift from the fielding team. Today only one of every ten is unearned. Oh, you'll hear about better surfaces and improved coaching and conditioning. Those are relatively minor factors. Artificial turf has added only a point or two to fielding percentages. Old-time teams may have lacked scouts, instructors and trainers, but they took fielding as seriously as the moderns do, maybe more so. No, that dramatic improvement in glove work comes overwhelmingly from the glove itself.

A trip through the Hall of Fame shows why. The first gloves you'll find in the downstairs trophy cases are crude, resembling work gloves or children's mittens—technically, gloves have separate fingers, mitts don't. They protected hands more than they caught balls. There are horsehide and calfskin gloves with single strands of lace between thumb and index finger, puffy catchers' mitts, pancake and three-fingered fielders' models. And finally, the lightweight cowhide and deerhide gloves of today: cavernous, comfy, elegantly laced creations variously described as *cestas,* fruit baskets and grocery carts.

Texas right fielder Ruben Sierra (opposite) is one of baseball's rising all-around stars. He uses a massive fielder's glove well, and then switches the ball to his real weapon—a throwing arm that tied for top honors with 17 assists in 1987.

OFF THE BAT

By the late 1870s catchers had moved to a perilous position directly behind the batter, but they had primitive protection in the form of gloves and masks. The catcher's permanent crouch—popularized by Buck Ewing—became standard by the 1890s.

Actually, gloves have been used in baseball from the beginning. There's some speculation, based on old correspondence, that gloves were used in the "Massachusetts Game," a forerunner of modern baseball. In 1869 a Cincinnati catcher, Doug Allison, supposedly had a saddle maker prepare him a mitt, and as early as 1872, advertisements recommended using gloves. In the first documented case of professional use, for an 1875 game in Boston—a year before the National League was founded—a St. Louis outfielder-first baseman, Charles C. Waitt, donned a pair of flesh-colored gloves with the fingers of the right hand cut out for throwing. Waitt was not an overnight sensation. Fans called him a sissy, opponents jeered, and historians are forever spelling his name "Waite."

Two years later, Albert G. Spalding switched from pitcher to first and adopted a black kid glove. Ever the entrepreneurs, he and his brother quickly began selling "Spalding's model" gloves at their sporting-goods store, advertising that "no catcher or player subject to sore hands should be without a pair of these gloves."

Nonetheless, the professional game remained substantially glove-less until the 1890s. The aristocrats who adapted baseball from rounders and cricket considered it "unmanly" to play with gloves, and the tough Irish and German immigrants who flooded the sport relished the bare-handed challenge.

In the 1880s the puff-pillow catcher's mitt appeared. There's debate as to whether Joe Gunson or Harry Decker invented it, but the New York Giants' Buck Ewing popularized it and improved it by adding padding and patches. In 1883 a Providence shortstop named Arthur Irwin was hit by a pitch that broke the third and fourth fingers on his left hand. To keep playing,

he had a shoemaker construct a padded glove in which the broken fingers were encased in a single sheath.

By 1900 most fielders used padded if extremely unsophisticated gloves. As a direct result, batting averages declined. According to the 1908 *Spalding Guide:* "It may be that no more .400 batters are likely to be born. It is almost certain that all batting will have its limitations, with the gloves now used by fielders and their speed. It is not true that unusual pitching has subordinated the batting so much as the thick glove has given the fielder the daring to undertake to stop or catch anything. By the thickness of its protection, a cushion is afforded which is far better than the cushion of the hand."

Other than their padding, however, early 20th-century gloves were only slightly better than older models. It was perfectly commonplace for a line drive to rip right through a glove's fingers or knock the glove off the fielder's hand. Bill Doak never enjoyed that sight. A Cardinal spitball pitcher, he felt his glove could be made more useful. Doak took some of the padding out, soaked the glove, folded over the thumb and fingers into a round mass, and wound rubber bands around it. A couple of days later he had what he wanted: a glove with a pocket.

In 1919 Doak sold Rawlings on his revolutionary idea. The Doak model introduced the following year resembled a cupped hand—a bare-bones glove with three laces for webbing and the smallest of pockets, created by building up the heel. The Doak model kept evolving and improving, yet served as a standard for many years.

"George Kelly showed me the first baseman's glove he used in his last season in the big leagues, 1932," an acquaintance named Tom Clark said in 1978. "A mere scrap of leather, it barely covered his large hand, had a sizable

By the 1890s umpires had joined catchers in wearing masks and chest protectors behind the plate. Catchers got shin guards in 1907, making headfirst slides into home ill advised.

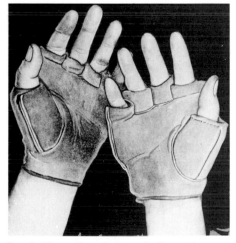

Baseball's earliest gloves—similar to those worn by gentlemen when driving buggies—did little to improve fielding. In 1875 outfielder Charles Waitt was the first player to wear a glove, but with Baltimore in 1882, he committed 22 errors in just 72 games. The team total was 490.

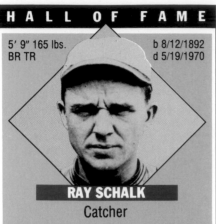

Ray Schalk seemed to be all over the infield. He was the first major league catcher to back up first base on infield ground balls, and he occasionally covered third base to make putouts. He even surprised a few runners by sneaking to second base to take throws from the outfield. He led the AL in putouts by a catcher for nine of his 17 years with the Chicago White Sox.

When Schalk reported to the White Sox in 1912, the team had to make a custom-fitted uniform for the 19-year-old, who at that time weighed only 155 pounds. But despite his youth and size, he quickly earned the respect of the Chicago pitchers. Eddie Cicotte, a dominant pitcher of the era, never pitched to another catcher after Schalk became a regular.

Schalk might have played for one of the biggest dynasties in the history of the game, but through no fault of his own, he wound up playing mostly for second-division teams. The White Sox won the 1917 World Series and returned in 1919. Schalk was one of the first to suspect that his teammates weren't giving an all-out effort in the 1919 Series. The scandal unfolded the next season, and the eight conspirators were permanently suspended, destroying the nucleus of the White Sox.

Schalk played until 1928 and managed in the minor leagues for several years, but he always refused to discuss the Black Sox scandal. He was elected to the Hall of Fame in 1955.

"Spittin' Bill" Doak threw his last major league pitch in 1929, but the glove he wore and helped design (right)—with its preformed, prelubricated pocket and reinforced webbing—stayed in production and earned Doak royalties until shortly before his death in 1954.

hole in its meager pocket and could not have weighed more than two or three ounces."

The stiff leather gloves used by old-time players had to be laboriously broken in and were used for years. You'd see guys sitting on the bench before a game, throwing ball after ball into the glove to form a pocket and get the right feel. When the game ended, they'd put their gloves in their back pockets. The typical player used three gloves. There was the "gamer" for competition, a practice glove, and another in reserve. Gloves were valuable equipment; in fact, the players had to pay for them. Nowadays players are flooded with a dozen or so free gloves from the companies they're contracted to. They're scattered around lockers like clothes in a teenager's room.

In the 1934 World Series, Detroit's Hank Greenberg unveiled a first-baseman's mitt with fish-net webbing that rose three inches above the fingers. "I was responsible for revolutionizing the shape of the glove," Greenberg states. The mitt was banned in 1939, but manufacturers soon introduced legal mitts and gloves with large webbings. After World War II, "Trapper" and "Snapper," first-baseman's gloves with elongated web panels, became the norm.

Alas, catchers struggled on. Working with a deeper pillow-style model that still forced them to catch pitches in the palm, receivers stuffed everything from metal to meat between their mitts and their palms. "Some guys used falsies," says Joe Garagiola. "After a tag play at home Walker Cooper's fell out and landed square on the plate. The next day he got at least 100 falsies in the mail." In the late 1940s Yogi Berra and Gus Niarhos played behind the plate for the Yankees. Niarhos caught just 142 games in three seasons with

New York, while Berra—who played 19 years for the Yanks—became a Hall of Famer, but they had one thing in common: they placed their index fingers outside the mitt. Berra is credited with introducing the new technique. It was typical of Yogi: a simple act born of a sophisticated baseball mind. Today most players keep the finger out, and some gloves have a finger loop on the back to accommodate it. "Keeping the index finger out creates an air pocket," says Bill Mazeroski. "When the ball hits the glove, it's cushioned."

In the 1980s Japanese manufacturers brought vibrant color and foreign competition to the U.S. baseball glove market as companies like Mizuno challenged stalwarts like Rawlings. Cardinal shortstop Ozzie Smith (above) says glove size "doesn't matter, as long as it's comfortable."

In 1960 Baltimore manager Paul Richards found that his receivers couldn't handle Hoyt Wilhelm's dancing knuckleball. Richards developed a huge mitt, 45 inches in circumference, the first with a hinged pocket. Opponents howled, and the rules committee reduced the mitt to 38 inches in 1965, but the stage was set for the Hundley-Bench model. Popularized by the Cubs' Randy Hundley and the Reds' Johnny Bench, the trimmed-down glove has a long pocket and a central hinge that makes the glove close upon impact. "Hundley had caught 160 games in 1968, and I asked him how he did it," says Bench. "He told me that the only way to last that long was to get your bare hand out of the way by using the hinged mitt." Changing gloves, Bench further modernized the position by catching one-handed like a squatting first baseman.

The fielder's best friend of all was the late Harry "Bud" Latina, Rawlings' chief glove designer for four decades. Baseball's legendary "Glove Doctor," Latina designed styles with deeper pockets, wonders of webbing, tight fit, and quick-closing action. Above all, Latina understood the ballplayer. When Achilles tendon problems slowed down Joe DiMaggio, Latina told him, "You've lost only a half-step, Joe, and I'll give it back to you."

Tools of the Trade

1883

1884

lthough gloves haven't been around as long as bats or balls, their evolution has been the most dramatic of the three. Two-bit workmen's gloves with cutout fingers in the 1880s, 100 years later they're $100 apiece and big enough to catch footballs. In between they've been padded, pocketed, webbed and widened, with innovative features from Bill Doak's landmark preformed pocket in 1919 to Rawlings' recent Spin-Stopper, said to reduce ball spin when the ball hits the glove.

1921

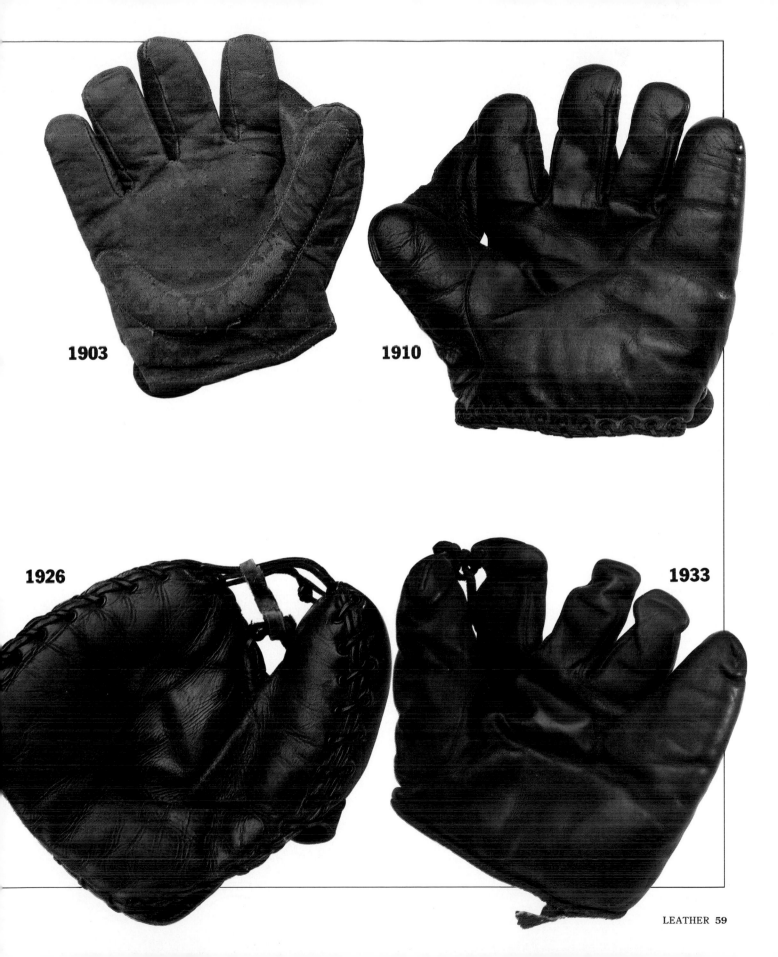

1903

1910

1926

1933

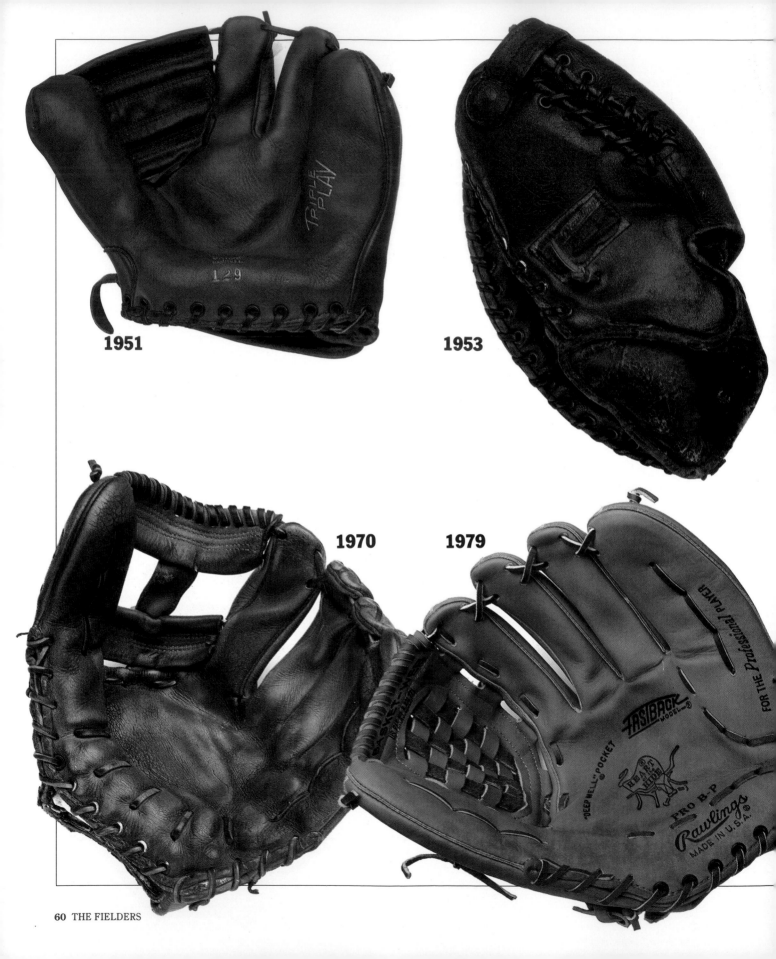

1951

1953

1970

1979

1960

1989

The drastic changes in the size and efficiency of gloves have made for some lively debate over the years. For example, what kind of miracles could Pie Traynor have worked in the 1920s if he'd had the advantage of the glove Brooks Robinson used in 1970. Or how brilliant would Ozzie Smith look shagging gounders with Honus Wagner's glove? The debate rages on.

Imagine having to catch Walter Johnson's fastball in a mitt with no webbing, or handling a hot smash with a glove barely bigger—and with less padding—than your own hand. Ah, progress.

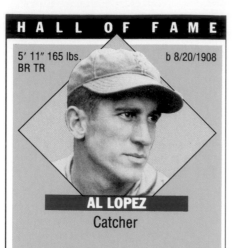

5' 11" 165 lbs. b 8/20/1908
BR TR

AL LOPEZ
Catcher

In 1925 an off-season team of major leaguers led by Walter Johnson barnstormed through Tampa, Florida. To boost attendance, they selected a local teenager to catch the "Big Train." They chose 16-year-old Alfonso Lopez. After the game, the strikeout artist told the kid, "Son, some day you're going to be a great catcher."

Three years later, when Al Lopez arrived in the Brooklyn Dodgers' locker room, manager Wilbert Robinson said: "They're sending me midgets. He ain't never gonna make a catcher. He's too small and skinny."

Walter Johnson proved to know more about catchers than Wilbert Robinson. Lopez caught for 19 major league seasons and set a record for games caught that wasn't broken until 1987—1,918 games for the Dodgers, Pittsburgh Pirates, Boston Braves and Cleveland Indians. He shared the NL record for having caught 100 games or more for 12 seasons until Cincinnati's Johnny Bench broke it in 1980. In 1941 he caught 114 games for the Pirates and didn't allow a passed ball.

In 1951, three years after his retirement as a player, Lopez started a 17-year career as one of the most respected and successful managers in the AL. He was the only manager to break the Yankees' streak of pennants from 1949 to 1964, leading the Cleveland Indians and the Chicago White Sox to the World Series in 1954 and 1959, respectively.

Whichever mitt Keith Hernandez puts his hand inside becomes the best first-baseman's mitt in baseball. One of the game's finest all-around players in the 1970s and 1980s, he says, "Defense is easy for me, but hitting is difficult."

DiMaggio switched to a newer, larger glove, whose increased reach gave him, in effect, another half step. "My father was a hard worker, had a knack for gloves, and loved baseball," says his son and successor, Rollie "Glove Man" Latina. "That was all it took."

In 1971 the younger Latina developed the latest major glove patent—the Fastback model, whose snug fit allows the fielder to push the glove away from his fingers while still gripping it tightly—in effect lengthening the glove while strengthening the hand.

Today, gloves personify glovemen. The pitcher's glove tends to be large enough to hide knuckleball and split-finger grips, baseballs, thumbtacks, Vaseline, sandpaper and pine tar. It's less a glove than a magician's bag. The catcher's mitt is oval, deep and well pocketed. It catches.

The first-baseman's mitt, which resembles a catcher's mitt but is slightly less padded, fairly cries out "stretch" to the big guy who wears it. Uniquely constructed, it grabs errant throws that hit anywhere on its surface, not just in the pocket or web. Walt Dropo, the Joe Palooka of the position in the 1950s, explains: "There are no errant fly balls."

Infielders' gloves are made with the fingers curving in toward the pocket. The second-baseman's glove is baseball's smallest, a cutie for the little fellow with nimble hands and feet who has to unload fast in the pivot. Joe "Little Red" Morgan used a second-baseman's glove so small it fit into a typical infielder's glove. "I got the idea from Nellie Fox," says Morgan, who needed to unload especially fast because of his average arm. "With a small glove, you know where the ball is all the time. The glove is the pocket."

The shortstop's glove is deeper, longer and stronger than his double-play partner's but not too padded—a versatile glove for the most versatile

The Cubs' Shawon Dunston is a spectacular, if erratic, shortstop with a tremendous throwing arm. In 1986 Dunston led NL shortstops— including Ozzie Smith— in putouts, assists and errors.

fielder. The third-baseman's glove has extra padding and solid webbing—a leather shield for the hot corner. Fingers bend out from the outfielder's big glove, and the pocket extends diagonally from heel to webbing.

A fielder's glove can measure a maximum of 12 inches in length and 7¾ inches across the palm, with webbing up to 4½ inches across the top and 5¾ inches deep. First-basemen's and catchers' mitts are slightly larger. These guidelines aren't well enforced, and the penalty for an over-sized glove is expulsion of the glove, not the player using it or the great catch he just made.

Outfielder Willie Mays got away with using an extra-long glove late in his career with the Giants. The White Sox' Carlton Fisk was suspected of using an extra-wide mitt to frame LaMarr Hoyt's outside pitches when Hoyt won the Cy Young award in 1983. Outfielders routinely wear 13-inch models. "The biggest glove I've ever seen is the one Luis Polonia used in Oakland," says Jim Lefebvre. "It was so big he could use it for a shopping basket."

Players constantly tinker with their gloves. Patching and padding—or unpadding—them are only part of the process. "When I was in the field, I wore a batting glove on my left hand and put adhesive tape on the little finger and thumb," says former American League infielder Greg Pryor. "There are finger loops in the fielder's glove where you slip in your little finger and thumb, so the tape gave me a snug fit. The glove felt like an extension of my hand rather than a foreign object. It didn't slip. That can be the difference between a ball getting away from you and an out."

St. Louis shortstop Ozzie Smith is not only the best gloveman in the game today but, almost unique among modern ballplayers, Smith has a sense of history. In fact, the "Wiz" displays a collection of old gloves at his St. Louis

Hank Greenberg's attempts to add length to the webbing of his mitt brought the disfavor of both Commissioner Kenesaw Mountain Landis and the Rules Committee. Greenberg's extended mitt was outlawed in 1939, and first-basemen's mitts were limited to 12 inches from top to bottom.

At 6' 4" and 200 pounds, Baltimore's Cal Ripken, Jr., is baseball's biggest shortstop, and as a result far from its quickest. But he compensates with outstanding anticipation and a great arm. The result has been four AL assists titles in his first seven years, including an AL-record 583 assists in 1984.

restaurant. "You had to be talented to use these gloves," says Smith. "They make you appreciate old ballplayers."

Smith is something of an old-fashioned gloveman himself. He uses the Trapp-Eze so-called six-finger model that Rawlings introduced in 1959, temporarily discontinued, and currently manufactures for about 50 major leaguers. With its small, tight webbing and stubby fingers bent in like the hand of an arthritis victim, the glove is constructed to catch the ball in the palm, the way fielders used to. "I like the feel," says Smith. "You don't get it in the web."

A palm-oriented glove virtually mandates a return to two-handed fielding, at least on routine plays. Despite his reputation for those diving and scooping one-handed stops he calls on in a pinch, Smith still makes most plays using two hands. "I always try to corral the ball and stay in front of it," he says. "Two hands are better than one."

Actually, the most significant change in fielding technique at all positions is the one-handed catch—and it's almost exclusively a creation of the catch-all glove. Early players had to field with two hands, the ball landing painfully in the palm of the glove hand. Moderns can catch one-handed, scarcely feeling the ball as it thuds into a monster web large enough to hold two baseballs. The one-handed catch used to be reserved for daredevils. A right-handed first baseman for seven teams from 1954 to 1965, Vic Power deliberately one-handed grounders to his right with men on base to line himself up for the throw to second. Another first baseman, Willie Montanez, who bounced around both leagues through the 1970s and 1980s, slapped at pop-ups like a butterfly chaser.

Explaining the demise of the .400 hitter, Ted Williams put it bluntly: the slider and the improved glove. "The deeper pockets have made it possible to catch everything you can get to," says Seattle third baseman Jim Presley. "There are more throwing errors now than actual fielding errors."

One-handed fielding is common practice now: you won't hear "hot dog" echo around the stadium unless Oakland's Rickey Henderson is "snatching" a fly with his deft, scythe-like motion. Almost every outfielder one-hands flies, and most infielders one-hand a good share of grounders. Even the most weathered fielding coaches admit wearily that a lot of tough chances can't be fielded any other way; players can reach farther using one hand than using two. Montreal infield coach Ron Hansen even recommends fielding many a routine grounder that way. "I prefer a one-handed style for middle infielders because you're usually moving to the ball," he says. "When you field one-handed moving in, you can switch the ball to your throwing hand as you're turning your body. The two-handed style fouls up your co-ordination. And one-handed, you can catch the ball in front of you, where you can see it. Two-handers tend to field the ball close to the body and lose sight of it."

Although some second basemen and pitchers have adopted smaller gloves, the big-glove, one-handed fielding style is plainly here to stay. Artificial turf makes one-handed fielding especially feasible. A player can get away with rushing slow rollers and one-handing them because on artificial turf, baseballs bounce uniformly. Toronto coach Mike Squires, a handy lefty who played every position but short and second, says that players have no choice but to one-hand many of the harder shots off the rug. "Take the line drive one-hopper on wet turf. There's no time to get two hands down. All you can do is protect yourself by sticking one hand down." Today's leather, he adds,

Great speed and a huge glove enable San Diego right fielder Tony Gwynn to catch just about everything that comes his way. A two-time Gold Glove winner, Gwynn led NL outfielders in putouts and total chances, and was second in assists in 1986. In August 1988 Gwynn earned a new challenge—center field.

Most catchers—like Boston's Rich Gedman (right)—in the post-Johnny Bench era have adopted Bench's one-handed catching method. Catching with one hand reduces injuries to the throwing hand but hardly makes catching a safe job. From 1982 through 1988, Gedman broke his right collarbone, left cheekbone and right foot, and also suffered injuries to his groin and left thumb.

Even with bigger gloves, proper communication between fielders is still essential in order to prevent situations like this one.

is more than adequate to the task. But not everyone likes modern gloves. "They're too big," says former outfielder Jimmy Piersall, now an instructor in the Cub system. "Players' hands aren't big enough to control them. They have a tough time opening them after a long run. When they charge a ground ball, it hits the heel of the glove or they can't get it out of the pocket." Cardinal coach Red Schoendienst worries about outfielders double-clutching as they try to dislodge a ball. "That's the difference between safe and out," he says.

"Gloves are too padded," says Mazeroski. "The ball hits and bounces out. I used to take the padding out of the heel. You want to catch the ball where you can feel it. I caught the ball on the last two fingers, with my bare hand beside the glove to widen it six inches or so. Then I'd roll the hand over on top of the ball and throw it." Maz got rid of the ball so fast he was known as "No Touch."

"The ball rolls around in the glove, and you can't turn the double play," says Tony Kubek, broadcaster and former Yankee shortstop. "Players also fall into what I call the 'artificial-surface habit' with their big gloves. They get used to taking balls off-balance because they bounce true on the rug. They switch to dirt, balls scoot on them, and they aren't in position. Guys going from turf to dirt look awful."

Kubek appreciates sensational stops as much as the next fellow, but he says one-handed fielding is getting out of hand. He sees many players stick out a casual glove, neglecting to get into position or watch the bouncing ball. "I blame the agents," says Kubek. "They're trying to protect their clients' stats, so they have them one-handing balls to avoid getting charged with an error."

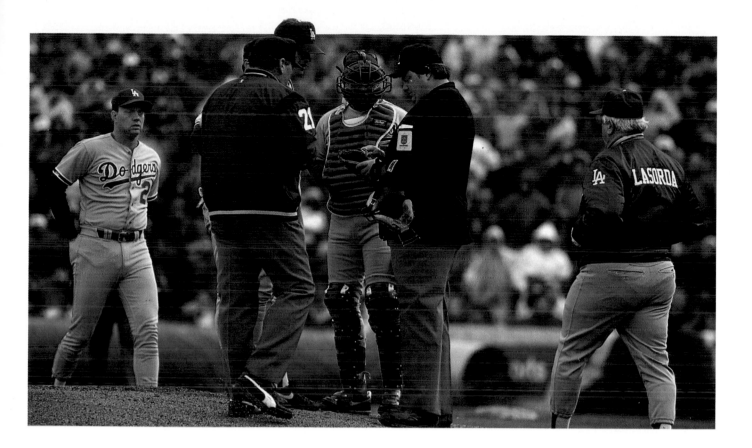

Even the hinged catcher's mitt has its critics. "It's a double-edged sword," insists Joe Garagiola, the Cardinal catcher in the 1946 World Series. "When the ball hits the hinge, it stays in the glove. That much is great. Catchers have never been better at framing, a technique to coax a strike call by keeping part of the glove in the strike zone while catching a pitch outside it. In the old days we caught a low pitch with the glove coming up. Now a Bob Boone can catch it with the glove going down. All the ump sees is the back of his hand, and it's in the strike zone. Boone can maneuver that glove so well the pitcher never looks wild.

"But there are problems, too. We were taught to always be in front of the ball. Nowadays catchers are reaching out for the pitch. Shifting has become obsolete, and they're missing a lot of pitches in the dirt. By catching everything one-handed, they also have to make an extra movement in getting the ball to their throwing hand. They don't have time to grip it with all four seams the way they're supposed to. I also don't like the one-handed tag Bench brought in. You should tag a runner with your glove and keep the ball in your bare hand about six inches back. I kid Johnny about how he ruined a lot of catchers by making everything look so easy."

"I might have created some laziness," says Bench, "but I also created a more mobile catcher. I didn't move much because I had a bad back. A good catcher will move as much as he has to. With the round mitt, the best a catcher could hope to do was knock down an outside pitch in the dirt. Using the hinged mitt, we could get it. Same with tags. The one-handed sweep is like the play a shortstop makes on a sliding runner. He needs the whole arm extension. If he made a two-handed tag, he'd lose three or four feet. In the 1987 Series Tony Pena tried to make a two-handed tag at the plate and missed."

A glove belonging to Dodger reliever Jay Howell became national news when Howell was ejected from Game 3 of the 1988 NL Championship Series for having pine tar on his glove. Howell explained to umpires Joe West (holding glove) and Harry Wendelstedt that he was only using the sticky substance to get a better grip on the ball in the wet conditions, but to no avail. Dodger manager Tommy Lasorda, third baseman Tracy Woodson (far left) and catcher Mike Scioscia were helpless spectators. Howell was suspended by Commissioner Bart Giamatti for two games.

Jim Hegan

Ask many an old-timer to name his favorite catcher, and he'll have a ready answer for you. He won't say Hall of Famers Bill Dickey, Mickey Cochrane, Yogi Berra or Johnny Bench. He'll say Jim Hegan. Unlike those other great catchers, Hegan hasn't made the Hall of Fame; his lifetime .228 batting average makes his induction to Cooperstown unlikely. But a catcher is primarily a fielder, and Hegan may have worked the plate better than anyone else.

He certainly had the physical tools. At 6' 2" and 195 pounds, Hegan was fast for a catcher and durable enough to work 105 or more games for ten years in a row as the Cleveland mainstay in the 1940s and 1950s. "I don't know if I've ever seen a better mechanical catcher," said Oriole scout Birdie Tebbetts, who was Hegan's backup in 1951 and 1952. "He caught everything they threw at him, had a great arm, and never missed a foul pop. He was a superior athlete who had been a high school football star and didn't have an ounce of flab on him."

Hegan grew up in Massachusetts idolizing fellow Bay Stater Cochrane and decided to be a catcher by the time he was 11. He started in 1938 with a Springfield, Massachusetts, team and made the grade with Cleveland in 1941. After 1942 Hegan was off for military service, returning to the Indians in 1946.

Unlike many of his peers, Hegan never settled into a predictable pattern of pitch selection. He called for hard-to-handle pitches—Bob Lemon's sinker and slider, Early Wynn's knuckler— with men on base. If a pitcher wanted to change his mind in the middle of a windup, no problem; Hegan could adjust. Batters became so frustrated guessing his pattern that they'd stalk back to the dugout after a strikeout cursing Hegan instead of the pitcher. The last time the Indians won the world championship—in 1948—manager Lou Boudreau paid the ultimate compliment to the ultimate backstop: "As much or more than any man, he was responsible for what we did." Quiet and abstemious, Hegan was not one to take credit for his team's performance. "The important thing is whether you get a good fast ball or a good curve. It's the pitcher's game; the catcher doesn't deserve either as much credit or as much blame as he usually gets for a pitcher's performance," he said.

But he could be much more expansive when talking strategy. Coaching for the Yankees in 1973, Hegan threw pitches in the dirt to young catcher Gerry Moses and told *New York Times* columnist Red Smith: "He wants to block a wild pitch and keep the ball in front of him. If his body is turned at an angle or if the mitt is, the ball can glance away and let runners advance. We don't want him to catch the wild pitch, just block it. He wants to be square on his knees with the mitt square between the knees and the meathand behind the mitt.

"Little things. You'd be surprised how many catchers don't know them. Like I ask them, on the double play that goes to the plate and then first base, what foot steps on the plate? The left foot does, and as you throw your stride takes you toward first so the man sliding home doesn't hit you."

Hegan finished his 17-season playing career in 1960 with the Chicago Cubs. He died in 1984 at 63. Bill Dickey summed up his career, "When you can catch like Hegan, you don't have to be able to hit."

Whether calling pitches, throwing out baserunners, handling pitchers, or blocking the plate as below against Boston's Hoot Evers, Jim Hegan set the defensive standard for all catchers who followed. Hegan retired in 1960, four years before his son Mike began his major league career with the Yankees—as a first baseman.

JIM HEGAN

Catcher
Cleveland Indians 1941–1942,
 1946–1957
Detroit Tigers 1958
Philadelphia Phillies 1958–1959
San Francisco Giants 1959
Chicago Cubs 1960

GAMES	**1,666**
FIELDING PERCENTAGE	
Career	.990
Season High	.997
PUTOUTS	
Career	7,506
Season High	661
PUTOUTS PER GAME	
Career	4.61
Season High	5.49
ASSISTS	
Career	703
Season High	76
ASSISTS PER GAME	
Career	.42
Season High	.54
CHANCES	
Career	8,300
Season High	729
CHANCES PER GAME	
Career	4.98
Season High	5.62
ERRORS PER GAME	
Career	.05
Season Low	.02
WORLD SERIES	**1948, 1954**

THE DURABLE DOZEN

Catching is baseball's answer to trench warfare. Foul tips, curves in the dirt, runners charging home plate, and squatting and rising more than 100 times each game are just a few of a catcher's normal hardships. But a few hardy souls have stuck it out behind the plate for long, successful careers, and new advances in physical conditioning have given baseball a new phenomenon—the 40-year-old catcher. Three of the top four catchers in games played were still active at the start of the 1989 season. Below are the top 12 in games played through 1988.

Player	Years Played	Games Played	Fielding Percentage
Bob Boone	1972–	2,056	.987
Al Lopez	1928–1947	1,918	.985
Jim Sundberg	1974–	1,854	.993
Carlton Fisk	1969–	1,838	.986
Rick Ferrell	1929–1947	1,806	.984
Gabby Hartnett	1922–1941	1,793	.984
Gary Carter	1974–	1,776	.991
Ted Simmons	1968–1988	1,772	.987
Johnny Bench	1967–1983	1,744	.990
Ray Schalk	1912–1929	1,726	.981
Bill Dickey	1928–1946	1,712	.988
Yogi Berra	1946–1965	1,696	.989

Brady Anderson was just one of a handful of speedy young outfielders that opened the 1989 season with the Orioles. In 1986 Anderson led the Class A Florida State League with a .997 fielding percentage and stole 44 bases.

The fact is there's no accepted orthodoxy on gloves or glove work, except maybe keeping your eye on the ball. White Sox scout Eddie Brinkman, a world-class shortstop in the 1960s and an outstanding infield coach in the 1980s, says players should get the largest modern gloves they can handle. On the other hand, a third baseman of recent vintage named Brooks Robinson used a smaller-than-average glove held together by adhesive tape, patches, and a tongue depressor to keep the thumb straight.

For every lackadaisical practice nurtured by the contemporary glove, there's a lalapalooza of a fielding play you rarely saw in the old days: an ice-cream-cone catch over the wall, a diving stop in short center, a behind-the-back grab on the mound. And the routine plays have never been so routine: 98 percent success ain't exactly butterfingers.

Like all lovers, players and their gloves have occasional spats. Wes Ferrell, a Red Sox pitcher in the 1930s, blamed a wild streak on his new glove. When manager Joe Cronin removed him from a game, Ferrell walked to the dugout yelling, "It's your fault!" at his glove. By the time he reached the bench, Ferrell had shredded the thing and left it for dead. Ted Williams responded to being picked off at second by kicking his glove until he reached his position in left field. Some players treat their gloves like dogs. "The old infielder Buddy Peterson used to put a rope around his glove and drag it around," says Milwaukee manager Tom Trebelhorn. "If he had a bad day, he'd tie it up and make it sit in front of his locker all night. The next day he'd go out to shortstop and talk to his glove: 'Behave today, damn it!' "

But mostly there's tender loving care. Players can break in their gloves as painstakingly as musicians tuning violins. Some performers just spit into

During the 1980s, when Velcro first appeared on baseball gloves, Baltimore pitcher Mike Boddicker decided to give a glove with a Velcro strap a try. In 1984 Boddicker's entire glove seemed made of Velcro, as he set an AL record with 49 putouts.

Mickey Mantle's glove almost always took a back seat to his bat, but one of Mantle's last great feats was in the field. In 1966, his final year as an outfielder, the 34-year-old Mantle played 97 games and handled 174 chances without an error.

their gloves or play them into shape. Others use baby oil, saddle soap or shaving cream; they say the lanolin in shaving cream makes the glove soft and pliable. "That keeps it moist but doesn't make it heavy," says San Francisco second baseman Robby Thompson.

"I was talking with Ed Brinkman before a game," said Kubek. "He was the kind of shortstop you listen to—a guy who set a major-league record with 7 errors in a season, and an American League record of 72 consecutive errorless games. Eddie was sitting on the bench with a styrofoam coffee cup in one hand and the glove in the other. Suddenly he started pouring coffee in his glove! 'This is the way I've always broken in my gloves: coffee, cream, a little sugar.' "

A few glove artisans are so respected they break in other players' gloves. Coach Bill Fahey soaks gloves in water and shaving cream for a week, watching over them daily. "That's the only reason he's coaching in the big leagues," says Bob Brenly. Willie Stargell, not content merely to be a Hall of Fame slugger and father confessor to the Pirates, was a glove masseur par excellence. "He would put the gloves in water, take them out, put two or three balls in the pocket, tie them with string, and let them dry for two days," says former teammate Bob Skinner. "After that he'd rub them with oil or shaving cream, then take them out to the bench and pound the leather with a bat. That would soften the leather and form it."

Most ballplayers left their gloves on the field when batting until 1954, when the rule changed. "Members of the offensive team shall carry all gloves and other equipment off the field and to the dugout while their team is at bat. No equipment shall be left lying on the field, either in fair or foul territory."

Right fielder Mel Ott never played a day in the minor leagues, or with any other major league team than the New York Giants. For more than two decades, he stopped baserunners in their tracks with the threat of his lightning-bolt throws, yet still averaged a remarkable 17 assists per 154-game season in his career.

Yankee great Joe DiMaggio was known for his long, graceful strides into the power alleys of Yankee Stadium, but he claimed he wasn't born a great outfielder. "I may have made a lot of catches look easy, but I worked very hard at becoming a solid center fielder," DiMaggio said.

"We always thought that throwing the glove was neat," says former outfielder Irv Noren. "We'd try to hit a certain spot, like delivering newspapers." Infielders were even more theatrical. Many an inning would end with a shortstop making a spectacular stop and throw, then delighting the crowd by chucking his glove over his shoulder—an early version of the celebratory spike or high five.

Base hits rarely bounced off discarded gloves, but there were some notable exceptions, one of which figured in a pennant race. On September 28, 1905, the Philadelphia Athletics and the Chicago White Sox played with first place at stake. The score was tied 2–2 in the seventh, with Athletics left fielder Topsy Hartsell on second, when Harry Davis slapped a liner to the left side. The ball hit the glove Hartsell had left in shallow left and the contact slowed the ball down. Hartsell scored ahead of Nixey Callahan's strong throw to give the Athletics a 3–2 victory. Philadelphia took two games out of three and won the AL pennant by two games over the White Sox.

There was a pattern to the tossed glove: the pitcher would drop his near the dugout, the catcher would take his mitt to the bench, the first and third basemen would place their gloves in foul territory near their bases, and the outfielders and middle infielders would throw theirs on the outfield grass.

Finding opponents' gloves, fielders couldn't resist the urge to play practical jokes. Some gloves would wind up under bases or stuffed with dirt. Red Sox shortstop Johnny Pesky, who enjoyed playing hearts, found the queen of spades in his glove. The skittish Yankee Phil Rizzuto would trot out to his glove and find everything from dead sparrows to dead rats in it.

The Giants' Bill Terry covered a lot of ground around first base. He led NL first basemen five times in assists and in 1930 set an NL record with at least one assist in 14 consecutive games.

You can borrow a ballplayer's bat, but don't ever touch his glove. "You go sticking your hands in a ballplayer's mitt and he breaks your jaw for you," promoter Julie Isaacson told magazine writer George Plimpton when he was preparing to pitch to big league all-stars. "He thinks maybe you'll throw him in a slump."

A player on an errorless streak will wear the same glove day after day, ignoring the holes or patching them with fresh strips of leather. Some slumping players will discard even a brand-new glove. "When Zoilo Versalles made an error, he would blame the glove and throw it away," says Seattle manager Jim Lefebvre, then a teammate of the star shortstop. "After awhile he went through so many gloves that he had to go to the store to get one even though he was under contract to the company. He went to a local department store and got one off the shelf. When the glove made the error, he got rid of it."

From 1956 to 1970 the two greatest glovemen in the history of their positions—second baseman Mazeroski and right fielder Roberto Clemente—started together for the Pirates. But what different gloves they used. "Clemente broke in a new glove every year," says Mazeroski. "It was just a habit he got into. I only used three or four in my career. My feeling was, 'This 'un's all right, I don't need a new one.' Once he tried to give my glove away. It was sitting in the dugout. It used to come apart a lot, and it had leather patches all over it. Clemente picked it up and threw it to a kid in the stands. The kid took one look at it and threw it back." ⚾

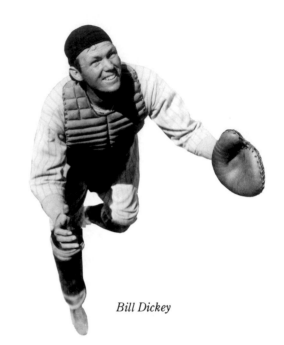

Bill Dickey

Backstops

The catcher is baseball's grunt, its foot soldier, the guy who does the work no one else wants to do. He is at once the game's most protected and abused player, wearing a suit of armor that can't possibly shelter him from a daily dose of assault and battery. If a foul tip isn't conking him on the mask, or worse yet, attacking his Adam's apple, then he's playing human bowling pin for an onrushing baserunner who wants a part of the plate the catcher is obligated to block. And in the unlikely event that he goes an entire game without being battered by balls or ballplayers, he still has to do 100 to 150 deep knee bends while wearing metal shackles from ankle to thigh.

Considering all the abuse they take in the field, catchers should be allowed to rest when their team is at bat. But throughout baseball history, catchers have been expected to be among the most potent hitters in the lineup. Greats like Mickey Cochrane, Bill Dickey, Josh Gibson, Yogi Berra and Johnny Bench could beat you from behind *and* beside the plate. But with million-dollar salaries sapping baseball's blue-collar image, fewer and fewer prospective stars want to don what Washington Senator Muddy Ruel once called the "tools of

ignorance" and set up shop behind home plate. Those who do can make it to the majors in a hurry. "I've said it for ten years: If you want to get to the big leagues, learn to catch," said Cal McLish, a scout for the Milwaukee Brewers.

The fact that 39-year-old Carlton Fisk and 40-year-old Bob Boone began the 1988 season as two of baseball's most sought after catchers attests to the shortage of talent at the position. And Detroit manager Sparky Anderson sees the pair as the last of their breed. "As soon as Fisk and Boone leave, it's over. You'll never see the great catchers again. There's too much money in this game to sit back there and take a beating."

Today, a catcher can get by without being much of a hitter if he's solid defensively, calls a good game, and is an adept handler of pitchers. The Dodgers' Rick Dempsey hits in the .230s, but his ability to get the most out of pitchers has kept him in the majors 20 years and counting. Texas' Jim Sundberg has never hit over .249 since becoming a major leaguer in 1974, but has six Gold Gloves and secured a $825,000 contract in 1987.

But if you're going to get by as a catcher on defensive skills, you've got to be tough, quick and

Mickey Cochrane (left) and Josh Gibson (above) are among the best all-around players the game has ever seen, and both had unusual speed for catchers. Walter Johnson said Gibson "catches so easy he might as well be in a rocking chair." Connie Mack didn't know "of any catcher who could out-run" Cochrane.

smart. First and foremost, you've got to do what the job title says—catch. Every single pitch. You've got to know the opposing hitters as well as you know your own pitchers, and then position your fielders accordingly. You've got to be able to get the ball from your glove to second base in about two seconds, and catch dizzying foul pops with a mitt designed for anything but catching dizzying foul pops. And you've got to have the concentration to field a one-hop bullet from 250 feet away while a 200-pound man barrels straight at you, and the strength not only to take his best shot, but to hold on to the ball as well.

Life behind the plate wasn't always so rough. Baseball's first catchers stood far behind home plate and caught the ball on the bounce until the 1870s, when a brave soul named Nat Hicks became the first to stand directly behind the batter. Hicks is also credited by some as being the first player to use a glove. In 1875 Fred W. Thayer adapted a fencing mask for the catcher's use. Hall of Famer Buck Ewing sentenced a century of catchers to chronic knee pain by going into a crouch in the 1880s, but the blow was softened by the appearance of padded chest protectors and mitts. In 1907

Only seven players in history have won three MVP awards, and two were catchers—the Yankees' Yogi Berra (above) and the Dodgers' Roy Campanella. Berra led AL catchers six times in double plays, including 25 in 1951.

Catchers are the last line of defense for their teams, and as a result sacrifice their bodies in order to stop runs from scoring. Detroit's Matt Nokes (above) took on Kansas City's George Brett and won, holding on to the ball as Brett tried to score from second on a single.

Roger Bresnahan, also a Hall of Fame catcher, completed the wardrobe with the invention of shin guards.

At 5′ 9″ and 200 pounds, the Giants' Bresnahan epitomized the durable, hard-nosed catcher with a rifle arm. He had startling speed for his size, stole 212 career bases and batted leadoff for manager John McGraw. But he was just one of the fine defensive catchers of the era. The Cubs' Johnny Kling led NL catchers in fielding percentage from 1902 through 1905, and threw out six Athletics' runners trying to steal in the 1910 World Series. Kling started a long tradition of excellent Cub catchers, and was followed by Jimmy Archer, who had an even better arm than Kling. In the AL, the Senators' Gabby Street became famous for catching a ball dropped from the top of the Washington Monument, then in 1909 set AL records with 210 assists, 18 double plays and 924 total chances.

Ray Schalk of the White Sox was the game's best defensive catcher for most of his career, which lasted from 1912 to 1929. By the time Schalk retired, three future Hall of Famers—Mickey Cochrane, Bill Dickey and Gabby Hartnett—had ushered in something of a golden age for catchers.

All great hitters, they played in 17 World Series between them. Both Cochrane and Dickey were smooth, stylish catchers and true team leaders. Cochrane set a major league record with a .993 fielding percentage in 1930, only to have it broken the following year by Dickey's .996 in a season that also saw Dickey go without committing a passed ball. Hartnett wasn't quite as pretty a catcher as the others, but he was every bit as sure-handed, and led the NL in fielding percentage a league-record seven times.

The 1940s and 1950s saw more emphasis placed on a catcher's defensive skills, and the era produced standouts like Cleveland's Jim Hegan, whose catching ability kept him in the majors 17 years despite a .228 lifetime average; Sherm Lollar, another great White Sox catcher, whose .992 career fielding percentage is the fourth best ever; and Buddy Rosar, who in 1946 became the first catcher ever to play an entire season of at least 100 games without committing an error, as he handled 605 chances flawlessly for the last-place Athletics. In 1957 Pete Daley of the Red Sox and Lou Berberet of the Senators matched Rosar's feat, and in 1958 the Yankees' Yogi Berra became the

Even Johnny Bench couldn't reach this wild throw which allowed the Cubs' Billy Williams to score. Cincinnati's Bench went the entire 1975 season—121 games—without allowing a passed ball.

Carlton Fisk has always been an unusually mobile catcher. As a rookie, in 1972, he led the AL in putouts, assists and chances. In 1985 he stole 17 bases.

last man to date to catch a perfect season—making no errors for a 1.000 fielding percentage.

Elston Howard followed Berra in the long line of great Yankee catchers, and ranks second all time in fielding percentage behind another power-hitting 1960s catcher, Detroit's Bill Freehan, a five-time Gold Glove winner. The Cubs' Randy Hundley was the best of the good field, no hit catchers, committed just four errors in 152 games in 1967, and in 1968 played in 160 games, still a major league record. Into the 1970s charged a group of aggressive and poised young catchers with power in their bats and arms, and among them was the man considered the best catcher in history, Johnny Bench of Cincinnati. Bench revolutionized the position. With him behind the plate no runner was safe, no matter where he was or how short his lead. Two of Bench's colleagues showed great promise but one found misfortune, the other tragedy. Cleveland's Ray Fosse was a 23-year-old phenom in 1970 when Cincinnati's Pete Rose flattened him in the All-Star Game, separating his shoulder to blunt what may have been a great career. Thurman Munson was the Yankees' team captain, and committed just one error in 125 games in 1971. Munson led New York

to three straight pennants from 1976 to 1978, but in August of 1979 he was killed in a plane crash.

Boone and Fisk began their careers in the early 1970s, but who will succeed them? A corps of young hopefuls like Milwaukee's B. J. Surhoff, San Diego's Benito Santiago and the Cubs' Damon Berryhill show promise, but the test of a great catcher is how well he's performing in his tenth season, not his first. They're just not making them like they used to. As usual, former Mets manager Casey Stengel put the problem in a nutshell. "I got one that can throw, but can't catch, and one that can catch but can't throw," Stengel said. "And one who can hit but can't do either."

Skills Beyond Measure

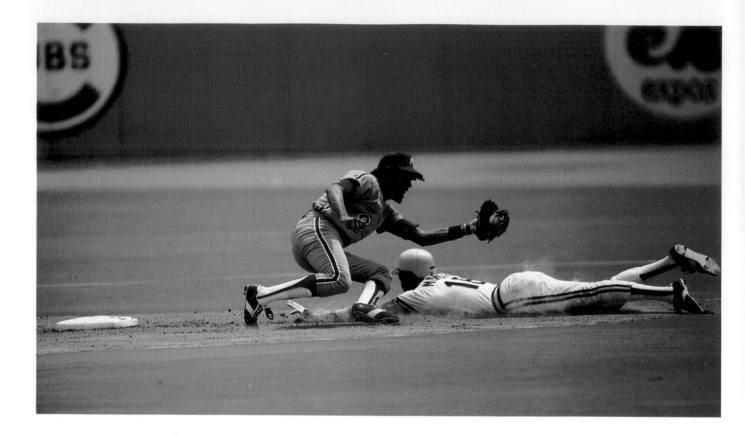

Manny Trillo led NL second basemen in assists from 1975 to 1978 but also led the league in errors twice. In 1982 Trillo set a major league record with 89 straight errorless games and posted the eighth best fielding percentage ever, .994, on five errors in 789 chances.

Even the best fielders—like Milwaukee's Robin Yount (preceding page)—drop the ball sometimes. Yount led AL shortstops with 489 assists and won a Gold Glove in 1982, then after shoulder surgery forced him to the outfield in 1985, he led the majors in 1986 with a .997 fielding percentage, committing just one error in 131 games.

othing in baseball is more deceptive than the fielding statistic. Not only are there no catchy fielding numbers, but even the most popular measures of fielding prowess are either misleading or incomplete or both. A player who makes few errors may also have no range, no arm, no knowledge of positioning. A good fielder, on the other hand, may commit errors because he reaches more batted balls and accepts tougher chances.

Take the most commonly cited fielding statistic, fielding percentage: determined by dividing the sum of putouts and assists by total chances, it's a fairly good measure of lifetime accomplishment but often a marginal seasonal stat, tending to reward players with good hands, toe-to-toe range, and terrible arms who field only those few balls they can reach. Former San Diego first baseman Steve Garvey is a case in point. "On sacrifice situations, we always used to bunt at him," says a former foe. "We knew he'd never throw to second." Fielding percentage has become increasingly meaningless as the differences between the best and worst averages have narrowed. How important is percentage when the best shortstops handle 98 out of every 100 chances and the worst handle 95?

Or consider total chances: figured by adding a player's putouts, assists and errors, it's considered a good measure of range. In 1868 the first great baseball reporter, Henry Chadwick, wrote, "The best player in a nine is he who makes the most good plays in a match, not the one who commits the fewest errors, and it is in the record of his good plays that we are to look for the most correct data for an estimate of his skill in the position he occupies."

Many modern observers agree. They note that the best players may average 200 to 300 more chances per season than the also-rans. Baseball

analyst Bill James' famous "range factor"—total chances minus errors divided by games—attempts to measure productive range on a daily basis.

But even James realizes that his creation depends on variables. A shortstop who plays on slow grass when a left-handed sinkerball pitcher is working will get plenty of ground balls hit his way. An equally good shortstop playing on artificial turf with a right-handed pitcher throwing high fastballs will spend the game watching speeded-up grounders skip by him or fly balls pass overhead. Similarly, an outfielder in a large park has a natural advantage over a fielder in a "bandbox." And infielders in the dead-ball era had a huge advantage over moderns.

Double plays ought to be indicators of an infield's performance. "What counts aren't the number of double plays," says St. Louis manager Whitey Herzog, "but the ones you should have had and missed." Indeed, teams with poor pitching staffs and weak fielders are bound to put more men on base, creating more double-play opportunities, than shut-'em-down rotations and eat-'em-up infields. In 1988 the White Sox were last in American League fielding percentage and ninth in earned run average but first in double plays.

For outfielders, assists—throws that contribute to an out—should tell the story. On the surface a good measure of an arm, assists can be misleading. Baserunners hesitate to advance on a fielder with a Roberto Clemente-style arm. An outfielder with a weak arm, however, is tempting to run on. Getting more throwing opportunities than other players, he may wind up leading the league in assists. Witness Ron LeFlore, who could barely throw across a puddle, pacing American League center fielders in assists in 1975

The best pitchers often make the best fielders, and Tom Seaver was no exception. Seaver was blessed with a blazing fastball, but he had to work a little harder on his defense and regularly used to go through 30-minute sessions of fielding practice.

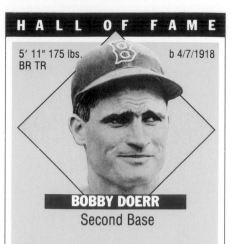

HALL OF FAME

5′ 11″ 175 lbs.
BR TR

b 4/7/1918

BOBBY DOERR
Second Base

Bobby Doerr played his entire major league career at second base for the Boston Red Sox, establishing a reputation for consistency in the field and at the plate few players of his era could match.

Breaking in with Boston in 1937, Doerr hit .224 and played 47 games at second base. He never hit under .258 or played fewer than 100 games a season at second base throughout the rest of his 14-year career.

As a fielder, Doerr was without peer, having led the league in fielding percentage at second base four times and tying for the lead two other seasons. He turned more double plays than any other second baseman in the AL five times and in 1948 fielded 414 consecutive chances without making an error, setting an AL record.

At the plate, Doerr provided the Red Sox with a capacity for power hitting unusual in a second baseman. He hit 27 home runs in a season twice during his career and drove in 100 or more runs six times, including a 120-RBI season in 1950, when he hit .294.

During his career, Doerr combined with such hitters as Ted Williams, Vern Stephens and Walt Dropo to give the Red Sox one of the hardest-hitting lineups in baseball. In 1950 the team's batting average was .302. The next year, after hitting .289 with 13 home runs, Doerr retired at 33. Doerr's longtime double-play partner, Johnny Pesky, said, "Doerr wasn't good, he was simply great."

Brooklyn's Jackie Robinson (above, with Boston's Stan Rojek) was a double-play whiz no matter which position he played. As a rookie in 1947, he led NL first basemen with 144, then moved to second, where he led the league in double plays from 1949 to 1952.

There are other, more arcane fielding numbers, such as "caught stealing," a newly popular yardstick for catchers that is determined by dividing the number of runners caught stealing by the total number of throws on attempted steals. The problem with this percentage is that it assumes baserunners steal only on catchers, not pitchers. In 1981, his last season with the Phillies, Bob Boone was known as SB-E2—baseball shorthand for "stolen base-error catcher"—because he made so many wild throws to second on steal situations. In 1982, Boone's first year with the Angels, his arm was the scourge of the AL. The difference wasn't improved throwing. Phillie pitchers had failed to hold baserunners close to the bag, forcing Boone to rush his throws. Angel pitchers did their job, giving Boone more time to throw.

For that matter, all stats seem to fail catchers. "Don't even think about assists," says Pittsburgh receiver Mike LaValliere. "You get those for throwing to first after you drop a third strike. I've seen guys with brick hands getting one assist after another. I don't like fielding percentages either. You get putouts because your pitcher struck someone out. And you can get errors for throwing the ball into center when pitchers failed to hold the runner or middle infielders couldn't pick the ball out of the dirt."

Authors John Thorn and Pete Palmer unveiled "defensive wins," the most famous of the new statistics, in *The Hidden Game of Baseball.* Their formula involves a little of everything—assists, errors, double plays, positioning factors, team totals, league averages, pine tar, neat's-foot oil. Alas, even this effort couldn't nail down such elusive yet crucial factors as great plays under maximum pressure.

For his part, Cardinal manager Herzog rejects fielding stats altogether. Not only are the usual standards unsatisfying, he claims, but they do not

measure the innumerable intangibles like positioning, signal calling and pitch selection. "There's no common denominator," says Herzog, "The only way to judge fielders is to watch them every day."

Herzog's view is typical. In fact, if you ask baseball people to evaluate fielders, the last thing they will cite is statistics. "The first thing I look for in an infielder is 'soft hands,' which describe a player who catches the ball without fighting it," says Montreal infield coach Ron Hansen. "You also watch how a guy approaches the ball. The easiest way to catch it is on a big hop, and the best players pick a spot where they'll get it. I like the tennis theory of standing straight up, with a little movement, as the ball is pitched. The crouching guy who moves forward is off-balance on a ball hit to the side."

"I'm always watching mechanics," says Dodger coach Joe Amalfitano. "Does the infielder have his glove in good position—away from his body—when the ball is pitched? Is he on the balls of his feet? Does he separate his hands as soon as he catches the ball, and is he simultaneously moving his feet in position to throw? Is the outfielder in ready position when the pitch is thrown? I'm always watching them on balls hit away from them. Say a ball is hit foul to right field; the leftfielder and centerfielder should be moving to their left. Also, all fielders should watch the barrel of the bat—the ball can't come off anything else.

"I'm not that concerned with outfield assists as much as having guys whose arms are so respected that they prevent runners from even trying to take an extra base." Late in his career Willie Mays' reputation kept some runners from advancing. He had spent years charging balls like an infielder.

Proper preparation can take a fielder only so far, as Kansas City third baseman Kevin Seitzer has shown. As a rookie in 1987, Seitzer led AL third basemen with 22 errors in 141 games. In 1988 he repeated his inauspicious title, this time booting 26.

Hands of Stone

Dick Stuart was born to be a designated hitter. Unfortunately, he was born too soon, for by the time the DH arrived in 1973, Stuart had retired, leaving behind a reputation as one of the worst fielders in baseball history.

Bad fielders not only remind us how tough it is to be a good fielder, they also provide the game with some of its best stories. Or at least they used to, until the DH came along and gave refuge to good hitters with hands of stone and feet of clay.

Stuart, whose nicknames included "Dr. Strangeglove," "Stone Fingers" and "the Boston Strangler," was an awful first baseman, but his 66 home runs in the minors in 1956 overshadowed his 30 errors at first base, and in 1958 he got a shot at the majors with Pittsburgh. He played in only 64 games that season but still managed to earn a tie for the league lead with 16 errors. For the next six years, Stuart led NL first basemen—then, after he was traded to the Red Sox in 1963—AL first basemen in errors. But like many awful fielders, Stuart recognized his lack of talent and had a sense of humor about it. The license plate on his car read *E3*. Once, during a game in which Stuart was having a particularly rough time in the field, a hot dog wrapper blew out of the stands and into Stuart's vicinity. He one-handed it on the fly and got a standing ovation.

But Stuart had nothing on Smead Jolley, who played something resembling outfield for the White Sox and the Red Sox in the early 1930s. While with Chicago, Jolley misplayed the same ball three times. First he let a grounder go through his legs, then, after the ball had bounced off the fence, it went through his legs on the return trip. When he finally ran the ball down, he heaved it over the catcher's head and into the stands. After being traded to Boston, Jolley was having all kinds of trouble with Fenway Park's left field, which at the time featured an incline toward the wall. Coaches drilled Jolley with fungo after fungo until he was about as good as he was going to get at catching fly balls running uphill. Well practiced, Jolley went smoothly up the hill after a fly ball during a game against Washington, but discovered he had overrun it. He started back down the hill, fell on his face, and got hit on the head with the ball. In the dugout, Jolley blamed his teammates and coaches. "Fine bunch, you guys. For ten days you teach me how to go up hill, but none of you have brains enough to teach me how to come down."

Pete Browning was one of baseball's first worst fielders. Browning, the Louisville slugger for whom the bat was named, made 44 errors in center field in 1886 for a .791 fielding percentage, an unofficial record. On paper, first baseman Zeke Bonura looked like a darn good fielder. In the 1930s, Bonura led AL first basemen in fielding percentage three times, but only because he would take a pass on balls that weren't thrown or hit directly at him. Bonura's theory that if you don't touch it you can't be held responsible for it worked, at least with official scorers. He wasn't so successful with managers. "This has got to be the worst

Zeke Bonura (above, fielding) wanted a $500 raise after hitting .345 for the White Sox in 1937. "But you were last in fielding," countered manager Jimmie Dykes. From then on Bonura rarely went near a ball he thought he might miss and in 1938 had the best fielding percentage of any AL first baseman.

first baseman who ever lived," said Chicago manager Jimmie Dykes. "He doesn't just let ground balls go by him. He doesn't wave at balls, he salutes them."

The rest of the worst included, but is hardly limited to: Brooklyn outfielder Babe Herman, who fought for years the claim that he was once hit on the head by a fly ball and who Dodger scout Fresco Thompson claimed wore a glove solely because it was league custom; Piano Legs Hickman, who made 86 errors in 120 games at third base for the 1900 New York Giants; and the infamous Marv Throneberry, chief bumbler of 1962 New York Mets. Once, during a birthday party for manager Casey Stengel, Throneberry complained that he hadn't been given a piece of cake. "We wuz gonna give you a piece, Marv," Stengel said, "but we wuz afraid you'd drop it."

Put a mitt on his hand and first baseman Dick Stuart was dangerous. In 1958, his rookie year, he ran down Pittsburgh catcher Bill Hall (above) and actually made the catch. Stuart also tied for the league high with 16 errors that season despite having played just 64 games.

Turning Two

The true test of a second baseman or a shortstop is his ability to turn the double play. Often the smallest players on the field, these middle infielders must catch another fielder's throw, tag the base for the first out, hurdle the oncoming baserunner who's built up a 30-yard head of steam, and get off a strong throw to first. Below are the second basemen and shortstops who have posted the ten best single-season double play totals in history, along with their teams' total double plays in that season.

SHORTSTOPS Player	Team	Year	Total DP's	Team DP's
Rick Burleson	Red Sox	1980	147	206
Roy Smalley	Twins	1979	144	203
Bobby Wine	Expos	1970	137	193
Lou Boudreau	Indians	1944	134	192
Spike Owen	Mariners	1986	133	191
Rafael Ramirez	Braves	1982	130	186
Roy McMillan	Reds	1954	129	194
Gene Alley	Pirates	1966	128	187
Hod Ford	Reds	1928	128	194
Vern Stephens	Red Sox	1949	128	207

SECOND BASEMEN Player	Team	Year	Total DP's	Team DP's
Bill Mazeroski	Pirates	1966	161	187
Gerry Priddy	Tigers	1950	150	194
Bill Mazeroski	Pirates	1961	144	187
Dave Cash	Phillies	1974	141	168
Nellie Fox	White Sox	1957	141	169
Buddy Myer	Senators	1935	138	186
Bill Mazeroski	Pirates	1962	138	177
Jerry Coleman	Yankees	1950	137	188
Jackie Robinson	Dodgers	1951	137	192
Red Schoendienst	Cardinals	1954	137	178

In fact, good glovemen at any position invariably seem to move like infielders. Watching their minor leaguers in play, Atlanta instructors Luke Appling and Phil Niekro scoffed when a pitcher caught a grounder with his knees locked and his eyes off the ball. "He was lucky to catch that," said the octogenarian Appling, a Hall of Fame shortstop. "He didn't move his feet," said Niekro, a knuckleballer whose fielding helped him join the 300-win club. "He didn't move his body."

"A player's feet and body movement are as important as his glove," Niekro said later. "You have to get to the ball quickly, with your body in position to throw, look at the fielder you're throwing to, and throw with a quick release. Jim Kaat wasn't fast, but he moved well and worked on his footwork. The pickoff, the throw to second—it's all footwork. You become an infielder, that's what you do."

Baseball hasn't had daily recognition of fielding in a quarter-century. Until the early 1960s, newspaper box scores listed each player's putouts and assists. These numbers described not only fielding performances, but also pitching performances. If a sinkerballer was working and his infielders were getting plenty of assists, you knew the pitcher was doing his job. The wire services decided to narrow the width and reduce the length of box scores. The Associated Press and United Press International dropped assists, putouts, and the names of fielders involved in double plays and triple plays. Now all we know about fielders from boxscores is who made the errors and which teams made double or triple plays.

There are some nonstatistical measures that are used to evaluate fielders. "Like the times we catchers have set up a hitter in a crucial situation so

that the pitcher could get him out," says Pittsburgh's LaValliere. "There's too much involved in that to put it into numbers."

"Range isn't really a stat—it's a thought," says Met second baseman Tim Teufel. "Ozzie Smith gets to more balls than other shortstops and deserves credit for especially tough chances. It's like diving: degree of difficulty should factor in."

"I think how you judge a ball is important," says Met left fielder Kevin McReynolds. "If you can't judge it, you can't get to it."

The true test of a second baseman seems to be how quick his hands are in turning the double play. "Bill Mazeroski has the quickest hands I've ever seen," says Royal Frank White, perhaps the best defensive second baseman since the Pirate great retired. Realizing Maz played his last game in 1972, White's interviewer asked him if he'd seen Mazeroski on film. "No, I'm talking about his hands right now," said White. "I've seen him fooling around with a ball. He has the quickest hands I've ever seen."

And yet the statistics mavens insist that fielding can be quantified. Their argument is not so much that existing statistics are perfect, but that they aren't properly weighted. Conceding that fielding percentage doesn't give due credit to a fielder's range, they argue that it can be a decent measure of career performance at some positions. That Brooks Robinson leads all third basemen with a .971 average is no accident, just as it's no coincidence that Larry Bowa and Ozzie Smith lead shortstops at .980 and .979, respectively.

Lots of career double plays is another indicator of a fine middle infielder. Mazeroski is first among second basemen with 1,706, and Luis Aparicio tops

Dependable if not flashy in the field, Steve Garvey led NL first basemen five times in fielding percentage—four times with the Dodgers, once with the Padres—and picked up four straight Gold Gloves from 1974 to 1977.

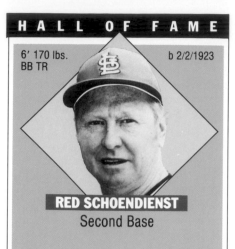

HALL OF FAME

6' 170 lbs.
BB TR

b 2/2/1923

RED SCHOENDIENST
Second Base

Four years after hitchhiking to St. Louis in 1942 for a tryout with the Cardinals, Red Schoendienst found a home at second base, where he emerged as one of the game's steadiest fielders and most consistent hitters during a career that spanned three decades.

Sporting freckles and a tuft of red hair, Schoendienst played outfield during his rookie year with the Cardinals in 1945. He moved to second base the next year, helping St. Louis win the pennant with his .281 batting average and his league-leading .983 fielding percentage.

Although Schoendienst played third base, shortstop and the outfield during his career, he was primarily a second baseman and led the NL in fielding percentage at that position six times. In 1956 he was traded to the New York Giants and the following year was traded to Milwaukee, where he collected 200 hits, posted a .309 batting average, and tied for the league lead in fielding percentage to help the Braves win the NL pennant.

Schoendienst returned to St. Louis as a player in 1961 and spent two years as an outstanding pinch hitter. He took over as manager of the Cardinals in 1965 and led them to NL championships in 1967, when they went on to beat the Red Sox and win the World Series, and in 1968. He managed the Cardinals until 1976, longer than anyone else has, and returned to the club as a coach in 1979.

Yankee shortstop Phil Rizzuto hurdled Cleveland's Bobby Avila (above) on his way to one of 113 double plays in 1951. Rizzuto started three double plays in the first six innings of Game 6 of the 1951 World Series against the Giants, and the Yankees won, 4–3.

all shortstops with 1,553. Assists per game indicate a middle infielder's ability in getting to a ball, catching it, and throwing out the batter. The record is admittedly era-, field-, and pitching-dependent: at 3.2 assists per game, the great Bill Mazeroski trails nearly a dozen old-time second basemen: and Oakland's underrated Glenn Hubbard, at 3.4, is the only active player on the top-ten list. Among active shortstops, only Ozzie Smith—fourth at 3.5—makes the list.

Assists are a better gauge of first basemen. A rangy first baseman racks them up—not only making the peg to the pitcher covering first, but nipping runners at second, third and home. A slow first baseman merely catches throws from other fielders. The Mets' Keith Hernandez and Red Sox star Bill Buckner are the all-time leaders with an average of .9 assists per game.

A pitcher's fielding—the 3–1 putout, fielding bunts and balls hit back to him—often passes unnoticed. The 1989 *American League Red Book* carried only one pitcher's fielding stats. The *National League Green Book* had none. Yet total chances are a good measure for moundsmen. In the course of a game, a nimble pitcher can easily get two or three of them. Nick Altrock, a White Sox star early in the century, averaged an astonishing 3.7 chances per game.

Some of the more visionary stat hounds favor a new measure: "exceptional defensive play" or "game-saving fielding play" that players could be eligible for in a day. Says former infielder Greg Pryor, "If there's a save for pitchers, there should be a save for fielders." Unfortunately, the elimination of the game-winning RBI in 1989 augurs poorly for a similar fielding number.

That doesn't deter the reformers. They point to available stats that either aren't kept or aren't heeded. "Total errors may not be meaningful, but

In 1942 Cleveland shortstop Lou Boudreau was also the team's manager, but those duties didn't stop the 24-year-old Boudreau from continuing to make plays in the field, like tagging out the Yankees' Buddy Rosar (12) trying to steal second. Boudreau, said sportswriter Rud Rennie, "can't run and his arm's no good, but he's the best shortstop in the game."

errors per game are," says Pryor. "A shortstop who makes an error every 10 to 15 games is doing a good job." An error every 40 or 50 games is something special. Kevin Elster set the shortstop mark with 88 straight errorless games in 1989 playing for the New York Mets. Joe Morgan set the second-base standard with 91 straight in 1977 and 1978. Yet the only streak familiar to most baseball fans is the 56-game hitting streak Joe DiMaggio had with the 1941 Yankees.

How about taking up Herzog on his suggestion to count "attempted double plays"? Each time the relay man throws to first, tabulate whether his team recorded a double play or had to settle for the force out.

Most ballplayers favor relieving a fielder of an error when a good throw caroms off the back of a sliding runner and allows him to take an extra base. They believe such a mishap should be recorded as a "team error." Same for a fly ball that drops untouched because no one called for it; that play normally is scored as a hit.

"Give an outfielder points for assists and subtract them for errors," says Jamie Quirk, who has played every position but pitcher and center field. Granted, the result ignores total chances and range, but it would logically credit fielders—especially left fielders and right fielders—for good hands and arms. For example, the NL assists-errors leaders among outfielders in 1988 were Kevin McReynolds (+14), Dale Murphy (+12), Phil Bradley (+11), Tom Brunansky (+9), and Andy Van Slyke (+8). Because center fielder Van Slyke already led the league with 422 chances, being one of the top five assists-errors leaders puts him among the NL's best outfielders. The AL leaders were Cory Snyder (+11), Pete Incaviglia (+10), Robin Yount (+10), Dan Gladden (+9), Kirby Puckett (+9), and Jesse Barfield (+8).

After the season he had in 1987, Dion James might be excused if he thought he could bring down any ball he could see. In his first season with Atlanta, James paced NL outfielders with a .996 fielding percentage on one error in 267 total chances.

BILL MAZEROSKI 2b

Bill Mazeroski

Bill Mazeroski, the legendary Pirate second baseman, had a right to be thrilled. He had just hit the only homer ever to end a World Series—the dramatic ninth-inning shot that beat the Yankees in 1960. People were snake-dancing down the streets of Pittsburgh and stalling trolleys by throwing tons of confetti out windows. Always a quiet guy, Maz had taken his wife to a hill to sit and take stock of what had happened. And as he reflected, Maz became less delirious. What a shame, he told friends later, that he'd be remembered for his bat rather than his glove.

Not that he couldn't bat. In his 17 years with the Pirates, Maz had 2,016 hits and at least ten homers six times—fine offensive output for a middle infielder. But it was his superb fielding that distinguished him from his peers. Maz set major league records for double plays by a second baseman in a season and for a career. He also has the most years leading the league in double plays with eight and assists with nine. Never mind that he played most of his home games on the rough turf of Forbes Field; his lifetime fielding percentage of .983 is sixth among all National Leaguers. As a pivotman Mazeroski was second to none. With nimble and strong legs, the 5' 11", 185-pound Mazeroski could reach the base well ahead of the throw and push off before the runner arrived. He believed that the most efficient way to make the pivot was to go straight at the runner. He hung in so tough that teammates called him "Tree Stump." When an opponent crashed into him, they had to bring out a stretcher—for the runner.

On one memorable occasion in the late 1960s, the Pirates were leading the Astros by a run with men on first and third and one out in the ninth. A Houston player hit a high hopper to shortstop Gene Alley, who made the only play possible by throwing to Maz for the force at second base. Girding for extra innings, the Pirates leaned back on the bench and conceded a run. Seconds later they realized the game was over; Maz had relayed to first in time for the double play.

"That was one of the best double plays I ever made," says Mazeroski. "everyone wound up on the ground. Alley fell down making the throw, I turned it with my feet in the air, and Donn Clendenon hit the ground stretching for the ball at first. I never had to wind up to throw, and that helped me a lot on the double play."

So did his sure hands. "I never worried about anything but catching the ball and throwing it to Maz," says Dick Groat, Mazeroski's shortstop from 1956 through 1962. "He'd make the double play after getting a perfect throw or a terrible one."

Mazeroski grew up bouncing rubber balls off walls by the hour. His first instructor was his father; the late Lew Mazeroski was himself a major league prospect when a lump of coal smashed his foot in a mining accident. Bill reported to his high school team in Tiltonsville, Ohio, as a freshman, and his coach, Al Barazio, told him, "I'm going to make a big leaguer out of you." Maz was headed for the big leagues when he was switched from shortstop to second base by none other than Branch Rickey, the father of the farm system. By the time he made his first All-Star team in 1958, the 21-year-old Mazeroski was already known as "Dazzlin' Maz" and "the Boy Bandit." Before the game, when the NL took fielding practice, stars from both leagues stopped to watch him—the fielding equivalent of watching Ted Williams hit. Maz went on to win eight Gold Gloves in a career that Bill James summed up in his *Historical Baseball Abstract:* "Bill Mazeroski's defensive statistics are probably the most impressive of any player at any position."

In 1956 nineteen-year-old rookie second baseman Bill Mazeroski (left) gave little notice of great things to come. He hit just .243 but did share in 56 double plays in only 81 games. In 1959 Mazeroski (below, taking the throw ahead of St. Louis' Joe Cunningham) and shortstop Dick Groat led the Pirates to a league-high 165 double plays.

BILL
MAZEROSKI

Second Base
Pittsburgh Pirates 1956–1972

GAMES	2,163
FIELDING PERCENTAGE	
Career	.983
Season High	.992
PUTOUTS	
Career *(7th all time)*	4,974
Season High	425
PUTOUTS PER GAME	
Career	2.38
Season High	2.74
ASSISTS	
Career *(5th all time)*	6,685
Season High	543
ASSISTS PER GAME	
Career	3.19
Season High	3.67
CHANCES	
Career *(7th all time)*	11,863
Season High	957
CHANCES PER GAME	
Career	5.48
Season High	6.23
ERRORS PER GAME	
Career	.10
Season Low	.05
DOUBLE PLAYS	
Career *(1st all time)*	1,706
Season High *(1st all time)*	161
WORLD SERIES	1960, 1971
GOLD GLOVES	1958, 1960–1961, 1963–1967

Being a small, quick-moving target enabled Luis Aparicio to elude the likes of Cleveland's Max Alvis and share in 1,553 career double plays, tops all time among shortstops. Aparicio played 18 years in the majors for the White Sox, the Orioles and the Red Sox, and he averaged 143 games a year at shortstop.

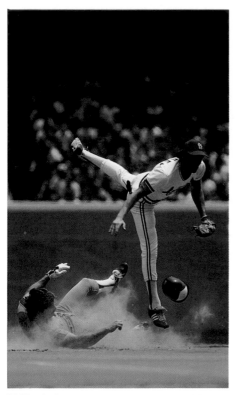

Utility infielders are valuable commodities, but since they play a lot of positions, they take their lumps from all sides. St. Louis' Mike Ramsey got upended by Montreal's 6' 3", 190-pound third baseman Larry Parrish, but in 1982 Ramsey's ability to play second, short, third and the outfield earned him a winner's share of the World Series pot.

Center fielder Puckett, who led the AL with 465 chances, was in a class by himself.

Some statisticians envision other measures of excellence for outfielders: the times a left fielder throws out a man trying to score from second on a single, and the times a right fielder retires a runner going from first to third. These feats are considered prime challenges for players at those positions. Right fielders have plenty of chances to make the long peg to third, because first basemen give batters an inviting hole between first and second by holding runners close to the bag. The left fielder gets the most chances to throw home because more balls are hit his way than to right, and because the center fielder is usually too deeply situated to make the play. What's more, the runner on second has to delay for a split second before running when a ground ball is hit to the left side of second base; that gives the left fielder more time to throw home.

Of course, some fielders throw so well that runners hesitate to advance on them. Statisticians have the answer to that, too. To a left fielder's assists to home plate, add the times runners stop at third on singles to left field; and to a right fielder's assists at third, add the times runners stop at second on base hits to right field.

Who leads these categories? Who knows, they've never been officially kept. The boldest numbers finders even tackle the least quantifiable position: catcher. A catcher's fielding percentage and errors would be more meaningful, many catchers say, if passed balls counted as errors as they once did. Today, a passed ball is charged to a catcher if he allows a runner to advance by muffing a pitch he should have caught. But passed balls, kept separately from errors, go little noted. "We get charged for errors on things that aren't

In a 1987 poll of AL managers, Toronto shortstop Tony Fernandez (left, hurdling Kansas City's John Wathan) was tabbed as having the best arm of any AL infielder. In his first five seasons in the majors, Fernandez won three Gold Gloves, and had led AL shortstops twice in putouts and once in assists and fielding percentage.

completely our fault, like a rushed throw when a pitcher was slow coming home," says LaValliere. "A passed ball is completely the catcher's fault. As far as I'm concerned, it's an error."

Another helpful indicator is the earned run averages of pitchers when they work with particular catchers. Kansas City's Bob Boone, who has caught more games than any other catcher in baseball history, invariably seems to get lower ERAs out of his pitchers than other catchers on his teams have. So there it is: a quantifiable figure for the most intangible of elements—calling a game.

But baseball loves its numbers and awards, and fielders surely deserve their certificates of merit. Since 1957 baseball's answer has been the annual Gold Glove awards. The honors go to the nine top fielders selected as the best at their positions. In the award's inaugural year, a nine-player major-league squad was chosen by a panel of 19 sportswriters. In 1958 the players took over the voting and began selecting nine-man teams for each league—on the condition that they couldn't vote for teammates. In 1965 coaches and managers became electors, with the same stipulation in effect to prevent team favoritism. Registered and copyrighted by the Rawlings Sporting Goods Company and awarded by *The Sporting News,* Gold Gloves are selected in the last month of the season and announced in a December issue of *The Sporting News.*

Still the only honor given fielders, the Gold Glove has become a respected feature of the game, even if pre-1957 glovemen are neglected. And generally, the cream rises to the top. The leading Gold Glove winners with 16 apiece are Hall of Fame third baseman Brooks Robinson and Jim Kaat,

The Mets liked Gregg Jefferies' bat so much that they selected him on the first round of the 1985 free-agent draft, but they can't seem to find a spot for his glove. In 1987 he hit .367 in Class AA but committed 35 errors at third and short. In Class AAA in 1988 he played second, short, third and the outfield, and made 27 errors.

In 1953 Brooklyn's Roy Campanella set a major league record with 807 putouts, one coming on a tag of the Giants' Daryl Spencer (above). Campanella was masterful around the plate—big, strong and quick. "He stood a big-boned five feet nine, with massive arms and torso, a sumo wrestler pared to catcher's size," wrote Dodger eulogist Roger Kahn.

Boston's Tony Armas (opposite, left) couldn't believe his eyes as Chicago catcher Joel Skinner took himself and all his equipment airborne in pursuit of an errant throw. Skinner caught almost everything that came his way in 1984, allowing just one passed ball in 64 games.

a slick-fielding left-hander who pitched in an unmatched 25 seasons. Willie Mays and Roberto Clemente head all outfielders with 12 Gold Gloves apiece; Keith Hernandez tops all first basemen with 11; and it's no accident that Ozzie Smith, Mark Belanger and Luis Aparicio, the best shortstops of the last three decades, have won nine, eight, and nine Gold Gloves, respectively.

The fact remains, although the casual spectator may take it for granted, fielding a batted ball is one of the most demanding and subtle skills in all of sport. Commenting on the difficulty of measuring the talents that make a great fielder—ironic in a sport that thrives on precise statistical computation—longtime manager Branch Rickey once remarked, "there is nothing on earth anybody can do with fielding."

Although there is no perfect, or even universally accepted, statistical measure for evaluating fielders, baseball analysts keep manipulating the available data to determine a ranking system. Among members of the Society for American Baseball Research, several formulas have been put forth, none of which is likely to find a niche in the record books anytime soon. Those infinitely complex findings, however, tend to agree with the instinctive judgment of sportswriters and fans alike. Just as every hitting formula seems to establish Babe Ruth and Ted Williams as baseball's greatest batters, so does one fielding measure after another rate one man as the most dominant gloveman ever—the dazzling Bill Mazeroski.

It appears, then, that Branch Rickey was wrong: there is something you can do about fielding. ◗

Keystone Cops

Hughie Critz

Second basemen don't get much respect. If they're really good, they earn such rave adjectives as "scrappy" and "hard-nosed." The infield's most physically challenging play—turning the double play while avoiding a blind-side hit—is their acid test. And since their defensive role is undervalued, they have to hit better than shortstops in order to justify their spot in the lineup.

If you want to make the highlight films, get yourself a flashy shortstop. But if you want to win ballgames, open your wallet for a second baseman.

Between 1976 and 1985, the Kansas City Royals won six American League West Division titles, using three different shortstops and just one second baseman—eight-time Gold Glove winner Frank White. The man who's played in more World Series than any other non-Yankee was a second baseman—Frankie Frisch, who played in eight fall classics with the New York Giants and the St. Louis Cardinals. And Giants manager Leo Durocher, a former shortstop, had this to say about his second basemen, Eddie Stanky: "He can't hit, he can't field, he can't run—all he can do is beat you."

To beat you consistently, a second baseman needs great range and anticipation, a better arm than most people think, quick feet and nerves of steel. Range is key, because second basemen play next to first basemen, customarily the slowest, least adept infielders who become tied to the corner of the diamond when holding a runner on base, leaving second basemen with huge gaps to cover both to their left and their right. Second basemen must be quick enough to charge drag bunts and slow rollers, then throw to first as their momentum carries them toward home plate. The Yankees' Billy Martin saved the 1952 World Series when, with the bases loaded and two outs in Brooklyn's half of the seventh and New York leading 4–2, Martin rushed forward to catch a pop-up first baseman Joe Collins had lost sight of. Two Dodger runners had already crossed the plate and another was on his way home when Martin snared the ball at about knee level.

Second basemen must be fast enough to race into the outfield to snare Texas Leaguers, often catching the ball over their shoulder while avoiding onrushing outfielders. They've got to be able to field grounders hit up the middle, then—all in one motion—wheel 180 degrees and get something on

their throw to first. And they've got to try to knock down anything hit in the hole to their left, since the throw to first is so short they often have time to recover and throw out the runner.

Because the second baseman has to make the play more often than anyone else, and because his role is the toughest, the double-play pivot can make or break his career. On a double-play grounder hit to the left side of the infield, the second baseman must take the throw while facing away from the oncoming runner, touch the bag, pivot toward first, and get off a strong throw while protecting himself from the runner, whose job it is to take him out. The ways of performing this ballet are varied: some straddle the bag and hurdle the runner; others go across the bag and keep going toward third; still others hit the bag and step back to avoid the runner. When Nellie Fox was a 19-year-old rookie with the 1947 Philadelphia Athletics, he asked a veteran second baseman what it took to be a great pivotman. "Kid, it's simple," came the reply. "All you need is the nerve of a tightrope walker, the guts of a burglar, and the grace of an adagio dancer." Fox went on to record 1,619 double plays, second best ever.

Cincinnati's Joe Morgan (above, with Willie Randolph of the Yankees) and Detroit's Charlie Gehringer (below) were similar second basemen—unspectacular but incredibly durable, dependable and efficient. Morgan is third all time in assists, just behind Gehringer, while Gehringer is fourth in total chances, just behind Morgan.

CHARLIE GEHRINGER, Tigers

Nellie Fox—all 5' 10" and 160 pounds of him—dodged and hurdled oncoming baserunners (like the A's Louis Limmer, above) from 1947 to 1965 without ever suffering a serious injury. From August 7, 1955, to September 3, 1960, Fox played in 798 consecutive games, a record for second basemen.

The undisputed king of the double play was Pittsburgh's Bill Mazeroski, whose 1,706 twin killings are the most ever for a middle infielder. But others gained fame for their ability to turn two, among them Hall of Famers Bobby Doerr, Charlie Gehringer, Eddie Collins and Red Schoendienst. And second basemen weren't always underappreciated. In 1889 jack-of-all-trades John Montgomery Ward, also a Hall of Famer, called second base "the prettiest position to play of the entire field. In the number of chances offered it is next to first base, and in the character of the work to be done and the opportunities for brilliant play and the exercise of judgment, it is unsurpassed."

Ward probably had in mind Bid McPhee, who set the standard for second basemen in the late 1800s the hard way—without a glove. McPhee didn't wear a glove until 1897, about ten years after they'd become popular, but he led his league nine times in fielding percentage. His .978 mark for Cincinnati in 1896 stood for 23 years, and his 529 putouts in 1886 is still a major league record.

Not far behind McPhee was Napoleon Lajoie, a man famous mostly for his ferocious hitting, who was one of the finest fielding second baseman of his time. At 6' 1" and 195 pounds, Lajoie was big both for his era and his position, but he was known for his grace in the field, and led the league in fielding percentage seven times. No one played more major league games at second base than Eddie Collins, and few ever played the position so well. Collins is the all-time major league leader at second base in putouts, assists and total chances, and led the AL in fielding percentage a record nine times.

With all the ground they have to cover, knowing the hitters is especially important for second basemen, and can turn tough plays into routine ones. One of the best at this was Detroit's Charlie Gehringer, who played 1920s and 1930s hitters so well that he rarely had to go very far to make a play, and earned the nickname "the Mechanical Man." One writer called Gehringer's defensive play "scientifically unsensational," but it was effective, and Gehringer led AL second basemen in fielding percentage seven times.

Solid second base play continued through the 1930s and 1940s, led by the likes of the Cubs' Billy Herman, who thought the entire playing field was

In 1987 second baseman Robby Thompson (above) and shortstop Jose Uribe led the Giants to a major-league-leading 183 double plays.

In six AL Championship Series—26 games and 134 total chances—Royal second baseman Frank White (above) made one error for a .993 fielding percentage.

his responsibility, and whose 466 putouts in 1933 are still an NL record; Oscar "Ski" Melillo, who played in obscurity with the St. Louis Browns but who holds the AL record for assists in a season with 572; and Boston's Bobby Doerr, who once handled 414 consecutive chances without an error.

In 1948 Brooklyn's Jackie Robinson moved from first to second base, and played it the way he did everything else on the field—aggressively and to win. Robinson led the NL in fielding percentage three times and sparked the Dodgers to six pennants in his ten-year career. The 1950s and 1960s belonged to Red Schoendienst of the Cardinals, Nellie Fox of the White Sox, and Bill Mazeroski of the Pirates, three of the best to ever drag their foot across the bag at second.

Second basemen seemed to get bigger and more powerful in the 1970s and 1980s, but stayed every bit as dependable defensively. Four-time Gold Glove winner Bobby Grich committed just five errors in 162 games in 1973 for a record .995 fielding percentage, then gave up the Gold Glove in 1977 to Frank White, who won eight in the next 11 years. In the National League, Philadelphia's Manny Trillo went 89 games and 479 chances without an error in 1982, then gave way to Chicago's Ryne Sandberg, who tied Tito Fuentes' NL fielding percentage mark in 1984, and won every NL Gold Glove from 1983 to 1988.

Second base continues to be one of baseball's lowest-profile positions, but its tenants probably like it that way. They just go out, do their jobs, and make champions. Every second baseman would like to hear said about him what Ty Cobb said about Charlie Gehringer: "He'd say hello at the start of spring training and goodbye at the end of the season, and the rest of the time he'd let his bat and glove do the talking for him."

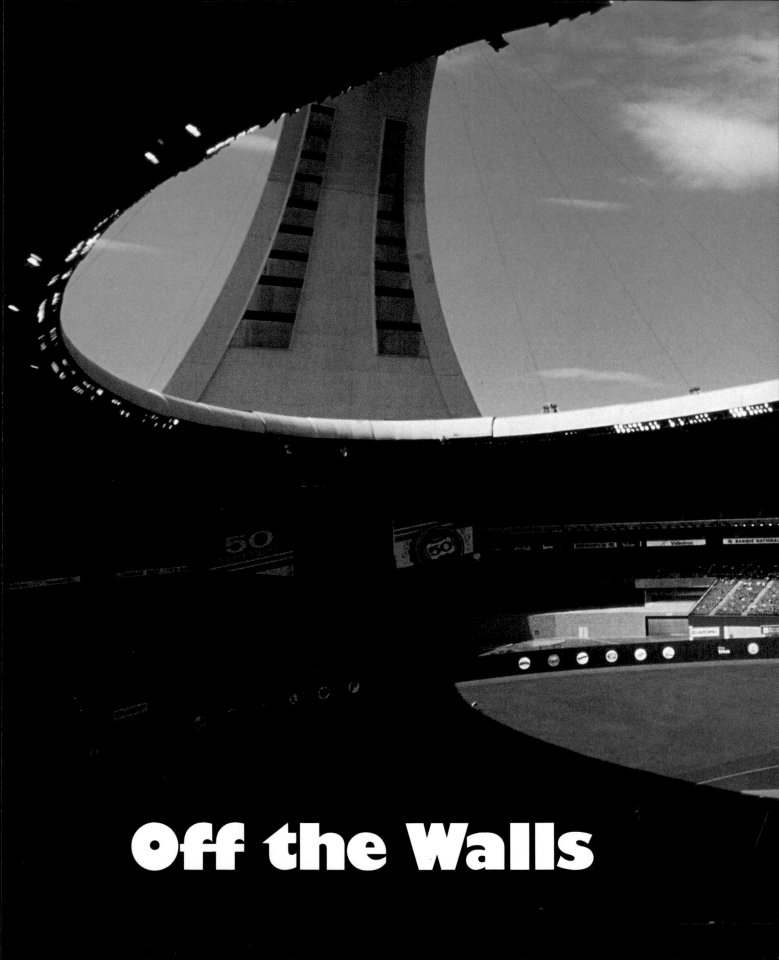

Off the Walls

From the day Pittsburgh's Forbes Field opened in 1909 (above) until it was demolished in 1971, it was one of baseball's roomiest parks. It was 462 feet to the deepest corner of center field, and 110 feet from home plate to the backstop.

Montreal's Olympic Stadium (preceding page), home of the Expos, features the largest retractable fabric roof in the world. The roof, made of a synthetic material used for bulletproof vests, covers 200,000 square feet, weighs 65 tons, and takes 45 minutes to open or close.

With the possible exception of golf, baseball has fewer restrictions on its playing surface than any major other sport. Aside from four bases 90 feet apart, foul lines at right angles, and a pitcher's mound 60 feet 6 inches from home plate, architects can pretty well design baseball stadiums at will. The perfection of the infield dimensions—the fact that a man can run those 90 feet in about the time a batted ball can be fielded and thrown to first, give or take a few critical microseconds—is balanced by the arbitrary spaciousness of the outfield. No wonder so many strange things happen once the ball is put in play.

This was especially so in baseball's infancy. The quintessential pastoral game, our national pastime was first played on open fields and meadows. Fair territory extended forever—and so did the possibilities for outfield play. Outfielders had to contend not only with endlessly rolling balls, but with sun and wind, gopher holes, furrows, mounds, hollows, plants, and clever hitters.

The unlimited playing field, to say nothing of the dead ball, discouraged batters from "swinging for the fences"—generally there weren't any—but encouraged them to place the ball between fielders—hence the prototypical turn-of-the-century hitter Wee Willie Keeler, whose adage "Hit 'em where they ain't" became a byword for savvy batsmen. Likewise, the best of fielders learned to master the fields they played on and to position themselves to thwart the hitters.

In those early days, the outfielder was aptly named: basemen tended to play close to their respective bags, and beyond them the endless expanse of fair territory was shared by just three men. Outfielders played far out,

Most ballparks built in the early 1900s stood side by side with industrial plants and factories, so some baseball cards of that era—like this one of Cincinnati pitcher Art Fromme from 1910—provided smokestacks as a backdrop.

because it was easier to run in on a fly ball or a bounding hit than it was to recover a ball hit over their heads. An outfielder had to be fleet of foot and strong of arm to succeed. The wiliest of fielders turned nature to their advantage. It was a typical 19th-century ploy to hide extra baseballs in the high grass. If a booming fly passed well overhead, the well prepared fielder could retreat a few steps, grab a ball from the weeds and fire it in. The imaginative Hall of Famer King Kelly used this ploy, and so did anyone who played for the great manager John McGraw when he managed the old Baltimore Orioles around the turn of the century.

The earliest ballparks made no provision for onlookers, but eventually clubs provided rows of benches along one or both of the baselines, open to the elements. More elaborate stands provided protection from sun and rain, but there was no attempt to use them to limit the scope of the playing field. Spectators were close to the field, ready and able to cheer or heckle the players, and baseballs that were hit into the seats were thrown back out to be played again. Wooden stands were relatively cheap to build, easy to repair, but always susceptible to the ravages of weather and fire.

The first enclosed baseball field to charge admission to spectators, the Union Grounds in Brooklyn, New York, was opened in 1862. Actually "enclosed" is a misleading term. Union Grounds and other wooden parks of that era offered covered seats behind the plate and along the first- and third-base lines and fences around the outfields. In cities these wooden parks were located on the outskirts, the better to benefit from low real estate prices. Small-town parks were often located in fields. In either case, there was generally plenty of wide open space to play in. The outer barriers were so far away—500 feet in the dead-ball era was not unusual—that the playing field,

Ebbets Field

On a plot of land notorious for its shanties and garbage-grazing pigs, a former ticket hawker built one of baseball's most beloved stadiums. Charles Hercules Ebbets was something of a baseball visionary, and when he gained majority ownership of the Brooklyn Dodgers in 1902, he began looking for a spot to build a new stadium.

He found a square block in the Pigtown section of Brooklyn, and bought the entire block, lot by lot. Ebbets Field was completed in 1913, and its inaugural event—an exhibition game between the Dodgers and the Yankees—hinted that it would be a haven for the unusual. First someone forgot the key to the gate of the center field bleachers, then the flag-raising ceremony hit a snag when someone forgot the flag, and the final gaffe came when it became clear that the stadium plans—which were lauded by sportswriters—failed to include a press box.

Ebbets Field played host to some of the most colorful teams, fans and incidents the game has seen. Casey Stengel, a favorite of Dodger fans since 1912, returned as a Pirate in 1918 to wild applause. Stengel doffed his cap to acknowledge the fans, and a sparrow flew out.

The golden age for the Dodgers and the fans was the 1940s and 1950s, when Brooklyn won seven pennants and their fans earned their reputation as baseball's most loyal, emotional and colorful. On September 16, 1940, a fan came out of the stands and attacked 6' 3", 240-pound umpire George Magerkurth. The Dodger faithful included Hilda Chester, who rang her cowbell loud and long in the bleachers, and the Dodger Sym-Phony, an informal brass band that played "Three Blind Mice" when the umpires took the field, until 1952, when a fourth umpire was added.

Dodger fans suffered the first of many colossal disappointments in the 1941 World Series. It was the ninth inning of Game 4 and the Dodgers led the Yankees 4–3 with two outs and the bases empty. Tommy Henrich swung and missed a Hugh Casey pitch for strike three, but catcher Mickey Owen dropped the ball and Henrich reached first safely. The Yankees went on to score four runs and win the game, and instead of being tied two and two in games, the Yankees led 3–1 and won the Series the next day.

On April 15, 1947, baseball's color line was broken in Ebbets Field as Jackie Robinson made his major league debut. Later that season, Brooklyn's Cookie Lavagetto broke up Floyd Bevens' World Series no-hitter—with two outs in the ninth of Game 4—with a two-run double for a 3–2 Brooklyn win. Still, the Yankees won the Series.

In 1952 the Yankees did it again when second baseman Billy Martin rushed in at the last instant to grab a bases-loaded pop-up in Game 7 of the World Series, saving a 4–2 win for New York. The Dodgers finally broke their string of five Series losses to the Yankees in 1955 when Johnny Podres shut out New York in Game 7.

Two years later it all came to an end. Ebbets Field was too small and run-down to be competitive anymore, and Dodger owner Walter O'Malley had his sights set on the West Coast. The Dodgers played their last game in Brooklyn on September 24, 1957, before just 6,702 fans. With the closing of Ebbets Field went a unique baseball experience, one where fans were close enough to the field to see the players' faces and hear their chatter. In *The Boys of Summer,* Roger Kahn wrote: "In the intimacy of Ebbets Field it was a short trip from the grandstand to the fantasy that you were in the game."

The most loyal, raucous fans in baseball could usually be found in the Ebbets Field bleachers (top left), and in 1941 the Dodgers gave fans something to cheer about, winning their first pennant since 1920. The first night game at Ebbets Field (left) came on June 15, 1938, and Cincinnati's Johnny Vander Meer made it memorable by pitching his second straight no-hitter. Ebbets Field (above) was among baseball's most lopsided ballparks.

Ebbets Field

Montgomery Street and
McKeever Place
Brooklyn, New York

Built 1913

Demolished 1960

Brooklyn Dodgers, NL
1913-1957

Seating Capacity
31,497

Style
Grass surface, Major League
Classic

Height of Outfield Fences
Left: 9 feet 10⅓ inches
Left center: 9 feet 10⅓
inches
Center: 9 feet 10⅓ inches to
15 feet
Right center: 9 to 19 feet
Right: 38 feet

Dugouts
Home: 1st base
Visitors: 3rd base

Bullpens
Foul territory
Home: right field side
Visitors: left field side

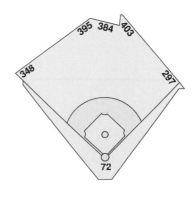

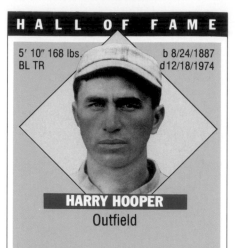

5' 10" 168 lbs.
BL TR

b 8/24/1887
d 12/18/1974

HARRY HOOPER
Outfield

Slick-fielding Harry Hooper, who played with the Boston Red Sox and the Chicago White Sox from 1909 to 1925, is overshadowed today by the other great outfielders of his era. But in his day, Hooper's peers recognized him as one of the game's best players. New York Giants manager John McGraw called him "one of the greatest outfielders that ever lived" and put Hooper in the same class with Tris Speaker and Ty Cobb.

McGraw's praise may have been inspired by Hooper's barehanded catch of a drive by the Giants' Larry Doyle that kept New York from winning the deciding game of the 1912 World Series. Playing right field alongside Speaker and Duffy Lewis in what was perhaps the greatest defensive outfield ever, Hooper helped the Red Sox win four World Series titles between 1912 and 1918.

Hooper's credentials as a fielder, which include 3,981 lifetime putouts and a career .966 fielding average, contributed to his selection for the Baseball Hall of Fame in 1971. But he was also an outstanding leadoff hitter, compiling a lifetime .281 batting average and collecting 2,466 hits.

As Red Sox captain in 1919, Hooper persuaded Boston manager Ed Barrow to put Babe Ruth, at the time a successful pitcher, in the outfield when he wasn't on the mound. Thus began Ruth's career as the Sultan of Swat.

Four hundred seats were added in front of the center field fence at tiny Baker Bowl for the 1915 World Series, but the hometown Phillies paid a high price for them. Harry Hooper homered into the temporary seats to win Game 5 and the Series for Boston.

for all intents and purposes, remained open, and outfielders rarely had to contend with baseballs bouncing off or going over the fence.

On April 12, 1909, Shibe Park, home to the Philadelphia Athletics and later known as Connie Mack Stadium, opened its gates and ushered in a new era. No longer was baseball to be played in parks and fields; now the correct generic term was "stadium." Before long, rustic wooden grandstands were replaced by concrete-and-steel palaces lined with columns, arched window openings, and even towers. By 1923 the major leagues had 14 more ornately decorated concrete-and-steel structures, and the wooden stadium was history.

The new parks were typically located near bus or trolley stops and had to be built to conform with existing streets and buildings. At first the playing fields in these parks resembled those within the older wooden structures. In Shibe Park the distance to the outfield walls was a reasonable 360 feet down the foul lines but a staggering 515 feet to straightaway center.

But by no stretch of the imagination were these downtown pleasure palaces indistinguishable from one another. Some, like Philadelphia's Baker Bowl, resemble huge rectangular sunken gardens. Others, notably Washington's Griffith Stadium and Brooklyn's Ebbets Field, featured sharply angled outfield corners that could make a baseball behave like a cue ball in a game of pocket billiards.

And nothing said that they had to remain the same from year to year. In 1909 Pittsburgh's Forbes Field started life open and spacious—360 and 375 feet down the left and right foul lines, respectively, and 462 feet to deepest center. New stands in 1925 cut more than 75 feet off the right field line, and

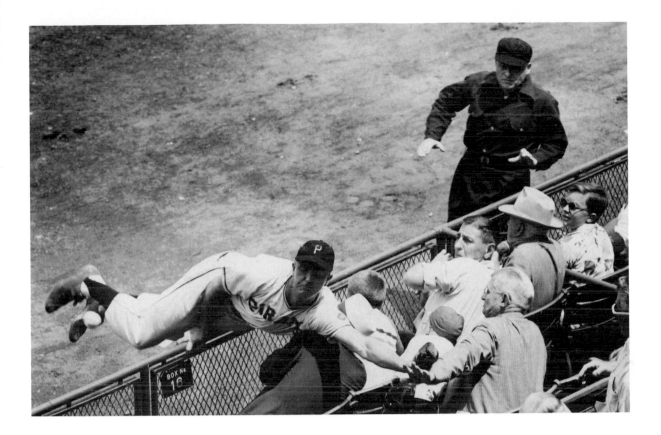

after World War II a short fence in left made home runs as easy as chip shots. Not surprisingly, the renovated stadium was named for home-team heroes, Greenberg Gardens in the beginning and Kiner's Korner a few years later.

The effect of these inner city parks on fielding was interesting. The wider the outfield expanses, the more baseball could be played along the old hit-and-run lines. There were innumerable triples, as well as an occasional inside-the-park home run. Baseball's most exciting hitting and fielding plays, the triple or the inside four-bagger represent 12 or 16 seconds of drama and chaos—the batter chugging around the base paths, the nine fielders setting up a regular bucket brigade of relaymen to stop him.

In the days of the dead ball and spacious parks where outfielders had to cover vast areas, there was a natural progression of hits: singles were far more common than doubles, doubles than triples, triples than home runs. From 1901 to 1929 the distribution of hits in the major leagues was 76.8 out of every 100 for singles, 15.2 for doubles, 5.3 for triples, 2.7 for homers. In 1988, by comparison, the ratios are 71.3, 17.6, 2.3. and 8.8. In 1912 Pittsburgh's Owen Wilson set a single-season record with 36 triples and the Pirates a 20th-century team record of 129. Many players who ended their careers by 1930 had more triples than homers, among them Ty Cobb, Honus Wagner, Shoeless Joe Jackson, Eddie Collins, Tris Speaker, George Sisler, Sam Crawford, and even Home Run Baker.

The dead ball that was used before 1920 merely added to the excitement. In enclosed fields outfielders had learned to play shallow, and balls hit over their heads or between them rolled to the deepest reaches of the park. With low scores the norm, baserunners felt it was worth their while to stretch an extra base out of a hit whenever possible. So the fans were regularly

Pittsburgh's Forbes Field was roomy all over, including foul territory. Pirate first baseman Jack "Stretch" Phillips made it all the way to the seats, then used every inch of his 6' 4" frame, but still couldn't reach this foul ball in a 1951 game against the Boston Braves.

Anaheim Stadium, home of the California Angels, is suburban, symmetrical, and relatively unremarkable, except for its 230-foot high tribute to the first letter of the alphabet (above). The stadium is known as "the Big-A," though the letter itself was moved into the parking lot in 1980.

treated to one of baseball's most exciting moments—a runner sliding into a base, a baseman taking the throw, a great cloud of dust, and the instant of anguish before the umpire's call.

In the 1920s things changed. Conscious of the crowd-pleasing possibilities of homers, baseball not only introduced a "lively" ball, it moved the outfield fences in. As a result, batters had a shorter shot to clear the fence, and fielders had less area to cover and a shorter throw to the infield. In 1929 major league home runs exceeded three-base hits for the first time. Plainly, a wonderful challenge in the field was disappearing.

But the new stadiums offered other challenges to fielding fans; these inner city parks were nothing if not idiosyncratic. Fielders had to learn how the ball would carom off walls, fences and screens. Brooklyn's Ebbets Field, opened in 1913, had a 38-foot fence and screen separating the park from Bedford Avenue in right and right center, and in short right field the foot of the wall slanted outward. The barrier was only 300 feet from home down the right field line, and balls were constantly bouncing off it in unpredictable directions. The best right fielders learned to play hits off the wall in spite of the angle and to hold batters to singles. Most famous of all was Pennsylvanian Carl Furillo, whose celebrated arm became known as the Reading Rifle.

Even weirder was Manhattan's Polo Grounds, the Giant's home from 1911 to 1957, the Yankees from 1913 to 1923, and the Mets in 1962 and 1963. The distances down the lines were an unnerving 257 to right and 279 to left. The bathtub-shaped structure curved out to 483 feet in straightaway center and nearly 450 feet in the power alleys. A Polo Grounds outfielder had two challenges: to learn the angles like a jai alai player and to cover the ground like a hare.

A Baseball Game at the Polo Grounds as seen from an airship—New York.

A lot of great players—including Hall of Famers Mel Ott, Hack Wilson and Freddie Lindstrom—have patrolled the Polo Grounds' vast center field, but the best was saved for last. Willie Mays became the Giants' center fielder in 1951, and moved with the team to San Francisco after the 1957 season.

Chicago's Wrigley Field, still the home of the Cubs, was built with short power alleys and a brick outfield fence that is now covered with ivy. In the spring balls slap off the wall and rip through the meager growth. By mid-summer a hit may actually be lost in the thick tapestry of vines. Other parks had outcropping stands or weirdly situated corners producing uncanny bounces. And not every fence was 38 feet tall. Most stadiums gave out-fielders an opportunity they never had in the pristine era—the chance to leap over a fence and rob the batter of a home run. In Yankee Stadium, opened in 1923 and ballyhooed as "The House That Ruth Built," there was a 3¾-foot fence just 295 feet down the right field line. Many a right fielder jumped high enough or reached over the wall to snag a would-be round-tripper. Indeed, almost every concrete-and-steel stadium had a fence under ten feet tall somewhere on the premises.

In 1935 baseball played its first game under the lights, in Cincinnati's Crosley Field. Other parks followed quickly, except for Wrigley Field, a holdout until 1988. As a result, fielders gazing skyward encountered yet another challenge. Though daylight has its problems—balls disappearing in and out of sun and cloud—glovemen found artificial lighting more uneven still. Even the best-lit parks leave parts of the field in darkness. Fielders lost balls in the glare, or they found them in the lights and lost them as they passed through dark spots. If a few bulbs were out, an arcing baseball might pass from light to dark to light and back to dark before settling into a fielder's glove—or into the outfield grass.

Until the 1960s, all stadiums had grass fields. Thanks to improved methods of groundskeeping and drainage, crews were constantly leveling off uneven spots—and reducing errors in the process. Clever groundskeepers

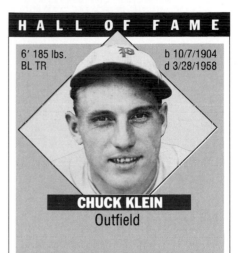

6' 185 lbs.
BL TR

b 10/7/1904
d 3/28/1958

CHUCK KLEIN
Outfield

In the year of the hitter, 1930, Chuck Klein was doing as well as any other batter, clubbing 40 home runs with 170 RBI and a .386 batting average for the Philadelphia Phillies.

However, during that same year, he set the modern major league record for outfield assists with 44. Klein had a few things going for him; 1930 was the best hitting year in baseball history, so naturally there were more opportunities to catch baserunners trying to advance. Klein also played half his games in Baker Bowl, where outfield fences were a cozy distance from home plate, making throws to the infield easy. Those same tin fences were pretty high and held in some line drives that might have been home runs elsewhere, putting more balls in play and adding a few more baserunners.

Most important, the Phillies pitching staff posted a horrendous 6.71 ERA. So even a right fielder in a game dominated by right-handed batters got a large portion of chances.

Known for his five-year assault on NL pitching, he led the league from 1929 to 1933 in at least one category every year and took the Triple Crown in 1933. Chuck Klein's most singular achievement may have been his fielding record, even though it brought small solace to a last-place club.

Klein completed his 17-year playing career in 1944. He was elected to the Hall of Fame in 1980.

Carl Furillo

Every other ballplayer has a throwing arm. Carl "the Reading Rifle" Furillo hid a long-range howitzer underneath his Brooklyn Dodgers uniform. It's September 21, 1949; the Dodgers are playing the St. Louis Cardinals. Stan Musial hits a high line drive to right. Marty Marion, who was on second, approaches third and is waved home. But Furillo catches Musial's drive off the wall, turns, and fires a perfect strike to catcher Roy Campanella, nailing Marion at the plate.

Two years later, on August 27, 1951, the Pittsburgh Pirates and the Dodgers are playing the first game of a doubleheader at Ebbets Field. Pirates pitcher Mel Queen is at bat in the third inning. Queen smacks what looks like a clean single off Dodgers pitcher Ralph Branca and lopes off down the baseline. Meanwhile, Furillo charges in on the ball and scoops it up like an infielder grabbing a grounder. His throw to first baseman Gil Hodges beats a startled Queen by two or three steps.

That's why they called him the Reading Rifle. From 1946 until 1960, Carl Furillo, a 6', 190-pound native of Stony Creek Mills, Pennsylvania, roamed right field for the Brooklyn and Los Angeles Dodgers. He used his magnificent throwing arm to break the heart of many a batter and baserunner. One writer noted, "So powerful were his pegs that most enemy runners refused to test them. If they did, they were usually gunned down like clay pigeons at a shooting range." Another called him "a ball hawk, the kind of natural outfielder who seems always to know almost from the crack of the bat where the ball is going."

While Furillo claimed that his throwing ability was "more God-given talent than anything else," he did study the art of throwing, much the same way that Ted Williams researched hitting. "I was always taught to use the arm, wrist, shoulder and body," Furillo said. "If you're throwing from center field you aim for the top of the pitcher's mound so that the ball will hit halfway between the mound and the plate. From right field you try to hit the cutoff man in the chest. You've got to get the ball out of your hand quickly. You have to charge the ball, come up with it and throw all in one motion."

Furillo grabbed the headlines with his miraculous throwing arm but he was also a solid hitter. His lifetime average was .299 and he won the NL batting title in 1953 with a .344 average. He hit over .300 five times, drove in more than 90 runs six times, and twice topped 100 RBI. However, he admitted, "I got more of a thrill out of throwing out a runner than I did getting a base hit. I used to love it. I really gloated on it."

Sadly, Furillo ended his playing days under a cloud. He was released by the Dodgers on May 17, 1960, but claimed he should have been put on the injured reserve list for 30 days, since he was injured. He sued the Dodgers for his full year's salary of $21,000—and won. When no other club picked him up, the 38-year-old said he had been blackballed. The Man with the Golden Arm was finished with baseball.

It seems ironic that an injury ended the Reading Rifle's playing career, for he had long been a fearless performer. Once, while playing the first game of a doubleheader, Furillo was spiked in the hand. He needed seven stitches. But he insisted on returning to the field and played the second game, rapping out two hits.

CARL FURILLO

Right Field
Brooklyn Dodgers 1946–1957
Los Angeles Dodgers 1958–1960

GAMES	**1,806**
FIELDING PERCENTAGE	
Career	**.980**
Season High	**.988**
PUTOUTS	
Career	**3,297**
Season High	**330**
PUTOUTS PER GAME	
Career	**1.93**
Season High	**2.54**
ASSISTS	
Career	**151**
Season High	**24**
ASSISTS PER GAME	
Career	**.09**
Season High	**.15**
CHANCES	
Career	**3,520**
Season High	**359**
CHANCES PER GAME	
Career	**2.06**
Season High	**2.81**
ERRORS PER GAME	
Career	**.04**
Season Low	**.02**
WORLD SERIES	**1947, 1949, 1952–1953, 1955–1956, 1959**

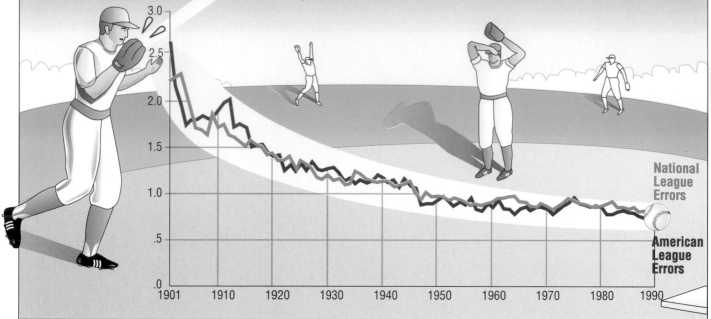

Decline of Errors

In 1876, the inaugural season of the National League, teams averaged about six errors a game each. By 1901, the year the American League began, that figure was under three a game, and in 1988 American League teams averaged just 0.74 errors a game, the lowest figure in history. Below is a look at the average number of errors—per team per game—from 1901 to 1988.

National League Errors

American League Errors

could be especially useful to the home team. If the infielders were sure-handed but sluggish, the groundkeeper could let infield grass grow high to slow down grounders; the Detroit crew is still famous for that practice. If a team had good bunters, the crew could "tilt" the ground near the foul lines to keep balls in fair territory; against a bunt-oriented visitor they'd tilt the foul lines away from fair territory. The most celebrated process of all was to water down the base paths to keep enemies from stealing. In 1962 San Francisco groundkeepers Jerry and Matty Schwab made a swamp of Candlestick Park when the Dodgers came to town for a late-season series and playoff. "Lake Candlestick" unnerved the visitors and helped the Giants win the pennant. The Schwabs were duly voted full shares of the World Series kitty.

Third-generation ballparks are loosely known as "superstadiums." Built in the last 30 years, these multisport colosseums typically accommodate 50,000 or more fans—the old concrete-and-steel stadiums averaged some 35,000—and often feature artificial playing surfaces. Modern parks are often built in the suburbs, and without city streets to define their dimensions, they're uniformly symmetrical—typically 330 feet down the lines and 400 to dead center, with eight to twelve-foot fences. Many are virtual carbon copies of each other; photos of Busch Memorial Stadium in St. Louis, Riverfront Stadium in Cincinnati, and Three Rivers Stadium in Pittsburgh are hard to identify. Five other modern stadiums—in Minneapolis, Seattle, Houston, Toronto and Montreal—are covered, either with permanent or movable domed roofs.

The effect these new stadiums have on the game is at best a mixed blessing. They are certainly commodious and comfortable for fans. Gone are

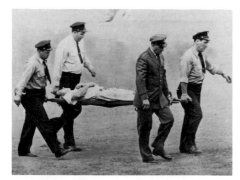

Brooklyn outfielder Pete Reiser was a superb talent with a nasty habit of running into the concrete wall in center field at Ebbets Field. In July 1942 Reiser was hitting .383 when he crashed into the wall, suffering a concussion and a fractured skull. "It felt like a hand grenade went off in my head," Reiser said.

the annoying pillars and columns that blocked the view of spectators unlucky enough to find themselves seated directly behind them. With most games played at night, gnats and mosquitoes hover high around the floodlights instead of chewing on people in the grandstands.

Things aren't so much improved for the players, however, and in many ways progress has been particularly pernicious to fielding. Indoor sports palaces use lights for both day and night games, and that artificial lighting can be very uneven, claim some players, because of harsh and inconsistent indoor backgrounds. Under such conditions, it's nothing for a fielder to lose a fly ball —or even a high-bouncing grounder—in the lights.

An outfielder is constantly playing the angles. He has to worry about balls that come off the walls on the fly and on the bounce, and no two chances are ever alike. He gets to know his home ballpark intimately, and he constantly studies and adapts to the characteristics of other parks in his league—high walls, low fences, hard concrete, sheet metal panels, padded cushions, bull-pen screens, and in Wrigley Field, at least, the infamous ivy tapestry.

Moving from one look-alike park to another, fielders understandably assume they can play them much the same way. An experienced player like Pete Rose knew better. "Whenever you play, you have to go out there and practice taking balls off the fence," he says. "Players don't realize that the ball caroms differently off the Atlanta fence from the Cincinnati fence from the Shea fence from the Philadelphia fence. You need fungo batters to hit balls into the corners and off the fences."

But the new stadiums aren't all bad. In most older fields, the grass grew right up to the outfield barriers, and even the most experienced fielders could

The ivy covering Wrigley Field's outfield walls may be lovely to look at, but it can produce nightmares for outfielders like St. Louis' Vince Coleman (above). Once Pirate great Roberto Clemente reached into the ivy to retrieve a ball, and came out throwing an empty paper cup.

Center fielder Fred Lynn's (below) specialty is making catches while bouncing off outfield walls. Lynn broke a rib crashing into a wall in 1982, and has often been sidelined by other injuries—from laryngitis to a broken toe—since his major league career began in 1974. Padded outfield fences in newer stadiums have encouraged outfielders to be more daring, so even a converted catcher like Pittsburgh's Brian Harper (right) could try to bring a home run back into the park.

Kansas City's Willie Wilson (opposite) has the speed to reach just about any ball that stays in the park, even if he has to bounce off the fence to do it. A Gold Glove winner in 1980, Wilson led AL outfielders in 1987 with a .997 fielding percentage on one error in 346 chances.

have nasty run-ins with walls they weren't expecting. The Dodgers' Pete Reiser nearly killed himself smashing into the Ebbets Field wall in 1942 and again in 1947. Today most fields have padded walls, and each new field is equipped with warning tracks. The point of the track is not so much visual, although it contrasts sharply with both natural or artificial grass, as it is audible. For a fielder backpeddling for a long fly, keeping his head up and his eye on the ball, the track gives a clear signal to the foot and to the ear the instant he steps on it. Still, he has to judge not only the arc and speed of the ball, but the angle and amount of room he has behind him.

At present there are basically two kinds of ballparks—multipurpose symmetrical stadiums, mostly in the National League, and older asymmetric parks, mostly in the American League. Teams understandably build rosters to suit their stadiums. The Boston Red Sox are constantly looking for right-handed sluggers to tee off in Fenway Park. The St. Louis Cardinals look for runners rather than home run hitters in cavernous Busch Stadium. Sadly, the fielding edge goes to teams built for the newer parks: speedsters cover ground better than sluggers.

The future looks a bit brighter. Reacting to massive revulsion against today's cookie-cutter look, the Minneapolis Metrodome and the Seattle Kingdome have recently erected 23-foot-high "blue monster" fences in right field; many a hit in these otherwise gloomy buildings becomes an adventure rather than a homer. Better still, stadium architects are planning baseball-only parks that will combine modern conveniences with ancient idiosyncracies. We can again expect to see short porches and tall walls, beeline throws and off-line caroms. We might even get to see some triples. ◗

The Longest Arm

Al Kaline

For millions of children on sandlot diamonds across the country, the two most chilling words in the language have always been "right field." It's bad enough that you've been the last kid picked when choosing up sides, but now you're stuck out in right field, baseball's answer to Alcatraz.

But if you stick it out, learn the position, and make the major leagues, you'll be in pretty fast company. For while right field is no man's land when you're a kid, in the majors it's the fastest ticket to the Hall of Fame. Unless, of course, you can pitch. Twenty right fielders have been enshrined in Cooperstown through 1989, including some of the game's greatest names—Babe Ruth, Hank Aaron, Mel Ott, Al Kaline and Roberto Clemente. And while most of these megastars were honored as sluggers, they were also talented outfielders playing a position whose importance is often underrated. The two men with the highest single-season home run totals in the history of the game—Roger Maris and Babe Ruth—were right fielders, and both were underrated defensively. Maris was the better right fielder of the two, and can lay claim to saving the 1962 World Series for the

Yankees. With two outs and a runner on first in the ninth inning of Game 7 and the Yankees clinging to a 1–0 lead, the Giants' Willie Mays drove a shot into the right center field gap. Maris raced over, cut the ball off, and threw a strike to second baseman Bobby Richardson, persuading the speedy Matty Alou to hold at third base. Willie McCovey then lined out to Richardson to end the Series.

As Maris showed, a right fielder's best friend is his throwing arm, and if it's strong and accurate, it can save his team a lot of runs over the course of a season. "More than any other position, he has to prevent runners from advancing," said former right fielder Ken Singleton, who led the majors with 20 assists for Montreal in 1973.

A right fielder with a good arm can stop runners from going from first to third on a single, persuade them not to stretch a double into a triple, and discourage them from scoring from second on a single. The right fielder has to make some of the longest throws in the game, often from the toughest positions. He must charge ground balls aggressively, but position himself so that his momentum carries him toward the base to which he is throwing. And because his throw to third is so long, he

Mets right fielder Darryl Strawberry is known mostly for his powerful bat, but his left arm can also be an intimidating weapon. In 1984 Strawberry tied for second among NL right fielders with 11 assists.

must be particularly adept at accurately playing the caroms of balls hit into the right field corner.

The most effective right fielders are those whose arms are so strong and accurate that base-runners stay put instead of challenging them. A case in point is Boston's Dwight Evans, acknowledged owner of one of baseball's best arms. Evans has never led AL outfielders in assists, but he has eight Gold Gloves to his credit. "Nobody goes from first to third on Dwight Evans," said 15-year veteran Enos Cabell. Sometimes runners are slow to learn, however, as with Jesse Barfield, who played his first 8½ seasons with Toronto before being traded to the Yankees in 1989. Barfield led AL outfielders in assists for three straight years, 1985 to 1987, before people stopped running on him.

In baseball's early days right field was something of a defensive desert, as most hitters were right-handed, and pitches were slow enough for them to pull almost everything to left. In fact, right field was often inhabited by pitchers who might be called on as relievers, as substitutions from the bench were illegal.

But by the early 1900s a few stars began to shine some light on the defensive possibilities in

Pittsburgh fans came to expect the extraordinary from Roberto Clemente, and they were rarely disappointed. Clemente often followed circus catches (above) with extraordinary throws, and led NL outfielders in assists a record five times.

Frank Robinson had a magical year in 1966, including a Triple Crown and this remarkable catch that came with two outs and two on in the bottom of the ninth and preserved the Orioles' 7–5 win over the Yankees.

right field. Since a right fielder's arm is so important, it's only natural that a right fielder be the first to dare to throw all the way home without an infielder's relay. Big Sam Thompson, who played with Detroit and Philadelphia of the NL from 1885 to 1898, also liked to crash through fences in pursuit of fly balls. Boston's Harry Hooper was the first great right fielder of the 20th century. Hooper's 344 career assists rank sixth on the all-time list, and he is the only Red Sox player to play on four world championship teams. Red Sox pitcher Smoky Joe Wood called Hooper the closest thing he ever saw as a fielder to Tris Speaker. But since Hooper played alongside Speaker in the Boston outfield, his defensive star didn't shine quite as brightly as it should have.

Detroit Tigers Sam Crawford and Ty Cobb swapped right and center field for a while, but each played right long enough to crack the record books, Cobb with an AL record of 12 double plays in 1907, and Crawford with a major-league-record .988 fielding percentage in 1905.

The Giants' Mel Ott is best known for his 511 home runs, but he was a wizard at playing the tricky right field wall in the Polo Grounds, and for two decades had runners looking over their shoulders and stopping at second. His 12 double plays in 1929 are still a 20th-century NL record. The following year, Phillies right fielder Chuck Klein had an amazing year at the plate, hitting .386 with 40 homers and 170 RBI, but he was even more amazing playing the short porch in Philadelphia's Baker Bowl. Klein threw out 44 runners from right in 1930, more than any other outfielder in the 20th century.

From Hooper to Jackie Jensen to Evans, the Red Sox have a long tradition of fine defensive right fielders, but two right fielders made their mark with Boston's other team, the Braves. In 1950 Tommy Holmes went the entire season—88 games—without an error. The next season Willard Marshall took over, and also played an errorless season, but his spanned 127 games.

From the mid-1950s to the mid-1970s, fans in each league got a chance to watch two of right field's true greats—Detroit's Al Kaline and Pittsburgh's Roberto Clemente. Both battled injuries throughout their careers, but both were spectacular outfielders. During his career, Kaline broke his jaw, his hand, his collarbone and his leg, but still

Tony Armas has a great throwing arm, but in 1982 he used his glove to set a major league record for right fielders with 11 putouts in one game.

Dave Winfield (above, left) is the only outfielder ever to win at least two Gold Gloves in each league—five with the Yankees, two with the Padres. Dwight Evans (right) has won eight—all with Boston.

managed to win ten Gold Gloves, and leads all right fielders in career putouts and total chances. At the ripe old age of 18, in a game against the White Sox, Kaline threw out one runner trying to stretch a single into a double, another trying to go from first to third on a single, and still another trying to score from second on a single. He led AL outfielders with 23 assists in 1958, but then baserunners stopped running on him, and their respect showed in his total of four assists the following season.

As good as Kaline was, in most people's minds Roberto Clemente was the greatest right fielder in baseball history. Clemente developed a cannon arm by throwing the javelin as a youth, and was the most graceful and acrobatic of right fielders. His speed was legendary, and he shocked fans and players alike once by running from right into short left center to field a bunt that had slipped through a hole at shortstop, then throwing out Houston's Walt Bond, who was trying to go from first to third. After seeing Clemente play in the 1971 World Series against Baltimore, Roger Angell wrote that Clemente, winner of 12 Gold Gloves, played "a kind of baseball that none of us had ever seen before—throwing and running

and hitting at something close to the level of absolute perfection."

Today's crop of right fielders includes such all-around stars as Barfield, Evans, San Diego's Tony Gwynn, Oakland's Dave Parker, and two New Yorkers—the Yankees' Dave Winfield and the Mets' Darryl Strawberry. They're big, aggressive outfielders who follow in Clemente's tradition of the cocky gunslinger ready to fire. "I've watched tapes of Clemente," said Pittsburgh's Andy Van Slyke. "He loved it when a guy challenged him. I try to be like that. There's nothing like the outfielder who tells the runner, 'I dare you to run.'"

Right field is an athlete's position, something that even author Bernard Malamud recognized in his novel *The Natural*. He called his hero Roy Hobbs and made him a right fielder.

How Hard is Fielding?

Cardinal shortstop Ozzie Smith (right) is known for his spectacular feats in the field, but he uses both hands to make the routine plays, and he makes just about all of them. In 1987 Smith led the NL in fielding percentage for the sixth time, tying Larry Bowa for the league record.

"PIE" TRAYNOR, CAPTAIN AND STAR THIRD BASEMAN OF THE SPEEDY PIRATE TEAM

Pittsburgh's Pie Traynor lowered the batting averages of numerous opponents with his sparkling play at third base in the 1920s and 1930s. "I'll bet he ruined more base hits for my club than any other two infielders in the game," said New York Giants manager John McGraw, himself an ex-third baseman.

When Philadelphia's Mike Schmidt (preceding page) retired in 1989, he left standards by which all future third basemen will be measured. He is the all-time NL leader at the position in assists and double plays.

F ielding is the last baseball skill learned and the first one forgotten. Watch a Little League game. When the ball is put in play, chaos invariably follows. Grounders bounce through legs like croquet balls through wickets. Throws ricochet around the infield like pinballs in a glass box. The most heartrending scene is a fly ball to the outfield. The little kid stationed out there comes charging in, only to find that the ball has bounced 15 feet behind him.

Now watch an old-timers' game. Some potbellied has-been can always be found to throw the ball over the plate, and plenty of other former studs are still strong enough to pole one out of the park. But let someone hit a pop-up or a simple grounder, and the old men in the field futilely huff after it or flail at it with gloves that no longer reach the ground.

Why should fielding skills be so fleeting? It's well established that glovework is the poor stepsister to hitting and pitching; she seems to don the glass slipper only when there's a game to be won. If fielding goes unrespected and largely uncompensated, it's no wonder players don't practice it enough.

But when you listen to baseball aficionados talking fielding—and they love to—you realize the situation is far more complicated than that. Fielding is a universe of theory and supposition, filled with black holes of debate and uncertainty. There's no consensus on what makes a good fielder, how to field, even how to teach fielding. That's why fielders learn late and forget early.

"What the really great infielders have is restraint," writes Louis D. Rubin, Jr., an author, publisher, and former baseball official. "An Ozzie Smith, a Brooks Robinson, a Luis Aparicio, a Marty Marion, a Frank White, a Pie Traynor seems not to hurry or strain to reach the ball; he is simply there

when the ball arrives, glove held low and waiting, and when he rises to throw it is done in one fluid motion, the ball is unleashed without fuss, always in time to beat the runner, yet seemingly never with excessive effort."

"The first thing I look for in a shortstop is soft hands," says the Cardinals' Ozzie Smith, the best shortstop in the game today. By "soft" Smith doesn't mean "weak": he means hands that will give with the hardest hit ground ball or line drive without giving it up. By contrast, "hard hands" simply deflect balls like rocks off a spatula. Smith's standard seems to make sense: what could be more important than catching the ball?

Not so fast, says former infielder Greg Pryor. "The first thing I look for is quick feet. If a boy has them, he can at least get to the ball. Then you can adjust to his inadequacies and teach the other skills: giving with the ball and getting in position. My number one goal between seasons was always to quicken my feet."

The one-handed catch has fitfully made its way into baseball practice, and there's general agreement about when to use it and when not to. Most baseball coaches still preach two-handing the routine plays and getting in front of the ball. Not Pryor: "Imagine trying to fence two-handed. Fielding two-handed is like fencing with a glove. If you get in front of the ball, you can't judge the bounce or give with it as well as you can to the side. The best fielders in the world are jai alai players, and you never see one catch a ball with the cesta in front of him."

Well, certainly Pryor teaches players by working on their weaknesses? Wrong again. "I say practice your strengths, and your weaknesses won't hurt as much." What's more, Pryor considers it a strength to do what comes naturally, even if it seems to go against established thinking. "Carney

Graig Nettles was in his early forties when he played with San Diego (above) in the mid-1980s, but in 1971, just his second full season, he set a major league record for third basemen with 412 assists for Cleveland. In 1973, with the Yankees, he came within two assists of tying his own record—which still stands.

Oakland's Carney Lansford is tough, agile and quick—everything you'd want in a third baseman. Although he is known mainly for his hitting, in 1979 Lansford posted the seventh best fielding percentage of all time among third basemen—.982—then led the AL again in 1987 and 1988.

Chicago's Luke Appling was a champion without a championship. He hit .310 lifetime and averaged 501 assists at shortstop per 154-game season, but in his career, which ran from 1930 to 1950, the White Sox never finished higher than third place.

Lansford, the Oakland third baseman, gets in a full crouch before every pitch. That's wrong, because you can't move to the side from a crouch. But if you had a stop-action film of Lansford, you'd probably see him straighten up when he has to. I used to have my hands straight out before every pitch. My teammate George Brett said I looked like a skinny bird in a love dance. But I brought my hands back in time. It's like all the weird stances you see hitters take; the best batters get in proper position before they swing."

Are fielders born or made? Granted, the best-coordinated infielder usually plays shortstop. From there he can easily switch to other positions. Mike Schmidt, the best all-around third baseman in baseball history, is a converted shortstop. So was the nonpareil second baseman Bill Mazeroski. Similarly, the best outfielder is generally stationed in center. He can always be redeployed elsewhere, like the Cubs' Andre Dawson moving to right and winning Gold Gloves there.

But if you speak to fielders, you'll find that even the best athletes among them benefited from long, arduous, and frequently ingenious labor. As a child, Ozzie Smith would lie on his back, throw a ball in the air, and try to catch it with his eyes closed. "There are a lot of times—say, when you're diving or fielding a bad hop—where you can't actually see the ball," he says. "Feeling is very important." The play that made Smith famous was essentially a blind-folded one. In 1978, Smith's first full season with the Padres, he ranged to his left in pursuit of a Jeff Burroughs grounder, dived for it, and then had to bare-hand the ball behind his back when it took a bad hop. When Smith bounced off the turf and threw out the runner, the sequence was flashed around the country on TV replays, and everyone learned about the Wizard of Oz.

Other fielding greats got an early jump on the ball—early in life, that is. Little Brooks Robinson threw golf balls off his door stoop in Little Rock, giving himself hard shots to his left and right, up and down. Al Kaline, the Tiger Hall of Fame right fielder with the rifle arm, fired rocks at the "O" on passing B & O freight cars. Jim Kaat, who won an unmatched 16 Gold Gloves as a pitcher, grew up listening to radio broadcasts of Detroit Tiger games. He got a kick out of the word pictures announcers painted of Bobby Shantz pitching for the Athletics, jumping into perfect fielding position. Kaat threw tennis balls off his garage door, bouncing forward and finishing with his glove in place the way he imagined Shantz doing. Brian Doyle and his twin brother Blake played full-swing pepper as kids. "If you dropped the ball or didn't hit it on the ground, the other guy got to slug you," says the the former Yankee infielder, who was the fielding star of the 1978 Series. "The drill taught you to have bat control and good hands." In Latin American countries there are dozens of impromptu catching games, hence the dominant Latin middle infielders. And you can bet that any klutz who made himself into an acceptable fielder has spent hours at solitary practice, as Greenberg did.

So it would seem that fielders are made rather than born. But Little League coaches beware—as we've seen, skills are often nurtured by youngsters originating their own drills. Some critics feel that Little League and Pee Wee routines stifle imagination and creativity. It's amazing how many big leaguers were never Little Leaguers.

What's the toughest play a player is likely to make in the course of a game? You'll be surprised at the range of answers. The most logical choice for infielders are the backhanded stabs that take them far from first base —behind third, in the hole between short and third, behind second—each

Known as "the Big Cat" for his quickness around first base, Montreal's Andres Galarraga was likened to the Dodgers' Gil Hodges—another great right-handed first baseman—by Cardinal manager Whitey Herzog. In 1987 Galarraga finished second to the Mets' Keith Hernandez in votes for the Gold Glove.

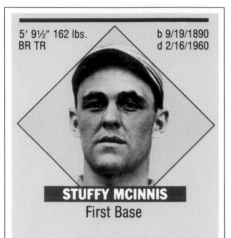

5' 9½" 162 lbs.   b 9/19/1890
BR TR   d 2/16/1960

STUFFY MCINNIS
First Base

The Philadelphia Athletics originally signed Stuffy McInnis as a middle infielder in 1909, but owner and manager Connie Mack had another idea of where to use the 18-year-old.

Common wisdom said that a first baseman should be tall so that infielders could have the largest target possible. Mack knew this, but needed a replacement for fading veteran Harry Davis and played the 5' 9½" McInnis at first for 97 games in 1911. Stuffy responded well to more time at the plate, winding up with a .321 average for the season, but he made 17 errors in the field.

He still had problems in 1912, making 27 errors in a full season, but he led the league in assists and putouts, and over the next 15 years compiled a .984 fielding percentage.

Playing in what was called the $100,000 infield with Eddie Collins, Jack Barry and "Home Run" Baker, McInnis started in two World Series in 1913 and 1914. Before the 1918 season, he was traded to the Boston Red Sox, helping them to their last world championship. While with the Sox in 1921 he made only one error and started a streak of 163 errorless games, unsurpassed until 1973, when Mike Hegan completed 178 games without an error.

A career .308 hitter with six different clubs, Stuffy McInnis had a leaping, diving, one-handed style that changed forever the way first base would be played.

Third base is a volatile position, even for sure-handed, strong-armed players like Chris Brown. In 1985, with the Giants, Brown paced NL third basemen with a .971 fielding percentage. In 1986 it dipped to .933.

requiring a pivot and long throw. Major league players don't always see it that way. "A two-hopper at third," says third base ace Graig Nettles. "You can't go in or back, and you don't get any perspective on the ball." Other third basemen fear the surprise bunt. "You have to field it one-handed, because you're moving at top speed," says Brooks Robinson. "If you field the ball with your left foot forward, you can throw right away, but it's awkward to bend down with your right foot forward. I always used a little stutter step to get the left foot in front."

"The toughest chances are slowly hit balls," says Toronto shortstop Tony Fernandez. "Hard hit ones become double plays. Slowly hit balls take spins and bounces, and you have to rush the throw."

Willie Randolph, the Los Angeles second baseman, agrees wholeheartedly. "The toughest play for a second baseman is a slow roller or a topper over the mound," he says. "If you're playing at regular depth, you have to run at full speed, catch the ball, and throw across your body sidearm and almost backwards. A lot of the time you have to field the ball on the short hop and bend over, which isn't easy, and it's tough to make an accurate throw when you're moving away from the bag. On top of everything else, you know you'll eat some turf, so you have to put both arms out when you fall."

"I had a lot of trouble at first base on balls hit to my right, but also with the pickoff throw," says Larry Parrish, who switched there in 1988 after several years as a third baseman and designated hitter for the Texas Rangers. "If the pitcher throws it off-line, you get caught flat-footed. A throw behind the runner is especially tough for a righthanded fielder like me. The coaches told me to step for the ball, as if I were taking the throw from third or short or second."

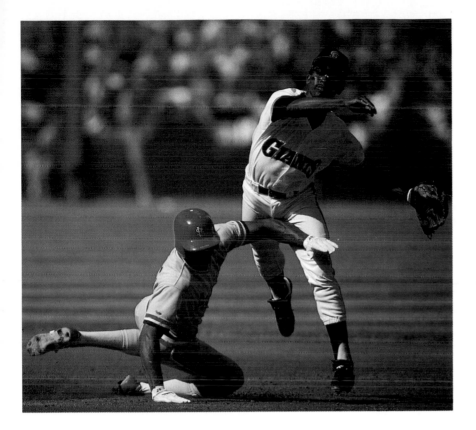

San Francisco shortstop Jose Uribe (left, throwing over St. Louis' Willie McGee) has earned a spot among the finest fielding shortstops of the 1980s. In 1986 he finished a close second in the NL to Ozzie Smith in fielding percentage—.978 to .977—and double plays—96 to 95.

Dave Van Gorder is a good catcher, but his fielding hasn't been enough to earn him much playing time in the majors. Although he led the Class AAA American Association in putouts and total chances in 1981 and 1983, he's never played more than 73 games in any of his five major league seasons.

Outfielders might be expected to fear long running catches, but almost to a man they cite the ball hit right at them. There's no angle, and the fielder may hesitate a second before committing himself—often a fatal second. "When they take a big swing and just get a piece of the ball, that's when you take a step back and have to rush in," says Royals center fielder Willie Wilson. Or vice versa. In the 1968 Series finale, the usually imperturbable Cardinal center fielder, Curt Flood, took a step in, only to see Jim Northrup's drive carry over his head for the decisive two-run triple. It can happen to anyone.

For a pitcher—coming out of his follow-through less than 20 yards away from the batter—there is nothing tougher than a line drive or a bouncing ball straight up the middle. Every pitcher knows about the sad case of Herb Score, a legendary fastballer who was never the same after being struck in the face by a line drive off the bat of Gil McDougald in 1957. Yet not every pitcher tries to follow through in perfect fielding position. "All they should be concerned about," says ex-catcher Tim McCarver, "is keeping the ball off the bat."

"A catcher's toughest play is tagging the runner after taking a throw from right field," says Toronto receiver Ernie Whitt. "It's a blind play, and you have to plant yourself and concentrate on catching the ball before you tag the guy. You want to give him part of the plate so that he'll slide. Then you take it away from him by collapsing your whole body in front of him. It's tough to move a guy who's sitting on his haunches."

In one memorable play, Whitt's teammate Buck Martinez took a throw from right fielder Jesse Barfield and suffered a broken right leg and a dislocated right ankle while tagging hard-sliding Phil Bradley of the Mariners.

Mickey Vernon

Smooth. Graceful. Rhythmic. Slick. He could play in a tuxedo. Such were descriptions of how Mickey Vernon performed at first base. Listless. Takes things too easy. Downright laziness. The affliction of vertical sleeping sickness. Such too were descriptions of Vernon in the field.

"Mickey is the ideal player to manage . . . always giving all he has," said Senators manager Bucky Harris, for whom Vernon played from 1939 to 1942 and from 1950 to 1954. "I think he's been underrated because his style at bat and in the field appear effortless. A lot of fans might misconstrue that as laziness. I'd like to have more 'lazy' players just like him."

James Barton "Mickey" Vernon had a flair around first base; he made it look easy. And he made it look easy for a long time. Vernon played in four decades—1939 to 1960—and spent much of his career with the Washington Senators, mostly under Harris. After retiring at age 42 he managed the Senators from 1961 to 1963.

A seven-time all-star, Vernon played 2,237 games at first base, a 20th-century record in the majors. "It was the only position I ever wanted to play," he said. And play it he did. No other American League first baseman has had more chances, 21,467, or putouts, 19,808. Of course many of those came on the tail end of groundouts. But Vernon also set AL marks for assists by a first baseman in a season, 155 in 1949, and a career, 1,448.

And he could hit. A .353 mark in 1946, his first season back from two years of service in the Navy in World War II, gave the lefty-swinging Vernon his first batting title, 11 points better than runner-up Ted Williams. He had never hit .300 before and didn't again until 1953. That's when he bested Al Rosen, .337 to .336, banging out two hits on the final day to deprive Rosen of the Triple Crown.

Yankee great Allie Reynolds said, "I pitch more carefully to Mickey than anyone else. He's not one of those powerful guys who is always looking down a pitcher's throat, but . . . You pitch him outside and he hits to left. Pitch him inside and he can put it out of the park."

Vernon retired just shy of 2,500 hits and led the AL in doubles three times. He didn't hit many home runs, but he provided the game-winning shot on Opening Day 1954. Besides the expected mobbing by teammates at home plate, he was greeted by a man in a suit. Vernon recalled the man saying: "It's okay, I'm a Secret Service man. The president wants to see you over at his box." The president was Dwight Eisenhower, who made it well known Vernon was his favorite player. "Nice going," was Ike's brief message for Mickey.

But fans remember him most for his fielding, like the day in May 1946 when he turned two *unassisted* double plays in one game for the Senators. Vernon spent 13½ seasons with the Washington Senators, perennial doormats of the AL, and he never played in a World Series. "But I really couldn't complain too much," he said years later. "You had to look at it this way: There were only eight first basemen in the American League . . . and you were one of them."

Mickey Vernon's career spanned five teams and four decades, but he never lost his superb feel for playing first base. "He played with a velvet touch, gliding around the bag as though engaged in a form of outdoor ballet," wrote Rich Westcott in Diamond Greats.

MICKEY VERNON

First Base
Washington Senators 1939–1948
Cleveland Indians 1949–1950
Washington Senators 1950–1955
Boston Red Sox 1956–1957
Cleveland Indians 1958
Milwaukee Braves 1959
Pittsburgh Pirates 1960

GAMES	**2,409**
FIELDING PERCENTAGE	
Career	.990
Season High	.994
PUTOUTS	
Career *(6th all time)*	19,808
Season High	1,438
PUTOUTS PER GAME	
Career	8.85
Season High	9.45
ASSISTS	
Career *(3rd all time)*	1,448
Season High *(6th all time)*	155
ASSISTS PER GAME	
Career	.65
Season High	1.01
CHANCES	
Career *(6th all time)*	21,467
Season High	1,607
CHANCES PER GAME	
Career	9.60
Season High	10.50
ERRORS PER GAME	
Career	.09
Season Low	.06
DOUBLE PLAYS	
Career *(1st all time)*	2,044
Season High *(6th all time)*	168

Kansas City catcher Larry Owen (above) has played just 171 games in the majors since his pro career started in 1977, so he's even more willing than most to sacrifice his body to keep a run from scoring, even against Texas' 225-pound Pete Incaviglia. Owen took the blow, but got the out.

Incredibly, Martinez hung on to the ball. But the play wasn't over. Dazed and lying on his back, Martinez saw batter Gorman Thomas heading for third, and got off a throw. It carried into left, but Martinez gamely hung on to take outfielder George Bell's return throw and tag out Thomas at the plate: a routine 9–2–7–2 double play if you're scoring.

But that isn't the play that worried former catcher Joe Garagiola most. "The toughest play for a catcher? Tying run on third and a knuckleballer on the mound. You aren't even thinking about catching the ball. All you want to do is make sure it doesn't get behind you."

No two infielders have the same system for preparing to field a ground ball. When he was a big league infielder in the late 1970s, Brian Doyle had a pre-pitch drill his Yankee teammates got a kick out of:

Spit twice.
Wipe mouth on the right shoulder.
Wipe mouth on the left shoulder.
Put right hand to the bill of the cap.
Take off glove and bring left hand to the bill of the cap.
Put the glove back on.
Pound the glove twice.

"It was a routine I used as a way to keep myself focused while I was waiting for the catcher's signal," says Doyle. "Then I'd watch the pitcher. I wanted to see the ball come out of his hand and its flight."

The Pittsburgh Pirates' Bill Mazeroski had fielding a ground ball down to an art. "I never wanted to move back on a ball unless I had to. If a ground ball was hit right at me, I'd charge it or at least take a stutter step. Then I'd catch

the ball on the little finger of my glove and flip it right over to my bare hand. I think it's softer that way than catching one-handed and covering up with the bare hand. Finally, I'd throw sidearm without winding up."

Mazeroski, who played in the era of natural grass, when ground balls could move unpredictably, held his bare hand next to the glove. These days, especially on artificial turf, balls bounce faster and higher but more predictably. The best current second baseman, Frank White of the Royals, holds his bare hand above the glove to trap unexpectedly high hops. "A lot of bad hops hit you on the chest or arm after bouncing over the glove," he says. "What I've been able to do with the grip is force the ball back into the glove with the palm of my right hand." Like Mazeroski, however, White is exceptionally aggressive. Most fielders take the easy hop and cradle the ball. White takes it on the short hop, pushing his glove forward. He plays the ball, not vice versa.

There's no consensus on how to execute baseball's most important fielding maneuver: pivoting on the double play. Mazeroski touched the bag with his right foot and stepped straight at the runner before making the throw. "My theory was that taking a step away from the runner would slow me down," he says. The Cardinals' Julian Javier, a Maz contemporary, chose to elude incoming runners; he wasn't known as the Phantom for nothing. Bobby Grich, an excellent second baseman from 1970 to 1986, always touched the bag with his left foot. "If my right foot were there, my momentum would be toward first too much, and I'd have trouble taking throws to my right," he says. Willie Randolph doesn't move at all: "I'm one of the few who pivot from a standstill. I don't need momentum, because I have a strong arm."

St. Louis second baseman Julian Javier (above, center) went low for this throw, but was at his best when hurdling oncoming runners. "Like a ghost. Dancing in the air," said teammate Dal Maxvill (above, left), who played alongside Javier from 1962 to 1971. Bucky Dent (below) led AL shortstops three times in fielding percentage and twice in double plays.

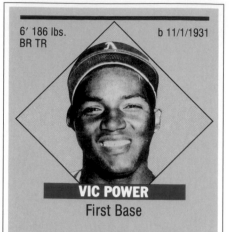

6' 186 lbs.
BR TR

b 11/1/1931

VIC POWER
First Base

Some people didn't like the way Vic Power played baseball. He caught everything one-handed, and held his bat straight down until the ball was pitched. They called him a showboat, and a loafer. He was a black player in the 1950s who refused to be silent in the face of heckling and abuse, so he saw plenty of beanballs and fights.

But Power was a marvelous first baseman. He won seven Gold Gloves in his career, and his lifetime .994 fielding percentage and .83 assists per game rank seventh and fourth, respectively, among first basemen. "I was born to play first base," he said. A vicious line-drive hitter, Power hit .284 lifetime.

Power signed with the Yankees in 1950, and hit .349 in Class AAA in 1953, but wasn't brought up to the majors despite the fact that two Yankees first basemen were sidelined in August. Black groups picketed Yankee Stadium, but Power stayed a minor leaguer, and New York didn't have a black player on its major league roster until Elston Howard in 1955.

In 1954 he was traded to the A's. He had his best year in 1955, hitting .319 and leading the AL in putouts, assists and double plays. Despite his reputation as a showboat, he won compliments from one man he played for. "He reminds me of Willie Mays," said A's manager Eddie Joost. "The way Willie sparks the Giants, that's the way Vic sparks the A's."

Cleveland's Rocky Colavito couldn't reach this Yogi Berra home run in 1958, but from September 6, 1964, to June 15, 1966, Colavito caught everything he could reach, establishing an AL record with 234 consecutive errorless games.

To Mets manager Davey Johnson, however, there are some constants in the pivot play. "It's like a bullfight," he told *The New York Times'* Joseph Durso. "The second baseman is the matador. His left leg is the red flag. The runner comes sliding in straight for it. He's the bull."

"You make the play with a series of steps, one, two, three," Johnson said. "You plant your left leg on the bag. You catch the ball, pivot on your left foot and step across the bag with your right foot. You plant the right foot on the other side, pivot on it and throw the ball while you raise your left leg and the runner slides under it. You're throwing the ball right through him, and he's not knocking you into left field."

Good outfielders play as shallow as they dare. The reason is simple: most fly balls and line drives are hit in front of them. The shallower they play, the more hits they'll steal—and the shorter their throws will be. Bobby Murcer, the former Yankee center fielder, offers another good reason for playing shallow: "It's harder to catch a ball coming in than going out. When you're running in, you're usually trying to catch a ball at your knees or lower. That's tougher to do than catching it at eye level, which you normally do when you're running back."

Boston right fielder Dwight Evans is always thinking ahead. "When there are runners on base, you always want to catch the ball lined up toward the base you're throwing to," he says. "With a runner on first, I'll actually circle around a base hit so that I'm facing third when I field it."

Most right-handed batters slice the ball toward the right field line against right-handed pitchers, but some right-handed batters drive shots up the gap. Evans has a book on every hitter he faces. "Three batters used to give me fits," he says. "Tony Oliva's hit would hook or sink or rise over my

Phil Bradley was third in the NL with 14 assists in 1988, then was traded from the Phillies to the Orioles, where he became part of one of baseball's best defensive outfields and a big reason for Baltimore's 1989 turnaround after 107 losses in 1988.

head—he made me feel like a fool. Cecil Cooper hit balls that took off to my right; you won't see that from other lefthanded hitters. Graig Nettles would hit balls with topspin or bite. You think it'll be easy, and you wind up diving."

"Catching the ball is only part of the job," says Joe Garagiola, who spent enough time behind National League plates in the post-World War II years to know. "One phase of baseball that's least appreciated by those who sign contracts is the ability to work a ballgame. A great joy for a catcher is finding out what works for a pitcher on a given day. Take the 1988 Series. In the last game Rick Dempsey did a wonderful job with Orel Hershiser. The best pitch Hershiser uses is a sinker, but for the first five innings it wasn't working. Dempsey had him changing speeds on his fastball and curve until he found the sinker in the sixth. From then on, no trouble."

Bob Boone, who has caught more games than anyone else in baseball history, uses a slightly different system. "I view pitching and catching as less of a science than an art form," he says. "You might have a pitcher who's having trouble with a breaking ball, so you'll throw them early when he won't get in trouble with one that hangs. You work up to a point where you can use them in pressure situations. The most important thing is to stay with the pitcher's strength, not the batter's weakness. But I can't explain what I do. Things happen. All of a sudden you're going with pitches you thought you'd never call."

Tim McCarver fully agrees. "It's more important for a catcher to know his pitcher than to know the hitter because even the best hitters won't get many hits off the best pitches. Steve Carlton thought of 'throwing through' the batter—literally playing catch with his catcher.

Left fielder Mike Greenwell (leaping) and center fielder Ellis Burks have joined right fielder Dwight Evans to give the Red Sox a fine defensive outfield. Boston was second in the AL in fielding in 1988, committing just 93 errors.

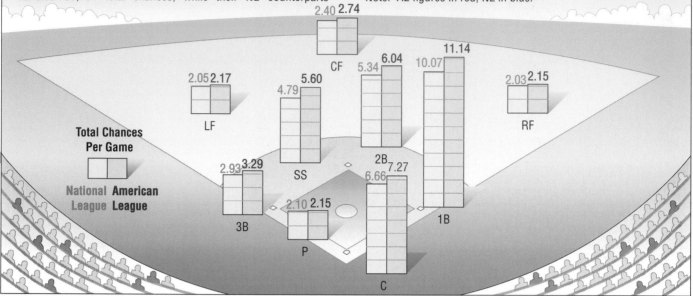

Where the Action Is

The number of chances—the combined total of all putouts, assists and errors—each fielder handles varies considerably from position to position. Below is a look at how many chances each position handled per game in 1988. American League fielders handled 85,784 total chances, while their NL counterparts handled 75,264. Seattle second baseman Harold Reynolds had 471 assists to lead the majors, San Francisco first baseman Will Clark led the majors with 1,492 putouts, and Pittsburgh third baseman Bobby Bonilla committed 32 errors, most in the majors. Note: AL figures in red, NL in blue.

CF 2.40 2.74
LF 2.05 2.17
RF 2.03 2.15
SS 4.79 5.60
2B 5.34 6.04
1B 10.07 11.14
3B 2.93 3.29
P 2.10 2.15
C 6.66 7.27

Total Chances Per Game

National League   American League

"A good defensive catcher can help a pitcher in so many ways. Sometimes just slapping down those signals with authority is a big plus. A tentative signal makes for a tentative pitch. A confident signal can make for a confident pitch, which may be successful even if it wasn't the textbook pitch you should have called. You also want to call your pitches briskly to establish a rhythm. As former pitcher Jim Kaat used to say, if you think long, you thing wrong."

On even counts a catcher will usually call a pitcher's best pitch. He doesn't want a pitcher to fall behind on the count. If he does, he'll almost have to throw his best pitch, and the batter will be waiting for it. If a pitcher is ahead on the count, he'll have options. The count is the fulcrum of the pitcher-batter relationship.

And the catcher is the fulcrum of the pitcher-catcher relationship. "It's been said that the pitcher's best friend is the double play," says former Oriole ace Jim Palmer. "But it's really the catcher. He's the guy you count on to come out and say the right thing."

When baseball people evaluate the best all-time fielders, they look for more than stats and skills. They ask other questions: How versatile was a player? How did he influence the play of his position? The most versatile fielder in baseball history was Pete Rose, who played 500 or more games at each of five positions: left and right field, and first, second and third bases. He was an all-star at each. In addition to leading the league in fielding percentage at four spots—no one else ever led at more than two—Rose is among the top three in career fielding percentage for outfielders with .9911. Perhaps most impressive, he made position changes swiftly and painlessly.

Some players have been their position's style setters. After the legendary Tris Speaker began playing shallow center for the Red Sox, and later

for the Indians early in the century, it became a test of mettle for every outfielder to edge as close as possible to the infield grass. Lately outfielders have become timid. They prefer to field balls on the bounce instead of being embarrassed by an occasional shot over their heads.

Mets first baseman Keith Hernandez, who will rush to the third-base side of the pitcher's mound while fielding bunts, has singlehandedly set a new standard for first basemen. No longer expected merely to take throws and field balls hit right at them, they now must cover more ground than a cattle rancher. Similarly, artificial turf has forced other infielders to roam freely. Phillies third baseman Mike Schmidt once chased an errant throw into right field. Ozzie Smith plays an exceptionally deep shortstop, confident that he has speed enough to run down slow grounders and still get the batter. Johnny Bench proved that catchers can be pretty agile blocks of granite. Superbly conditioned backstops Bob Boone and Carlton Fisk have dared their peers to do what used to be considered self-destructive: catch well into their forties.

Fielding is a democratic art, and ballplayers have special respect for little-known teammates who enter games as late-inning defensive replacements. "The toughest fielding job is being inserted in the ninth inning of a 1–0 game at short or second," says former Yankee shortstop Tony Kubek. "If you pinch hit, it's do or die. Not with defense. You're in there to catch everything hit at or near you. You can't make a mistake. You can be as loose as you want, but you're expected to be perfect." Says Pryor, the quintessential utilityman, "I took special pride in not making errors that cost runs." The toughest fielding job over the course of a season may be switching to an unfamiliar position. Mickey Stanley moved from center to short for the

His great throwing arm overshadowed the fact that Reds catcher Johnny Bench covered a lot of ground around home plate. After leading NL catchers in putouts and assists during his rookie year, 1968, the 21-year-old Bench asked Ted Williams to autograph a ball for him. Williams signed it, "To a Hall of Famer, for sure." In 1989 Williams was proved right.

When it comes to right of way, Kansas City outfielder Mike Brewer (17)—whose major league career lasted 12 games—had to defer to second baseman Frank White, one of the best to ever play the position. In 1988, at the age of 38, White played 148 games at second and did not make an error on a ground ball—all four of his errors came on throws.

1968 World Series—a rare and unusually challenging change of venue. The toughest switch made on a more regular basis seems to be moving from anywhere to third base. There's just no preparation for those hard shots. "I was like a fish out of water," says Mazeroski, who played third only ten times. "The ball came off the bat differently and got to me faster than when I played second. At third I felt like I had to hurry my throws because it was so far to first base, and I wound up throwing the ball away."

The best fielding plays are frequently the most improbable. "The bases were loaded with one out in the ninth inning and we were protecting a one-run lead," says Brian Doyle, recalling a game he played with Columbus in the International League, "when John Shelby hit a grounder up the middle. I came over from my second-base position, fielding the ball and without looking threw behind my back to the shortstop, who relayed to first for the game-ending double play. Doc Edwards, the Rochester manager, said he's seen the play made only twice before—by my brothers Blake and Denny."

Even tougher than the blind throw is the blind stab. Ozzie Smith wasn't the only one to turn that trick. Schmidt caught a grounder behind his back when he was moving toward the hole while the ball was curving toward the line. Yankee pitcher Dave Righetti made a 180-degree turn on his follow-through and fielded Luis Salazar's smash between his legs. "All I was trying to do," says Righetti, "was protect myself."

History has its share of barehanded catches too, like the clutch stab Red Sox right fielder Harry Hooper made in the finale of the 1912 World Series, falling into a mass of fans in brand-new Fenway Park's temporary right field bleachers. Willie Mays made a number of gloveless grabs, including one of a Roberto Clemente line drive in Forbes Field's

deep center, which Pittsburgh executive Branch Rickey called the greatest play he'd ever seen.

Some plays are mental gems. On September 23, 1908, the Giants Al Bridwell singled home the apparent game-winning run against the Cubs, but Chicago second baseman Johnny Evers noticed that base-runner Fred Merkle hadn't touched second. Evers procured a ball, stepped on second, appealed the run, and won a replay of the entire game. As it happened, the Cubs and Giants finished the season tied for first, and the replayed game, won by the Cubs, decided the pennant. Merkle's careless performance earned him the unshakable nickname "Bonehead," while Evers' alertness decided a pennant and, mind you, he never even touched a batted ball.

The final criterion for excellence seems to be visibility: the great play with a title at stake. There have been many spectacular October catches, but arguably nothing as athletic and astonishing as the one Ron Swoboda made on October 15, 1969. The Mets were leading the Orioles two games to one in the World Series with a one-run lead in the ninth inning of Game 4. With Orioles on first and third and one out, Brooks Robinson hit a sinking liner to right center. The only player anywhere near the ball was Swoboda, a lumbering right fielder and the very symbol of historic Mets futility, better known for tripping over bases and locking himself in cages than making balletic catches. The 57,367 fans in attendance at Shea Stadium held their breath and feared the worst: the ball rolling to the wall, two runs scoring, and the heavily favored Orioles squaring the Series. Swoboda had other ideas. Instead of trying to play the ball on a bounce and holding the damage to one run, he raced headlong across the outfield grass and dived parallel to the ground.

Pete Rose played in All-Star Games at five positions: second base, right field, left field, third base and first base. With the Phillies, Rose played first base—every day (above). In 1980, at the age of 39, Rose played in all 162 games, and led NL first basemen in assists and fielding percentage.

Dodger left fielder Kirk Gibson tripped but still managed to make the catch on this drive by the Mets' Mookie Wilson in Game 3 of the 1988 NL Championship Series. The Mets won the game, 8–4, but Gibson won Game 4 with a homer, and L.A. won the Series in seven.

Incredibly, Swoboda backhanded the ball in the webbing of his glove, and almost as improbably, he hung onto the ball after landing with a thud. Frank Robinson tagged up at third and scored the tying run, but the Mets won in extra innings and took the Series the next day. Ron Swoboda had kept the dream alive.

Not even Swoboda had expected to make the catch. "It hit way out near the end of my web," he said. "Fortunately, that's the best spot for a baseball to hit on a diving catch. If it hits solidly in the pocket, there's a good chance your hand will jar it out when it hits the ground. This time all I got was a face full of dirt."

Few people on hand would accept his unduly modest explanation. "The greatest catch I ever saw," said Hall of Fame center fielder Mickey Mantle. "The toughest play in baseball," says former second baseman Joe Morgan, "is a diving, backhanded catch by an outfielder."

Especially when the whole world is watching. ⚾

U.S. players can lay claim to most of the great catches of all time, but a majority of major leaguers in a 1983 poll picked a 1981 catch by Japan's Masafumi Yamamori (opposite) as the greatest they'd ever seen. The Hankyu Braves' Yamamori climbed the left field fence, balanced himself on the wooden railing, and backhanded a drive by Sumio Hirota of the Lotte Orions.

FIRST BASE.

Scoop

Hal Chase

First base has been the site of some of baseball's rudest awakenings. Many of the game's greatest stars have been shifted to first late in their careers, thinking that anyone who could stand still and catch a baseball could play there, only to find that playing first is quite a bit tougher than it looks. Yankee great Joe DiMaggio, one of the most talented and mobile center fielders of all time, played exactly one game there in 1950, then categorically refused to ever play there again. Frank Robinson, an outfielder by trade, played first occasionally with Baltimore in the late 1960s and early 1970s. When asked how he liked it, he replied, "You can have it."

The list of players who've played first late in their careers reads like a Hall of Fame welcome wagon: Hank Aaron, Willie Mays, Carl Yastrzemski, Stan Musial, Ernie Banks and Mickey Mantle. Boog Powell, Dick Stuart, George Scott, Don Mincher and Lee May were typical of the big, power-hitting first basemen of the 1960s. But first base has a rich tradition of fine two-way players, men who've combined the size and mobility it takes to be truly great at the position.

In 1929 six of baseball's 16 starting first basemen were headed for the Hall of Fame—Bill Terry, Jim Bottomley, George Sisler and George Kelly in the NL, Lou Gehrig and Jimmie Foxx in the AL. All were good fielders, with Terry, Sisler and Kelly ranking among the all-time best. And almost 60 years later, first base had again developed a strong case for being baseball's most glamorous position. Picking first basemen for the 1987 All-Star Game was an absurd task. Of the 26 starting first basemen in baseball, 15 drove in at least 89 runs, and 18 hit at least 20 homers. Included in this group were some master fielders like Kent Hrbek of the Twins, Don Mattingly of the Yankees, Pete O'Brien of the Rangers, Eddie Murray of the Orioles, and the incomparable Keith Hernandez of the Mets.

The current group of multitalented first basemen have all the tools needed to play the position effectively—quickness, agility, range and flexibility. First basemen need to be quick enough to get to the bag in plenty of time to set themselves for throws from other infielders. When they get there, that's when the fun begins. Throws arrive in the dirt, up the line and over their heads, and a good play can save two bases and a couple of

Willie McCovey's 6' 4" frame and seemingly endless reach earned him the nickname "Stretch" and a reputation as one of the best first basemen of the 1960s and 1970s. "On ground balls hit down to the second baseman, there's no need to throw," wrote Jim Murray in the Los Angeles Times. *"The second baseman just hands it to Willie."*

A truly complete player, Yankees slugger Don Mattingly led AL first basemen in fielding percentage from 1984 to 1987.

runs. Range is important because, like third basemen, first basemen protect a foul line, and knocking down balls hit down the line provides another two-base save. Also, the greater a first baseman's range, the farther to the right his second baseman can play.

And while he doesn't often have to throw to other bases, the throws he's called on to make are some of the toughest in the infield. His throw to the pitcher covering first on the 3-1 play on a bunt or a ground ball to the right of the bag is a delicate art, as he must lead the throw to an on-the-move pitcher. Sometimes it's an underhand pitch; sometimes it's a short strike.

First base is the only position—besides perhaps pitcher—where it's an advantage to be left-handed, since left-handers can face the rest of the infield with their foot on the bag, and they don't have to pivot before throwing to second or third. But that still doesn't make a throw to third after fielding a bunt easy. The 3-6-3 double play demands speed, accuracy and perfect timing, and is one of the toughest plays in the game. A first baseman must field the grounder cleanly, make a strong, accurate throw to the shortstop with the runner in

In 1918 Baseball Magazine *called the Browns' George Sisler a "fielder of consummate ability," and Sisler proved it by leading the AL in assists six times.*

Brooklyn's Gil Hodges was agile, but above all strong, especially in his hands. "Gil wears a glove at first because it's fashionable," said Pee Wee Reese, Hodges' teammate from 1947 to 1958. "With those hands he doesn't really need one."

his line of fire, then race back to the bag in time to take the return throw.

The acknowledged masters of this, and most other plays at first, are Hal Chase and Keith Hernandez. The two players could hardly be more different, both in time and temperament. Chase was probably the crookedest ballplayer in an era when the competition for that title was fierce, while Hernandez is a model ballplayer, a team leader and an all-around nice guy. But each redefined the position.

Chase played with five teams from 1905 to 1919, an era when defense was still the most important aspect of baseball. He played first base all over the infield, ranging to areas where no first baseman had gone before, and his plays are the stuff of legend. Stories are told of Chase's unassisted double plays in which he would race forward to catch a bunt before it hit the ground, then pursue and catch a runner trying to scramble back to third. Chase led AL first basemen in errors a record five times, but many came on balls no other first baseman would even get to, and on throws other infielders couldn't handle. As a measure of his effort, he shares the record with two other

great first basemen—George Sisler and the Athletics' Ferris Fain.

Players speak in hushed tones of Hernandez's defensive play. In a game after he was traded from St. Louis to the Mets in 1983, Hernandez turned in a mind-boggling 3-6-3 double play, several acrobatic saves on throws, and other merely good plays. The Mets' Ed Lynch said, "I'd say it was the greatest game I've ever seen him play. Except he does it all the time." Winner of 11 straight Gold Gloves and still counting, Hernandez is the all-time leader among first basemen in assists per game.

Between Chase and Hernandez have come some pretty good gloves, and some are far from household names. Following Chase at first for the Giants was no picnic, but George Kelly handled it beautifully, and showed the value of a strong-armed first baseman when he ended the 1921 World Series by gunning down Aaron Ward at third to end a spectacular 4-3-5 double play.

Stuffy McInnis of the Boston Red Sox committed just one error in 1921, while Washington's Joe Judge led the AL five times in fielding percentage, and in 1920 saved Walter Johnson's only

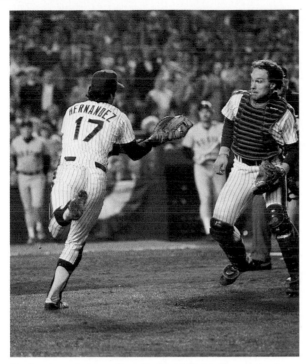

On bunts and slow rollers the Mets' Keith Hernandez is a catcher's—in this case Gary Carter's—best friend.

Owner of three Gold Gloves, Eddie Murray made one error in 991 total chances in 1981—a .999 percentage.

no-hitter by robbing Boston's Harry Hooper of a hit to end the game.

In 1949 Cleveland's Mickey Vernon was in on 168 double plays, which would have been a major league record except that the Athletics' Ferris Fain turned in an unheard-of 194, still the most by a first baseman in a single season. To prove it was no fluke, Fain turned in 192 twin killings in 1950, the second highest total ever. Brooklyn's Gil Hodges began his major league career as a catcher, but when Roy Campanella arrived, Hodges was switched to first, and started a Dodger tradition of fielding excellence there. Big, powerful and smooth, Hodges won three Gold Gloves as part of a great infield that included Jackie Robinson, Pee Wee Reese and Billy Cox. Hodges was followed by Wes Parker, who played first for the West Coast Dodgers from 1964 to 1972. Parker committed just 47 errors in nine years, and his .996 career fielding percentage was baseball's best until his successor, Steve Garvey, had a career that was a fraction of a percentage point better. After heading south for San Diego in 1983, Garvey turned in baseball's only perfect season at first in 1984, handling 1,319 chances without an error.

Sometimes one mishandled play can effectively mar the career of any great fielder, but few have suffered more than Bill Buckner. In Game 6 of the 1986 World Series, Buckner, hobbled by injured legs, let a ground ball go through his legs, allowing the winning run to score for the Mets, who then went on to win Game 7. Buckner was a fine first baseman and holds four of the five best single-season assist totals of all time. But when people think of him, they think of that one botched play.

When thinking of using first base as a repository for the worst glove in the lineup, managers would do well to heed the advice Eddie Murray offered his fellow first basemen: "You can't hide from the baseball; the ball will find you."

Between the Lines

Before the amplified preliminaries, before the umpire calls "Play ball," a knowing baseball fan can watch some of the most important members of the home team at work. Unnoticed by TV cameras, sportswriters and most spectators, the ground crew tends to the last details of preparing the field for play. But in order for baseball's impressively paid superstars to strut and fret through their nine-act performance, full credit has to go to the groundskeeper and his supporting cast for setting the stage. "A good groundskeeper," commented Cleveland's legendary player-manager Lou Boudreau, "can help you win a dozen games a year. He is the tenth man in the lineup."

The tenth man for the Baltimore Orioles, head groundskeeper Pat Santarone, is looking up at the overcast summer sky and scowling. "We are the shower stall of the American League," he says. Santarone has been driving his crew of 25 workers through 100-hour weeks to cope with record rains during the 1989 season. The crew ranges from college students toiling part-time for minimum wage to Santarone's right-hand man Paul Zwaska, who holds a degree in agronomy from the University of Wisconsin. Some do nothing but move and remove the tarp that protects the field against excess water. In dry weather, the crew may spend whole days playing Wiffleball in the bullpen or reading. Even before an expected deluge, two crew members sit in foul ground behind third base, debating the merits of a Henry James novel.

Umpires in Baltimore's Memorial Stadium get nice, bright outfield foul lines (opposite) to help with their calls. The foul lines are made of wood planks embedded in the dirt, and are painted with whitewash daily.

Chicago's Wrigley Field is one of baseball's most cherished monuments, in part because of its unique ivy-covered walls. But the ivy only dates back to 1937, while the surface of the field has been bluegrass since the stadium was built in 1914. In 1929 Cubs fans (above) flung their hats in appreciation of their hometown NL champs.

But this is no slack day. Since 7 a.m., the crew has been moving the infield tarpaulin, which can weigh tons when sodden, on and off the field. The tarp is folded and rolled onto a single metal tube 27 feet long and 30 inches in diameter. It is a chess match with nature, played on a grand scale. If sudden rain hits, the crew can move the tarp into position in less than 90 seconds. Santarone, a compact man with crystal blue eyes and Marine sergeant's demeanor, says the record is 14 moves in one day. The crew doesn't call it quits until after games end, usually around 11 p.m., their long days devoted to keeping the field in pristine condition.

"The average homeowner asks, 'What do I have to do to get a lawn like that? ' Well, you have to spend a lot of money and acquire a lot of knowledge," says Santarone, one of the top figures in his field. For 17 years he apprenticed in the minor leagues at Elmira, New York, where his father was groundskeeper before him. As part of the business of surviving during the Depression, the Santarones put goats to pasture on the field. One of young Pat's chores was to pick up the droppings before games. Since then he has received more formal training at places like Cornell University. In 1968 rookie Orioles manager Earl Weaver, just promoted from Elmira, persuaded the team brass to call up his old colleague Santarone.

But this field resists both Santarone's efforts and the weight of his 37 years' experience. Puddles have gathered on the crushed shale path that forms the quarter-mile warning track next to the outfield fence. The "warning" is audible to outfielders on the run. The shale makes a crunching noise when you step on it. Today it makes little noise and feels like walking in breakfast cereal with lots of milk. "As soon as you get this," Santarone says, "you know you'll have five plays in a game when players go end-over-end."

Maintaining a baseball field is anything but a routine job. Of the 26 major league teams, 16 still play on natural grass surfaces. Their groundskeepers contend with challenges ranging from drought to vandalism. Legendary Kansas City groundskeeper George "Sod God" Toma can attest to the pressures of the job. When weighing job offers in 1957, Toma chose the Kansas City Athletics over the New York Yankees' farm club in Denver, even though the Yankees promised him a promotion to the big leagues by 1959. "It was a rockpile," said Toma of the A's diamond. "A hayfield . . . I thought, 'This park is so bad and Yankee Stadium is pretty nice. Maybe I can mess up Yankee Stadium, but no way can I mess up this place.'"

He proved himself wrong. Early in the 1958 season, he watched his crops of bluegrass and Bermuda grass fail in succession. The field at Municipal Stadium looked like "shredded wheat," according to *Sports Illustrated.* "The writers and announcers were really on me," recalled Toma. "They wanted to run me out of town."

The problems a groundskeeper faces are not limited to the grass itself; they may start belowground. The subsurface at Milwaukee's County Stadium, for example, is built on drainage tiles beneath 18 inches of clay. Baltimore's Memorial Stadium is built right on top of the type of red clay that occurs naturally throughout Maryland. "This site used to be a clay mine," grumbles Santarone. "It's got terrible drainage, lousy percolation. We just depend on gravity now. The worst percolation you can have is with clay." Some fields have elaborate drainage systems that consist of underground pipes. Great percolation, Santarone might say. Baltimore's new stadium, scheduled to open early in the 1990s, will include a subterranean mechanical

Washington's Griffith Stadium was the site of some creative groundskeeping. In order to help the Senators' traditionally slow runners, the path from home plate to first base was sculpted to go downhill.

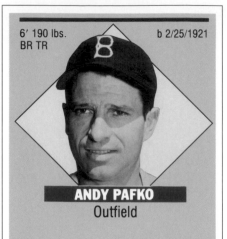

6' 190 lbs.
BR TR

b 2/25/1921

ANDY PAFKO
Outfield

In his 17-year career, it was almost as common to see Andy Pafko horizontal as vertical, going after fly balls for the Cubs, Dodgers and Braves.

From 1943 to 1959, besides brief stints at third base, he patrolled NL outfields with a style he compared to "Pete Rose sliding into base head first."

Playing a big role in Chicago's last pennant, in 1945, Pafko led senior circuit outfielders in fielding percentage while knocking in 110 runs. After four consecutive All-Star years for the Cubs from 1947 to 1950, he was traded to the Brooklyn Dodgers during the 1951 season, completing an outfield already containing Duke Snider and Carl Furillo, and adding to a fearsome lineup that included Jackie Robinson, Roy Campanella, Gil Hodges and Pee Wee Reese. It was Pafko who chased Bobby Thomson's ninth-inning, line-drive homer that won the three-game NL playoff that year for the New York Giants.

Disappointing as that loss was, "Handy Andy" saw plenty of World Series action afterwards, playing in the fall classic for the Dodgers the next year and for the Milwaukee Braves in their 1957 and 1958 glory years.

A lifetime .285 hitter with 213 home runs, Pafko had his best statistics in 1950, when he hit .304 with only 32 strikeouts and 36 homers, placing him second behind Ralph Kiner for league honors that year.

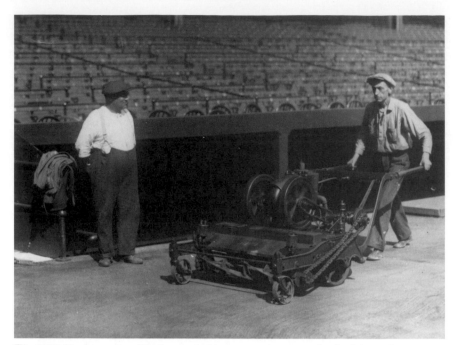

The 1927 Yankees—possibly the greatest team ever—were coming back home to Yankee Stadium for Game 3 of the World Series, so groundskeepers hauled out state-of-the-art mowing and raking equipment to get the field in perfect condition. Yankee pitcher Herb Pennock followed suit, and was perfect for seven innings on the way to an 8–1 win over the Pirates.

suction system. "It will probably suck three inches of rain in two minutes," says Santarone.

The stadium will have a state-of-the-art natural grass system called Prescription Athletic Turf (PAT), developed by Dr. William Daniel of Purdue University. The subsurface is graded and covered with a huge plastic sheet, punctuated by a network of perforated pipes. Six inches of peat gravel is poured over the tubes, and is then covered with a foot of special sand and, finally, a layer of sod.

For the fielder, a well-planned drainage system is critical. During a World Series game at Yankee Stadium in 1951, Mickey Mantle tripped over a drain pipe while chasing a long ball off the bat of Willie Mays. The resulting torn knee cartilage kept Mantle out of the rest of the Series.

Grasses employed for baseball include Kentucky bluegrass, Bermuda grass, and ryegrass. Bermuda grass tolerates heat well and is used in southern stadiums. Bluegrass is dominant elsewhere. Fast-growing ryegrass, once common, is now reserved for repairing rough patches. To prevent a blight such as fungus leaf spot from wiping out his entire crop, Santarone grows five different breeds of bluegrass on one field. Bluegrass also has the advantage of producing many blades of grass from one seed. "Sometimes it gets very thick, and you actually have to thin it out," says Santarone. But one disadvantage of bluegrass is that it grows slowly.

Most teams start their seasons with a fresh layer of sod, lovingly prepared in the weeks before Opening Day. During the season, the grass generally must be mowed daily, and it is cut to heights ranging from one-half inch to three times that long. The Detroit Tigers, historically a slow-footed team,

are known to grow a shaggy field to protect defenders with limited range. Gold Glove perennials such as Brooks Robinson and Mark Belanger preferred a surface as smooth as a pool table. "And Boog Powell never gave a damn," says Santarone of the Orioles' easygoing first baseman in the 1970s.

But the groundskeeper is a lot more than a man who mows the grass. Kansas City's Toma has said, "He's a doctor, when the grass gets sick. He's a pharmacist, preparing chemicals. He's a dietician, prescribing the right food, adding minerals like iron and zinc . . . we're weathermen—we've got to know when to water, when not to water."

Groundskeepers are also preoccupied with dirt—not only the soil under the grass, but the base paths, the pitcher's mound, and the batters' boxes. Ballfield "dirt" is a mixture of loam, clay, and peat or sand. At Memorial Stadium, the recipe calls for 7 percent sand, 7 percent clay, and the rest silt loam. Once applied, this soil has to be groomed daily. Santarone's crew begins each day by dragging a homemade device called a spiker across the infield and the warning track. A spiker is simply a plank with nails driven through it, weighted and dragged behind a tractor. "It levels the infield, smooths it down," says Santarone. The crew then pulls steel nets over the surface as a final refinement to remove stones and lumps that could cause bad hops. The nets are the same used every five innings in a game, when the crew gets to trot out on the field. Groundskeepers are particularly aware of lips that can gather when windblown dirt accumulates at the edge of the outfield grass.

The pitcher's mound, the batters' boxes, and the area around home plate are made of hard clay. When Santarone learned his favorite Maryland

The opening of Houston's Astrodome in 1965—and the inauguration of artificial turf—ushered in a new, less complicated era for groundskeepers. They spent less time watering and more time on costume design.

Carl Yastrzemski

When Carl Yastrzemski joined the Boston Red Sox in 1961, Ted Williams wasn't the only figure casting a shadow over him. More foreboding perhaps was the Green Monster, the left field wall at Fenway Park. But by the time he was through in 1983, Yaz had bettered many of Williams' feats, and had thoroughly tamed the famed 37-foot structure.

"When you heard [the ball] hit the cement wall," Yastrzemski said, referring to the bottom 15 feet of the Green Monster, "you stayed back a ways because it came off hard. Above the cement you had squares of tin with rivets in them. If the ball hit the tin, it made a thud and the ball dropped straight down. If it hit the rivets, it could do anything, come straight down, shoot to the side."

Yaz used this knowledge to win seven Gold Gloves and lead AL outfielders in assists a record seven times. The last of his assist titles came in 1977, when Yastrzemski threw out 16 baserunners in 140 games in the outfield—and didn't commit a single error. And this after spending most of the previous four seasons as a first baseman.

Born on New York's Long Island in 1939, Yastrzemski attended Notre Dame for a year before signing with Boston in 1958, reportedly receiving a $100,000 bonus. He was a middle infielder his first year in the minors, then became an outfielder, and was groomed to replace Williams.

Yaz started slowly both offensively and defensively, but in his second season he led AL outfielders with 15 assists, and a year later hit .321 for the first of three batting titles. His second came in 1967, the year he won the Triple Crown, with 44 home runs, 121 RBI and a .326 average, along with league-high totals of 189 hits, 112 runs scored, 360 total bases and a .622 slugging percentage; this performance resulted in a slew of accolades: AL Most Valuable Player, Sporting News Major League Player of the Year, Sports Illustrated Sportsman of the Year, Associated Press Male Athlete of the Year. All that and Boston's first pennant in 21 years. Yastrzemski hit .400 and played flawless defense in the Red Sox' seven-game World Series loss to the St. Louis Cardinals.

When the Red Sox returned to the postseason, in 1975, Yaz again displayed all-around talents before a national audience. Another seven-game Series setback, this one to the Cincinnati Reds, followed an AL Championship Series sweep of the Oakland A's, who were coming off three consecutive World Series victories.

"What I remember most about the playoff was that I went out to left field and made all the defensive plays after not playing left field most of the season," said Yastrzemski, discounting his .455 average in the three games. "I threw out Bert Campaneris and Sal Bando at third in the second game, then Reggie Jackson twice at second in the clincher.

"I remember Jackson hitting a ball in Oakland down the line. I backhanded it and threw him out at second. Then in the eighth inning, I went diving for Jackson's ball and held him to a single. Dick Drago got the next hitter to hit into a double play and we won it." The 36-year-old Yaz had played only eight games in left that season.

He retired at 44 as the only AL player in history to collect both 400 home runs and 3,000 hits, and was inducted into the Hall of Fame in 1989, his first year of eligibility.

No matter.

"The thing I remember most," he said, "is defense."

Carl Yastrzemski made a lot of great catches in his 23-year career, but few were more celebrated than the one that robbed Cincinnati's Johnny Bench of a home run in the 1969 All-Star Game (left). Eight years later Yaz robbed Carlos May of an extra base hit (below) in the shadow of Yankee Stadium's monument row.

CARL
YASTRZEMSKI

Left Field
Boston Red Sox 1961–1983
Hall of Fame 1989

GAMES (2nd all time)	3,308

FIELDING PERCENTAGE	
Career	.981
Season High	1.000

PUTOUTS	
Career	3,941
Season High	372

PUTOUTS PER GAME	
Career	1.90
Season High	2.51

ASSISTS	
Career	195
Season High	19

ASSISTS PER GAME	
Career	.09
Season High	.13

CHANCES	
Career	4,218
Season High	402

CHANCES PER GAME	
Career	2.03
Season High	2.72

ERRORS PER GAME	
Career	.04
Season Low	.00

DOUBLE PLAYS	
Career	30
Season High	4

WORLD SERIES	1967, 1975

GOLD GLOVES	1963, 1965, 1967–1969, 1971, 1977

MOST VALUABLE PLAYER	1967

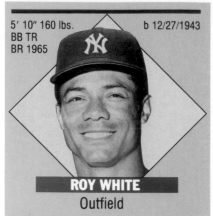

ROY WHITE
Outfield

5' 10" 160 lbs.
BB TR
BR 1965
b 12/27/1943

In 1963 Roy White was the worst second baseman in the Carolina League. By 1971 he was the best left fielder in the majors.

Even though he struggled as an infielder, White was solid at the plate, and in 1965 led his league in at-bats, runs scored, hits, triples and total bases, and was named MVP. At the end of the season, the Yankees brought him up to the majors. But by July 1967 he was back in the minors.

After the 1967 season he was once again a Yankee. In 1968, his first full season in the majors, he was moved to left field, a position manager Ralph Houk told him was his for keeps. "It wasn't easy at first," he said, "but it was mine."

Through reading books and observing hitters, White became an expert at field positioning. Houk described White as "the best left fielder the Yanks have had in my experience, which covers 22 years." In 1971 White led the majors with a 1.000 fielding percentage—errorless on 314 chances in 145 games.

White was as consistent at the plate as he was in the field, hitting .267 or better ten times in his 12 full seasons. He was a valued clutch hitter, and in 1978, the last of the three World Series in a row in which he played, he hit a homer, belted four RBI, and stole two bases.

From 1980 to 1982, White played for Tokyo's Yomiuri Giants. In 1983 "the Dependable Yankee" returned as a coach to the team he had already served so well as a player for 15 years.

clay supplier was closing, he ordered 100 tons. It's now stockpiled beneath the bleachers. Alongside are mounds of untreated earth, waiting to be sifted through vibrating screens to produce infield topsoil.

The pitcher's mound is designed to withstand the pressure of hard throwers and to give pitchers' spikes a firm grip. But pitchers have been known to make their own contributions. The Milwaukee Braves' Lew Burdette once called groundsmen on the field between pitches. He wanted a hole dug in front of the rubber to make his sinker more effective. The job complete, Burdette pitched his way out of a jam. Boston's Roger Clemens and Oakland's Bob Welch excavate veritable foxholes during games. Both drive the fastidious Santarone mildly insane: "You could bring a pick and shovel up to the mound before a game and say, 'Here, use this, you'll get the same results.' "

Groundskeepers also have to put up with the grumbling of players who earn as much as $2 million annually. After an error-filled game in Yankee Stadium on May 24, 1986, Don Mattingly seethed, "They ought to blow this infield up. It's the worst in the league." Owner George Steinbrenner's response was typical. He simply called in another body from the bullpen of humanity. In this case, it was groundskeeper Roger Bossard, lured from the White Sox, who supervised the revamping of Yankee Stadium's infield with a new clay mixture.

The foul lines and other markings are usually made with lime. Powdered chalk and marble dust can also be applied. In Memorial Stadium, the foul lines are painted from the infield edges to the foul poles. The reason: the outfield foul line is composed of four-by-four lengths of wood embedded in the earth.

Even when the materials are right, things can still go wrong. Although water is essential for growing grass, it can also create problems, like trying to keep three acres of Kentucky bluegrass trimmed to less than one inch. Well-watered grass grows fast, and it causes even Santarone's high-tech mower to rip up lumps of mud. A moist base path is a little easier to deal with, since the crew can add calcined clay, a heat-treated substance that absorbs about 100 times its weight in moisture. But groundskeepers also have to face fussy infielders. When playing for the Milwaukee Brewers, first baseman George Scott would round up groundskeeper Harry Gill at the slightest hint of dampness around his bag. "We ain't growing parsnips around here," the Boomer would grumble. "We're playing baseball."

The greatest weapon against precipitation is also a field's number-two enemy: the tarpaulin. Santarone seems to have a love-hate relationship with his. "You get diseases, funguses under a tarp. It's the best incubator in the world." The Baltimore Orioles' tarp measures 170 feet square, costs $40,000, lasts about four years, and is constructed from white, rubber-covered nylon. Why white? "A dark tarp will burn your grass in no time flat," he explains.

The most damage is wreaked on baseball fields by other users. Harry Gill of Milwaukee once had to contend with an infield that had been compacted four inches by a crowd at a Rolling Stones concert. To make the grass green again, Gill had to shoot nitrogen gas under the surface.

And every groundskeeper has football disaster stories. Santarone's happened to occur just days before the 1971 World Series opener. It was the groundskeeper's equivalent of the tenor developing laryngitis minutes before the climactic aria: "We played Pittsburgh right after three pro-football

Getting the 170-foot-square, nylon tarp at Baltimore's Memorial Stadium onto the field takes 25 members of the groundskeeping crew, all working at the same speed—flat-out fast. Head groundskeeper Pat Santarone said his crew once put the tarp on the field and took it off nine times during a 1970 game.

Groundskeepers must wonder why they bother to outline the batter's box and smooth out the dirt around home plate before a game. Invariably, the leadoff batter in the top of the first rubs out the chalk lines, then digs his own personal hitting ditch.

games, every one played in a thunderstorm. We went out there and leveled the field. It was ugly and we lost, but not because of the field. There wasn't a bad hop in the whole series." Kirk Gibson, then with Detroit, pouted after the Tigers' 1986 Opening Day in Cleveland because football markings were still evident on the field: "This outfield is assorted grass with dyed dirt. A one-year-old could do a better job than this."

Even more annoying than football or natural disasters to Santarone are today's slovenly players. Santarone's crew is responsible for cleaning the dugouts. "Dugouts today look like a huge picnic area instead of a baseball dugout. It looks like a pigpen. It isn't that the players are sloppier, but they eat more during the game. I can remember when you didn't dare eat one peanut. The manager might tell you to change your clothes and go on home. Now you look at the floor, it's littered with paper cups and sunflower husks. Their mothers or wives must follow them around at home to clean up after them."

Groundskeepers also have a variety of methods for treating the field to favor the home team. Tactics on the Army Corps of Engineers scale include tilting foul lines to encourage or deter bunts, steamrolling outfield grass to make baseballs skitter for extra-base hits, fiddling with the mound height, and distributing entire beaches of loose sand. Hall of Famers like Ty Cobb have not been above such tricks. "Ty was sly," recalled Neil Conway, Detroit Tigers groundskeeper for 30 years. "When a slugging club would come to Detroit, Ty would have me install temporary bleachers in the outfield so that balls hit out there would be ground-rule doubles instead of homers. When the regulation stands were only half full Ty made the

Fenway Park (above) took its name from its location in a section of Boston known as The Fens, a marshy, low-lying area. Fenway's original infield grass was transplanted from the Huntington Avenue Baseball Grounds, where the Red Sox played from 1901 to 1911.

whole ground crew sit in the temporary seats so the umpires wouldn't have them removed."

Some of the tricks are simple yet deceptive adjustments in grass height. For a club that likes to bunt, the groundskeeper may leave the infield grass a tad longer than usual, which can slow the ball—and the fielders—just enough to ensure a hit.

If the team's third baseman is a little shaky with his glove, the groundskeeper can mow the grass in front of the base to slant toward the foul line, causing balls to go foul. These accommodations mean a lot to players; many pennant-winning teams have voted to give the groundskeeper a three-quarter share in World Series money.

The most famous example of field chicanery occurred in 1962, when the powerful, plodding San Francisco Giants and the spray-hitting, speedy Los Angeles Dodgers faced off down the pennant stretch. The architects of what came to be called "groundskeeping by deceit" were the father-son team of Matty and Jerry Schwab. Before a big series with the Dodgers, Jerry recalled, "Dad and I were out at Candlestick before dawn . . . We were installing a speed trap." To deter Wills and other speedsters, the Schwabs dug a pit measuring 5 by 15 feet just outside first base. They filled it with a spongy mixture of sand, peat moss and water so that potential base stealers could not get a good jump off the base. The umpires caught on before the game even began. Perhaps they saw Dodger first baseman Ron Fairly building sand castles near his position.

They ordered the Schwabs out for repairs. They brought more of their swamp mix and watered it down at length. "What could you do," remembered Tommy Davis, the 1962 batting champion. "It was their park. They were

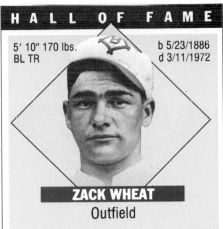

ZACK WHEAT
Outfield

Casey Stengel said he was the greatest left fielder the NL ever had, next to Stan Musial. And the most graceful left-handed hitter. But when Zack Wheat was brought up to the Brooklyn Dodgers late in the 1909 season, he arrived with a lowly .246 batting average. After playing the final 26 games of the season, Wheat had earned a .304 average and a spot on the Brooklyn roster he kept for 18 years.

He was probably the quietest Dodger; he rarely argued with opposing players or with his teammates, and he never argued with the umpires. He played in more games than any other Dodger, but was never ejected from one.

Wheat was adept in the field, and seemed to position himself just right for all the hitters, including left-handers such as Edd Roush, who liked to hit the ball deep to left. In 1914 he led the league in putouts, and in 1922 he had the NL's best fielding average. Branch Rickey called Wheat "the best outfielder Brooklyn ever had."

A solid hitter, Wheat had a 29-game hitting streak in 1916, one of the Dodgers' championship seasons. Two years later, he earned the NL batting title with a .335 average. In 2,410 games, Wheat collected 2,884 hits and a lifetime .317 batting average.

Wheat was released from the Dodgers after the 1926 season, and still holds Brooklyn records for at-bats, hits, singles, doubles, triples, total bases and extra-base hits. He was unanimously elected to the Hall of Fame in 1959.

At Baltimore's Memorial Stadium, homemade steel mesh dragnets are used ten minutes before game time to remove any bumps raised during infield practice. During a game they are brought out again after every five innings.

going to get away with anything." The Dodgers stole no bases and lost 11–2. By moonlight, the Schwabs undid their dirty work. The unnerved Dodgers lost the next two anyway. The press howled. "They found two abalone under second base," wrote *Los Angeles Times* columnist Jim Murray. Giants manager Alvin Dark became known as the Swamp Fox.

With the stage set for a Dodger-Giants playoff, the world's eyes—and those of umpire Jocko Conlan—were firmly on the Schwabs. So they changed tactics, spreading sand everywhere until the infield looked "like a sandy beach well above the high water mark," as *The New York Times* commented. The umpires ordered the field watered. Gladly, replied Matty. He told Jerry, "Get out there and make a lake." When the umpires finally complained, Matty shrugged, "New man on the job. We'll get this cleaned up." Out came the wheelbarrows of sand. The Giants won 8–0 and went on to take the playoff series 2–1. ◐

Detroit's Tiger Stadium (opposite) has a long history of groundskeeping trickery. For Ty Cobb, who played there from 1907 to 1926, groundskeepers watered down the area in front of home plate—known as Cobb's Lake—to prevent his bunts from reaching opposing fielders before Cobb could reach first base.

Zack Wheat

The Hitter's Spot

I f you're a slugger whose glovework leaves something to be desired, then left field is for you. Left field is where the Mickey Hatchers of the world go—outfielders who turn every fly ball into an adventure, who when they rear back to throw put all infielders on alert.

Sure, there have been some good, even great left fielders. But most of them either played on teams whose other two outfielders were so good that left was the only spot available, or were moved to center or right when their fielding prowess was discovered. Left fielders have the shortest throws of any outfield position and give way to the center fielder on just about any ball he can reach. Since their throw to third is so short, they don't have to be as proficient as right fielders on balls hit into the outfield corner. The only way a runner can get a triple out of a ball hit down the left field line is if the left fielder in question botches it totally.

Many of the records held by left fielders are records for futility and ineptitude. The lowest fielding percentage by a 20th-century National League outfielder belongs to Mike Donlin, left fielder for Cincinnati in 1903. Donlin committed

25 errors that season on his way to an even .900 mark. St. Louis' Lou Brock had great speed, but his hands made him a true left fielder, and he led National League outfielders in errors a record seven times. Left fielder Edward Beecher committed an unprecedented 55 errors in 1890 for Buffalo of the short-lived Players' League, and left fielder Roy Johnson set an American League mark for outfield errors in a season with 31 for the 1929 Detroit Tigers.

Still, with right-handed hitters in the majority, left fielders see their fair share of action, and since their arms are usually the outfield's weakest, they also see a lot of action as baserunners round third and head for home with impunity. But left field has been the site of some of the most important catches in history, including memorable World Series grabs by two Dodgers—Al Gionfriddo in 1947 and Sandy Amoros in 1955—and Oakland's Joe Rudi in 1972.

A number of left fielders in the early 1900s deserve mention for their defensive skills, among them Jimmy Sheckard, who played on four Cubs' pennant-winners between 1906 and 1910. Sheckard was a lifetime .275 hitter, but also had 36 as-

In 1981 A's left fielder Rickey Henderson won a title usually held by center fielders—he led the AL in putouts. In 1985 he became a Yankee and a center fielder.

Gary Matthews led his Class AA league in fielding percentage in 1971, then came to the majors and tied for the NL lead in errors three times.

Cardinal left fielder Lou Brock ran faster and jumped higher than just about any other player in the 1960s and 1970s—he just couldn't field. Brock led NL outfielders in errors a record seven times.

sists in 1903 for Brooklyn, still a 20th-century record for left fielders, and made just one error in four World Series.

Then there was Pittsburgh's Fred Clarke, a Hall of Famer and one of the game's first great player-managers. Clarke was steady and spectacular. He led National League left fielders nine times in fielding percentage, and also set a left field record with 362 putouts in 1909.

The man considered by many the best left fielder of the first half of the 20th century was Brooklyn's Zack Wheat. But Wheat had formidable competition from Duffy Lewis of the Red Sox. Lewis led American League left fielders in assists in each of his first four seasons in the major leagues, 1910 to 1913, and with center fielder Tris Speaker and right fielder Harry Hooper formed what many call the game's greatest defensive outfield. Lewis' 207 career assists are still tops among American League left fielders.

Several fine outfielders in the 1920s and 1930s spent a good portion of their careers in left field, like Hall of Famers Chick Hafey and Al Simmons. Hafey played left for the Cardinals from 1927 to 1931 and used his rifle arm to lead National

Kansas City's Bo Jackson may be the best athlete ever to play baseball, much less left field. In 1989 Jackson uncorked a 300-foot throw in Seattle to nail Harold Reynolds at home. "I was there. I was the one thrown out. I've seen it on replay. And I still don't believe it," Reynolds said.

League left fielders twice in assists. Simmons, who was one of the game's greatest hitters, played left field for three teams from 1928 to 1938, and set a record for left fielders with a .986 career fielding percentage.

Danny Litwhiler was the personification of a baseball journeyman, playing with four teams in 11 years and being traded in the middle of a season three separate times. But in 1942, as the Phillies' left fielder, Litwhiler did something that no other outfielder had done before— he played at least 150 games without committing a single error. Litwhiler handled 317 chances flawlessly, and it was 23 years before another outfielder— Cleveland's Rocky Colavito —matched his feat.

The great Yankee teams of the late 1940s and early 1950s had a locker room full of stars, so it's not too surprising that their left fielder—Gene Woodling—went largely unnoticed. But Woodling was solid in left for New York, and led all American League outfielders in fielding percentage in 1952 and 1953.

On the other side of town, in 1952, Andy Pafko was working his magic in left field for the Brooklyn Dodgers. A great outfielder, Pafko wound up in left in deference to the defensive brilliance of center fielder Duke Snider and right fielder Carl Furillo. Pafko made one of his most brilliant catches in Game 5 of the 1952 World Series. He fell into the right field stands at Yankee Stadium to save two runs in the second inning of a game the Dodgers won, 6–5 in 11 innings. The man he robbed? Gene Woodling.

Few stadiums ask as much of a left fielder as Fenway Park. Boston's Carl Yastrzemski may not have been as great a hitter as the man he succeeded in left field—Ted Williams—but no one played Fenway's Green Monster better than Yaz did. In the 1960s and 1970s Yastrzemski had rivals in left like the Yankees' Roy White, who turned in an errorless season in 1971—Yaz had his in 1977—and Oakland's Joe Rudi, whose .991 career fielding percentage is tops among full-time left fielders.

Speed came to left field a few years later in the person of Kansas City's Willie Wilson and Oakland's Rickey Henderson. Both moved to center field in later years, but each player made his mark in left, especially Wilson, who in 1980

Brooklyn's Andy Pafko (left) couldn't reach this Gil McDougald home run in Game 1 of the 1952 World Series against the Yankees, but got a measure of revenge later in the game by throwing out McDougald when he tried to go from first to third on a single.

shattered the major league records for left fielders with 482 putouts and 497 total chances. Wilson won the Gold Glove in 1980; Henderson followed in the strike-shortened season of 1981 as he led all American League outfielders with 327 putouts.

The state of the art in left field in the 1980s belonged in the National League to the Mets' Kevin McReynolds, who led National League outfielders in 1988 with 18 assists. But there's a guy over in the American League that just might change the way people think about left fielders for good. His name is Bo Jackson.

Oakland slugger Jose Canseco improved his fielding quickly. In 1986, his first full season, Canseco played left field, led the AL with 14 errors, and had just four assists. In 1987 he cut his errors to seven and upped his assists to 12. In 1988 he was promoted to right field.

Playing the Field

There's a direct correlation between the ascendance of hitting and pitching and the decline of new ideas in fielding. When Babe Ruth and the lively ball got going in 1920, managers turned their attention away from the guys with the gloves. And the thinking about fielding has remained pretty much frozen in place ever since. In fairness, many innovations had already been made. Baseball's pioneers invented lasting stratagems like pickoffs, cutoffs, backing up outfielders, and relays. Some really wacky practices—catching balls with caps, tripping baserunners, hiding extra balls in the grass—had been legislated out of existence. The condition most conducive to creative thinking—all-night bull sessions on trains and in shared hotel rooms—gave way to thought-sapping jet travel across time lines and single rooms. And ever more mechanical scouting changed strategy from an art to a computerized science.

Even so, it's amazing how few fielding ideas have been developed in the last six or seven decades. Dick Bartell, a fine National League shortstop in the 1930s, began covering third when opposing teams tried to sacrifice a runner over from second. These days that strategy has a fancy name: "the wheel play." Bartell also began the practice of coordinating pickoffs on a silent count with his pitchers.

Connie Mack deserves credit simply for continuing to think when other skippers weren't: Ty Cobb, probably the savviest player of his era, finished

It's tough to get noticed when you play in the same division as Ozzie Smith and alongside six-time Gold Glove winner Ryne Sandberg, but Cub shortstop Shawon Dunston (opposite) is opening some eyes. In 1988 he paced National League shortstops with 257 putouts.

Against the pull-hitting Ted Williams in 1946, Cleveland manager and shortstop Lou Boudreau pulled all four of his infielders and two of his outfielders to the right side of second base. The shift frustrated Williams throughout the season, though he had one major victory against it—an inside-the-park home run to left field that clinched the 1946 pennant for Boston.

his playing days with the 1927–1928 Philadelphia Athletics. One day Mack waved to him from the dugout to move over in the outfield. At first Cobb ignored the signal; then, just to humor the old man, he moved over. The batter hit a fly ball directly to him, and Cobb became a believer.

The most famous fielding alignment, of course, is the Williams Shift. Noting that Ted Williams pulled almost everything thrown at him, Cleveland manager Lou Boudreau began using three and even four infielders to the right of second base when Williams came to the plate. Teddy Ballgame laughed at the shift and batted .342 during the 1946 season, his first year back from World War II service. In the 1946 World Series, however, the Cardinals adapted the shift and held Williams to just five singles in seven games.

Later a reverse shift, with three men to the left of second, was introduced against right-handed pull hitters. "When the Cubs' Hank Sauer was hitting, we'd shift so far over I'd be in the shortstop's hole," says former Cardinal second baseman Red Schoendienst.

Well-traveled manager Gene Mauch occasionally used a five-man infield: with the bases loaded and the tying run on third in the ninth inning, Mauch sometimes brought in the right fielder to play between second and first. Dick Williams and Tommy Lasorda have had their second baseman charge the plate when an opposing batter threatened to lay down a sacrifice bunt; that way the first baseman could do what comes naturally: stay on his bag and not throw. And in very rare situations—for example, against a slugger who never hits grounders to the opposite side—a few managers have used four-man outfields.

There have been a few less obvious changes. In the 1920s, as long as the bases were empty, Cleveland outfielders routinely caught fly balls and

Second baseman Robby Thompson (above, left) and first baseman Will Clark carry two of the Giants' most important bats. But when the mitts go on, the talk turns to defense. In 1987 they helped set a team record with 183 double plays.

On June 30, 1989, Chicago's Ryne Sandberg played his 1,000th career game, qualifying him for the major league record book. His .988 career fielding percentage is the highest ever for a second baseman by a margin of four points. He's also led the league four times in assists.

immediately threw to home plate. "It kept their arms in good shape and they were able to throw out plenty of base runners just from forming the habit of throwing the ball as soon as they caught it," said Hall of Fame center fielder Tris Speaker. Today outfielders play catch between innings. "An outfielder may go through seven or eight innings without having to make a throw," said Mauch, "but the game may depend on his making a good one in the ninth. He's got a better chance to do it if he's warmed up a little bit through the game."

Forget about the pitcher-batter confrontation at a game, and just watch the fielders. There's magic out there. Consider the man in center field, standing alone in the middle of the outfield. From his spot, the center fielder commands a splendid view of the game and its participants. "You're in charge of the whole outfield," says former major leaguer Bob Bailor. "You can run as far as you want and throw as far as you want—as long as you hit the cutoff man. It's like you're a kid in your backyard again."

At the other end of the field is the catcher. His position is unique: squatting instead of standing, stationed in foul rather than fair territory, wearing heavy equipment, calling the signals instead of reacting to them, he's a figure as solid and stolid as Rodin's Thinker. "The infield is like a steel net held in the hand of the catcher," wrote the scholar and critic Jacques Barzun.

Pregame practice is a landscape of images. Playing catch on the sidelines, ballplayers air out their arms with ever-longer throws that never seem to drop. "Here's one of the primary attractions of baseball," relief pitcher Dan Quisenberry said one day. "It soothes the mind and rewards the spirit. It's always fun. I guess it brings back what we were like when we were kids." During batting practice a first baseman takes throws behind a protective

ROY McMILLAN   shortstop

The Light Hitters

Good field, no hit is a tag that can land you in the minors year after year, or, as in Dal Maxvill's case, land you on three world championship teams. It all depends on just how good your glove is, and how well equipped the rest of the lineup is to compensate for your bad bat.

Maxvill came along in the hitting-poor 1960s, when the larger strike zone, the slider, and new, pitcher-friendly ballparks conspired to frustrate hitters and convinced some managers that sacrificing a spot in the lineup for a really good shortstop made sense. Maxvill played 14 years in the majors —11 with the Cardinals—and compiled a lifetime batting average of .217, the fifth lowest of all time among players with at least 2,500 at-bats. He played on Cardinal pennant-winners in 1964, 1967 and 1968, and was an even worse hitter in the World Series—.115 including a zero-for-22 performance in 1968. But he didn't commit an error in any of those Series, all of which went seven games.

Maxvill, who hit just six home runs in 3,443 at-bats, was far from the only good field, no hit shortstop in the 1960s. Baltimore's Mark Belanger hit .228 lifetime, but his glove made him a valuable member of four Oriole pennant-winners. Belanger won eight Gold Gloves, yet in 1968 he was a disaster at the plate, hitting .208 with 114 strikeouts in 472 at-bats. Bobby Wine's 12-year career yielded a .215 batting average, but in 1970 he set an NL record for double plays by a shortstop with 137 for Montreal.

In the early days of the 20th century—the dead-ball era—it was catchers who appeared able to secure a spot in the lineup without being able to hit their weight. Bill Bergen lasted 11 years in the majors despite a .170 lifetime average that made him the only player in history to earn at least 2,500 at-bats and hit below .200. Bergen's bat was completely punchless, and he hit just two home runs in 947 games. Some dead-ball-era catchers hung on despite their lousy hitting because they were the favored catchers of great pitchers. Lou Criger broke into the majors with the Cleveland Spiders in 1896, and soon became a favorite of the immortal Cy Young. When Young went to St. Louis, Criger came along, and when Young decided to jump to Boston of the newly formed American League, Criger was part of the deal. Riding Young's broad coattails, Criger played 16 years despite a .221 lifetime average.

And then there was Eddie Brinkman. A shortstop whose major league career spanned 15 years, Brinkman was a lifetime .209 hitter when Ted Williams became his manager with the Senators in 1969. Williams talked hitting, Brinkman listened, and his batting average soared to .266, 37 points higher than his previous best. He followed that with a .262 year in 1970, but then was traded to Detroit and reverted to past form, hitting .228. His glove remained golden, however, and in 1972 he went 72 games without an error, a major league record that lasted until it was broken in 1989 by another light hitter—the Mets' Kevin Elster, who hit .214 in 1988, his first full season in the majors.

But Brinkman wasn't always a light hitter. In high school in Cincinnati, he was the best hitter on a team that included another pretty good hitter— Pete Rose. "He was our home run hitter," Rose said. "Ed hit the long ball."

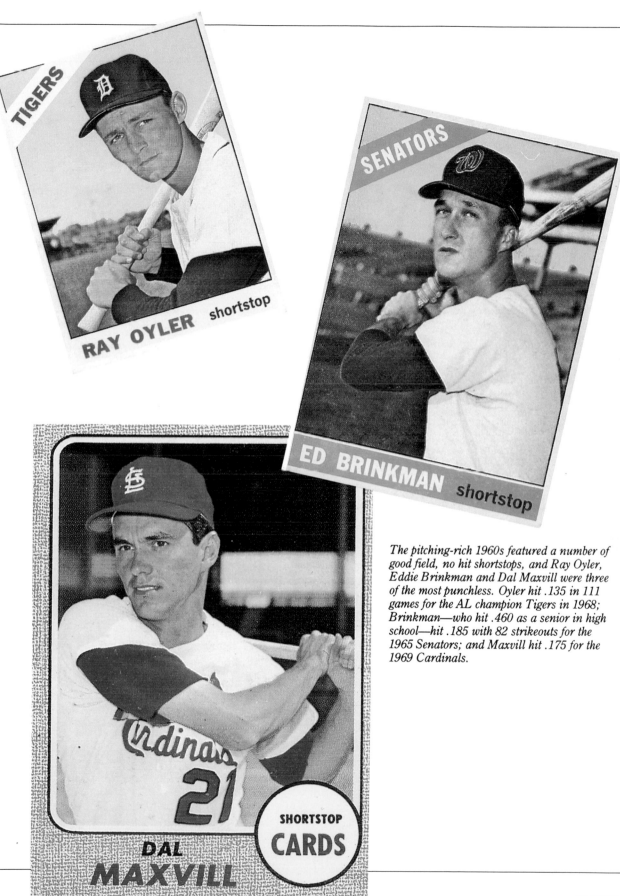

TIGERS

RAY OYLER shortstop

SENATORS

ED BRINKMAN shortstop

DAL MAXVILL

SHORTSTOP
CARDS

The pitching-rich 1960s featured a number of good field, no hit shortstops, and Ray Oyler, Eddie Brinkman and Dal Maxvill were three of the most punchless. Oyler hit .135 in 111 games for the AL champion Tigers in 1968; Brinkman—who hit .460 as a senior in high school—hit .185 with 82 strikeouts for the 1965 Senators; and Maxvill hit .175 for the 1969 Cardinals.

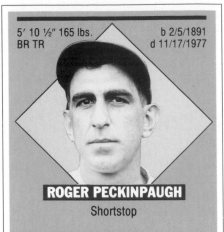

5' 10 ½" 165 lbs.　　　b 2/5/1891
BR TR　　　　　　　　d 11/17/1977

ROGER PECKINPAUGH
Shortstop

During the 1925 World Series, Roger Peckinpaugh booted, muffed and miscued his way into the record books. Known as a solid fielder, the Washington shortstop was capping off a season in which his .294 batting average and exceptional fielding earned him the AL's MVP award. But the World Series against Pittsburgh turned his dream season into a nightmare. He committed rally-sustaining errors in Games 2 and 6, and his two late-inning errors in Game 7 ensured Pittsburgh's win. His eight errors remain a World Series record.

The error-laden Series sticks out like a sore thumb against the rest of Peckinpaugh's career. He broke into the majors with Cleveland in 1910 and was traded to the Yankees in 1913. The next year, at 23, he entered the record books for the first time when he became the youngest manager in history. He continued his shortstop duties for New York, and consistently set league-leading numbers for his position. In 1916, 1918 and 1919, he led AL shortstops in assists, and in 1917 he led them in double plays with 84. He was with the Yankees when they won their first pennant in 1921, but they failed to win the Series, and Peckinpaugh was traded to Washington.

Peckinpaugh continued playing until 1927. But 50 years after the fact, those eight errors still haunted him. "It upset me then, and it still does today," he said in the 1970s. "Because after my long career, the first thing people ask is, 'What about the 1925 World Series?' "

In 1988 San Diego's 23-year-old Benito Santiago authored a new chapter in defense behind the plate by throwing from his knees—and caught 45 percent of runners who tried to steal.

screen. In the outfield players stand idly, caps askew, throwing gloves at flies over their heads like schoolboys.

And now for the action. The naked eye can't pick up the adjustments and subtleties of a pitcher's or hitter's craft, but the sight of fielders in motion quickens the pulse. A ball is hit to deep center, and everyone gasps, wondering if the celebrated gazelle out there—a Garry Maddox, a Paul Blair, a Gary Pettis—will run it down. A batter slaps a hard grounder to deep short, where the Cardinals' Ozzie Smith makes an improbable diving stop and a jack-in-the-box snap to his feet and throw to first. Short and center: the ultimate baseball athletes.

On some plays all nine fielders are in motion, contracting and expanding like color chips in a kaleidoscope. With a man on first and no outs, the batter lays down a sacrifice bunt. Pitcher, catcher, first and third basemen converge on the ball. The shortstop covers second, the second baseman covers first, and outfielders race in to back up the bases. Scarcely a game proceeds without a bunter challenging fielders to get the lead runner.

With another runner on first, a batter lines a shot up the gap in right center. The right fielder and center fielder chase the ball, one to field it, the other to yell where to throw it. The second baseman, backed by the shortstop, scampers into right center for the relay. The third baseman tends to his base, the first baseman stands at the mound for a possible cutoff, and the pitcher backs up the catcher at the plate. As the lead runner streaks around third, the second baseman takes the outfielder's throw and reaches back for the long relay. Ball and runner and catcher fuse in a cloud of dust, the umpire pauses before raising his arm, and . . .

"They talk about hitting and pitching being contagious," says Oakland's Mike Gallego, "but the most contagious part of baseball is defense."

And that's why we celebrate fielding.

But enough talk. Now it's time to take the field: to spend a season with a promising young shortstop, to gauge the changes in strategy, to have some fun with fielding. On April 22, 1988, Walter Weiss, a 24-year-old shortstop for the Oakland Athletics, played for the first time in Chicago's Comiskey Park. His appearance there was not unlike that of a presidential candidate touring a primary state. Though only a rookie, Weiss had already been declared something of a standard-bearer. In a risky deal that brought pitcher Bob Welch to Oakland, the A's had traded their starting shortstop, Alfredo Griffin, to the Los Angeles Dodgers and promoted Weiss, whose major league experience consisted of 16 games.

A rookie shortstop playing for a contender undergoes baseball's quintessential baptism by fire. Weiss had survived the early games, but now he was beginning his first extended road trip. Would he play the field, or would the field play him?

Weiss was fortunate enough to be managed by Tony La Russa. Young, law-school-trained, respected as a "communicator," La Russa had handled four of the previous five AL Rookies of the Year. In spring training La Russa wisely told Weiss to catch ground balls, make double plays and ignore his stats. That was a good thing, because in 1985 in Modesto, California, Weiss batted .197 with seven errors.

Weiss had an on-field support system, too. The A's had imported veteran second baseman Glenn Hubbard from Atlanta to play second and call

Some shortstops take longer than others to get comfortable at the position. The Dodgers' Alfredo Griffin led the AL in errors from 1979 to 1982 while with Toronto, then went to Oakland and won a Gold Glove in 1985. When the A's traded Griffin to L.A. in 1988, he helped steady a fine Dodger pitching staff that stopped the A's cold in the World Series.

Shortstop Greg Gagne (above, with second baseman Wally Backman) helped Minnesota set an all-time record with just 84 errors in 1988. Gagne's strong arm allows him to play deep on the Metrodome's artificial surface.

infield signals. With another veteran, Carney Lansford, at third, Weiss would have fewer responsibilities than the average shortstop. He also benefited from perhaps the finest coaching staff in the majors, including infield coach Jim Lefebvre, who left at the end of the season to manage the Seattle Mariners, and hitting coach Bob Watson, who went on to become assistant general manager of the Houston Astros. In spring training the staff didn't swamp Weiss with intricacies like relays, cutoffs, and positioning on double steals. "You never want to overcoach a player," said Lefebvre. "You over-feed a youngster, and he starts worrying about things. Just make sure his glove is oiled, and let him play." About all the coaches did was give Weiss plenty of grounders. That was fine with him. "No two ground balls are alike," he said before the Chicago series, "so I take as many as possible. I'm a big believer in repetition: Familiarity breeds comfortability."

Before every series, the Athletics' manager, coaches, starting pitchers, and up-the-middle players—catcher, second baseman, shortstop, center fielder—discuss a report on the other team prepared by an advance scout. This is a comparatively modern practice in baseball. Before the leagues expanded to ten teams apiece in 1961 and 1962 and 12 teams in 1969, players tended to keep their own mental books on the seven teams they were constantly facing. Old-time catchers especially relied on instant recall. "I can't remember your name," Hall of Famer Bill Dickey told one Joe Gantenbein, a hitter he'd faced years earlier, "but I know we used to pitch you high and outside."

Yankee manager Casey Stengel stayed ahead of the game. Back in 1957 Stengel had coach Frank Crosetti keeping charts on other AL teams and scout

Larry Bowa (above, avoiding a sliding Garry Templeton) has the best career fielding percentage, .980, of any shortstop in history. And in his only World Series appearance, Bowa played errorless ball and started seven double plays—a Series record—as the 1980 Phillies beat the Royals in six games.

Rudy York tailing the Yanks' next foe. Former Yankee shortstop Tony Kubek recalled one of Stengel's briefings: "Before a Friday night game, Casey called a meeting at the Lord Baltimore Hotel. Connie Johnson was going to pitch against us, and Rudy went over what he was throwing. We wanted to know about their hitters too, so we kept asking Rudy, 'How do you play this guy?' "

Today scouting is a much more scientific process. Scouts come armed with computer readouts on recent performance and "tendencies": what a player is hitting against a certain pitcher, how he's doing in day games and night games, how he performs in various parks to name a few. The A's were relying on one of the best advance scouts in the business, Mike Squires. Having seen the White Sox play an earlier series, Squires had charted every pitch: what was thrown, what was hit on what count, whether it was in the strike zone, whether it was a routine grounder or a fly or a hard-hit ball. As they huddled in Chicago, the A's asked Squires for still more information. "We discussed things like who pulls the ball, who doesn't, whether they'll hit and run or steal," says Squires, who became a Toronto coach at season's end. Squires' observations were supplemented with handwritten notes kept over the years by coaches Rene Lachemann and Dave Duncan.

Some teams swear by scouting reports. "They're a check on your memory," said the late Kansas City manager Dick Howser. "Here's what I mean. Every fielder remembers the hit that beat him. 'Last time through, this guy beat me on a hit up the middle,' a shortstop will say, arguing in favor of moving to his left when the hitter comes up. But the charts will show that most of the time the guy pulls the ball. Percentages don't lie, and we play them."

Rabbit Maranville

Baseball is full of Rabbit Maranville stories. Like the time he woke Pittsburgh manager Bill McKechnie at 4 a.m. just to tell him that all his players were in. Or the time he swam, fully clothed, across the Charles River in Boston simply because he didn't feel like walking a few blocks to the nearest bridge.

Maranville played in 2,670 games, had 10,078 official at-bats, and successfully handled—at shortstop—12,493 chances in the field during his major league career, but he's often remembered more for his antics than his ability. Though you're more likely to hear about his drinking, carousing and practical jokes, in his day Maranville was considered second only to the great Honus Wagner among defensive shortstops.

Walter James Maranville was the son of a Massachusetts policeman, and quickly developed a lifelong love affair with baseball. He joined the Boston Braves at the end of the 1912 season, and became their regular shortstop the following season. In 1914 Maranville was an unlikely slugger on one of baseball's most unlikely world champions, manager George Stallings' "Miracle Braves." Boston trailed the Giants by 11½ games on July 15, then proceeded to win 61 of their last 77 games to win the NL pennant going away. Maranville hit just .246, but led the Braves with 78 RBI, and was a wizard in the field. One story attributes his nickname to his ability to cover ground in the field, and in the miracle season Maranville set a major league record for total chances by a shortstop with 1,046, a record that was tied in 1922 by Dave Bancroft. Maranville then hit .308 in the Braves' four-game World Series sweep over Philadelphia.

Maranville quickly became one of baseball's most popular players, and was famous for his vest-pocket catches, a precursor to Willie Mays' basket catches. The Rabbit would catch pop flies at his belt, sometimes even banking them off his stomach first. He played with the enthusiasm of a child, and even some of his more annoying stunts, like tagging runners out and then sitting on top of them, usually failed to rile his opponents.

In 1921 Maranville was traded to Pittsburgh, where he had his best seasons at the plate, hitting .294 in 1921 and .295 in 1922. In July of 1925 he was hired as manager of the Cubs, but following a spree of practical jokes, including a late-night ice water raid on his own players, he was relieved of command after 53 games. His drinking led to more legendary escapades, but eventually took its toll on his play. In 1927 he was sent to the minors, and made a vow to quit drinking. "I'm on the water wagon for good and the guy don't live who can bump me off," Maranville said. He started his comeback by helping the 1928 Cardinals win the NL pennant, then in 1930 had one of his best seasons, hitting .281 and leading NL shortstops in fielding percentage.

Maranville was still going strong at age 42 when he broke his leg sliding into home during an exhibition game in the spring of 1934, missed the entire season, and played just 23 games in 1935 before retiring. When he heard of Maranville's sliding mishap, humorist Will Rogers summed up the feelings of most fans. "When Rabbit Maranville breaks his leg at the opening of the season," Rogers wrote, "that constitutes America's greatest crisis."

RABBIT
MARANVILLE

Shortstop
Boston Braves 1912–1920
Pittsburgh Pirates 1921–1924
Chicago Cubs 1925
Brooklyn Dodgers 1926
St. Louis Cardinals 1927–1928
Boston Braves 1929–1933, 1935
Hall of Fame 1954

GAMES	**2,670**
FIELDING PERCENTAGE	
Career	**.952**
Season High	**.969**
PUTOUTS	
Career *(1st all time)*	**5,139**
Season High *(4th all time)*	**407**
PUTOUTS PER GAME	
Career *(3rd all time)*	**2.39**
Season High	**2.76**
ASSISTS	
Career *(3rd all time)*	**7,354**
Season High *(9th all time)*	**574**
ASSISTS PER GAME	
Career	**3.42**
Season High	**3.73**
CHANCES	
Career *(2nd all time)*	**13,124**
Season High *(1st all time)*	**1,046**
CHANCES PER GAME	
Career *(6th all time)*	**6.10**
Season High	**6.79**
ERRORS PER GAME	
Career	**.29**
Season Low	**.17**
DOUBLE PLAYS	
Career *(10th all time)*	**1,183**
Season High	**104**
WORLD SERIES	**1914, 1928**

Streaks of Greatness

Although it wasn't as widely heralded as Joe DiMaggio's 56-game hitting streak or Orel Hershiser's 59-inning scoreless pitching streak, New York Mets' Kevin Elster put together a record 88-game errorless streak by a shortstop, which ended on May 9, 1989. Elster shattered the previous record of 72 games without an error set for shortstops in 1972 by Detroit's Eddie Brinkman. Below, by position, are the current records for errorless-game streaks in the major leagues.

Position	Player	Team	Errorless Games	Dates of Streak	Chances Handled
1B	Steve Garvey	Dodgers	193	June 26, 1983-Apr. 14, 1985	1,623
2B	Joe Morgan	Reds	91	July 6, 1977-Apr. 22, 1976	410
SS	Kevin Elster	Mets	88	July 19, 1988-May 9, 1989	294
3B	Jim Davenport	Giants	97	July 29, 1966-Apr. 28, 1968	209
OF	Brian Downing	Angels	244	May 25, 1981-July 21, 1983	471
C	Yogi Berra	Yankees	148	July 28, 1957-May 10, 1959	950
P	Paul Lindblad	A's, Rangers	385	Aug. 27, 1966-Apr. 30, 1974	126

But Howser gave some leeway. His own second baseman and field leader, Frank White, says, "I don't pay much attention to scouting reports because they might be a few days old and the hitter might be trying something new. A lot of scouting reports are based on how a pitcher was doing on a given day. Some managers will make you follow the charts; a good one will give you some freedom. That's why I don't look to the manager and fielding coach, who aren't on the field. I'll speak to the pitcher and catcher to see how the hitter is being pitched. I'll also make some adjustments on my own from studying the hitters."

The A's consider both the charts and player input. "We expect Walt to contribute in time," said Duncan. "We say, 'Two steps in the hole on this guy, up the middle on this guy,' and Walt will say, 'I'd like to shade this guy up the middle more and this guy to pull.' "

The final step in pregame preparation is batting and fielding practice. During batting practice a shortstop routinely stands at his position, taking fungo hits from a coach between pitches to the batter. In later infield drills he makes numerous throws to the bases and takes at least seven rounds of grounders: one right at him, one to his left, one to his right, three to start double plays, and a ball at him as he runs toward the plate. Unfortunately, the wet Comiskey Park infield was covered by a tarp, and practice was called off. Well, no matter: Weiss had taken grounders thousands of times and wouldn't miss this once.

It didn't take long to change his mind. With one out and runners on first and third in the Chicago half of the first inning, Ivan Calderon hit a high fly to short center. It looked for all the world like a "can of corn"—baseball parlance for a catch as easy as a tin can falling from a high shelf into a grocer's apron.

Schooled that in-betweeners are always the outfielder's ball, Weiss deferred to center fielder Stan Javier. Unfortunately, Javier was stationed deep, and the wind kept blowing the ball in. Javier raced in, in, in—and dropped the ball next to the spot where Weiss had backpedaled in short left center. "That was a tough decision for Walt in this park," said La Russa. "The wind was blowing hard and batting practice was called off, so he had no chance to take batted balls before the game."

Minnesota third baseman Gary Gaetti (above, tagging Baltimore's Alan Wiggins) won three straight Gold Gloves from 1986 to 1988, and in 1987 set a Twins' record with 47 straight errorless games.

Rookie shortstops are always going to make mistakes, but these days they arrive in the big leagues especially vulnerable. Thirty or forty years ago a team might have 25 farm clubs, and a player would spend five or six years in the minors developing his skills. Today a club might have only five lower-level teams, and players are routinely rushed up. Weiss had spent three seasons in the minors but played only 46 games at Triple-A Tacoma, the highest level. No wonder La Russa sounded so patient.

With the score tied 3–3 in the sixth, Weiss showed both how far he had come and how much he could still improve. First, he made a sparkling play on Greg Walker's hard grounder. Then he booted Carlton Fisk's slow nubber. Like many rookies, Weiss was sharper on a do-or-die play than a tricky dribbler that caught him off-balance.

An inning later, score still tied, La Russa sent in a pinch hitter for Weiss. At the time he was batting under .200 for the season and had been retired twice on weak grounders to second. Despite La Russa's assurances that "Walt could hit .100 and still keep his job," Weiss was preoccupied by his slow start at the plate. Was he taking his hitting woes into the field? Not likely. "I think the biggest challenge is to concentrate over 162 games," said Weiss.

Unlike many infielders, Oakland shortstop Walt Weiss doesn't wear a batting glove under his fielding glove. "It makes the fielding glove feel too loose," Weiss said. "It stays tighter when your hand is next to the glove. Plus, I like the feel."

"I have a system. When the catcher throws the ball to second at the start of every inning, that's when I forget about hitting, I consciously think, 'Let's play defense.'"

As the season progressed, the A's gave Weiss numerous pointers—not force-feeding them, but ladling them as slowly as if they were hot soup. When left fielder Dave Parker fielded a single and threw it toward second, Weiss wasn't in proper cutoff position. The throw eluded the second and first basemen, the runner reached second, and eventually scored the winning run. The following day the coaches drilled Weiss on this simple but critical play.

On other occasions Weiss got pointers before bad habits started. "Notice how the runner took off on a 2–0 pitch to Donnie Hill?" La Russa asked Weiss in the Chicago series. "That's not a stolen-base situation; it's a hit-and-run. In a situation like that, hold your position longer. Go toward the hitter before cutting over to second."

Weiss was making other adjustments on his own. "There's only so much we can tell a guy," White Sox scout Eddie Brinkman said while evaluating Weiss. "You get a feel for the game when you're on the field that someone on the bench wouldn't have. Besides, you have to be prepared to move on each pitch, depending on what's been called. You have to delay until the last second so you won't tip off the batter. There's no time to look to the dugout."

Weiss was building up a considerable mental file. He'd been tutored on the 14 American League fields—how the grass was high in Detroit and Chicago, even in Boston, New York and Oakland— but he had to discover for himself that the grass in Anaheim was higher than expected. He also had to learn the tendencies of new AL baserunners pretty much on his own. And hitters' habits would take all season to digest. The usual rookie notion is to play

Weiss showed unusual poise in 1988, handling the job of starting shortstop for a pennant contender in his rookie season. "He's a natural—so quick and fluid with those soft hands," said one AL scout. "And he's fundamentally very sound."

power hitters to pull, spray hitters to go up the middle, and everyone to pull more on a 3–1 count than on 0–2. Weiss discovered quickly that all hitters don't conform to this orthodoxy; the performance of most hitters, in fact, owes as much to who's pitching as to who's at the plate.

Weiss learned quickly. After the All-Star break he made only one error, hiked his average up to .250, and won the AL Rookie of the Year award—the fifth in the past six seasons for manager Tony La Russa. The A's won the American League's West Division, and La Russa said Weiss' play was the critical ingredient in the title.

In the AL playoffs against the Red Sox, Weiss drove in the winning run in Game 2 and had a pair of hits to help Oakland win Game 4. Even so, Weiss outdid himself fielding in Game 3. In the first inning he charged a slow bouncer and effortlessly threw out the runner. With the A's leading 6–5 in the third, one out and a runner on third, Weiss leaped over diving baserunner Jody Reed to complete an inning-ending double play, squelching the potential tying run. Finally, with a runner on first and one out in the eighth inning, Weiss rocketed to the right field side of second base to reach Ellis Burks' grounder and flipped a backwards peg to second baseman Mike Gallego for the force.

All in all, fielding was well served. ◖

Weiss had his problems early in his rookie season, but his fielding sparked the A's past Boston in the 1988 AL Championship Series.

SHORT STOP
TOWNSEND GUN CO.
1514 FARNAM
OMAHA.

Captain Infield

Honus Wagner

Shortstops get nicknamed to death. There's Scooter, Skeeter, Slats and Creepy. There's Pee Wee and the Wizard, not to mention most of the animal kingdom: Rabbit, the Rooster, Crazy Horse, the Chicken, the Flea and, oh yes, the Gnat.

It comes with the territory. Shortstops are probably the highest-profile fielders in the game. The old baseball axiom says that in order for a team to be successful, it must be strong up the middle, and the shortstop is the fulcrum of that strength. A good shortstop must do everything.

He has to make the longest, toughest throws of any infielder. Because of how deep he plays and how far he is from first base, he's got to have the infield's quickest release, but his arm must also have the power to get the ball to first from deep in the hole, and to beat runners to the plate from short left field. A shortstop must have the range to turn grounders in the hole or up the middle into rally-killing double plays, the quickness to charge slow rollers, and the speed to take command on bloopers down the left-field line. He must be not only the best athlete in the infield, but also its most knowledgeable member, as a

half step in the right direction as the pitch is thrown makes a bigger difference at short than anywhere else.

Outside of the pitcher, and maybe the catcher, the shortstop is the most important player on the field. And yet, there was a time when he didn't even exist. Rounders, the English game after which baseball was patterned, had just eight players, and it wasn't until 1845 that D. L. Adams of the New York Knickerbockers became baseball's first shortstop, and it took 11 more years before Brooklyn's Dickey Pearce became the first shortstop to play in the infield. But once the shortstop infiltrated the infield, he took over.

After George Wright, baseball's first great shortstop, retired in 1882 to become a sporting goods manufacturer, Jack Glasscock claimed the title "King of the Shortstops." Glasscock led the league six times in fielding percentage, and was noted for his outstanding range. Bobby Wallace was a major leaguer for 25 years, from 1894 to 1918, and is credited with being the first shortstop to field a grounder and throw in one uninterrupted motion. Wallace averaged 6.1 chances per game, fifth on the all-time list, and in

Cardinal shortstop Marty Marion was such a great fielder that in 1944, despite a .267 batting average, he was named the National League's MVP. Yankee catcher Bill Dickey called him "a regular floating ghost."

The year 1950 saw a changing of the guard in Chicago, as one great White Sox shortstop, Luke Appling (above, left), gave way to another, Chico Carrasquel. The team didn't lose a step, however: with Appling in 1949, Chicago turned 180 double plays; in 1950 with Carrasquel, 181.

1953 he became one of the first players to be named to the Hall of Fame primarily on the strength of his fielding.

There have been many shortstops who've played the position with more grace than Honus Wagner, but few who've played it more effectively. At 5' 11" and 200 pounds, Wagner was huge for a shortstop of his day, but he had great range and an aggressive attitude when it came to ground balls. While Wagner gave way to Rabbit Maranville in the National League, Everett Scott led the way for American League shortstops in the 1910s and 1920s. He played with strong teams like the Red Sox from 1914 to 1921 and the Yankees from 1922 to 1925, and his mediocre hitting was overlooked because of his fine glovework. Scott may not have had terrific range, but the balls he got to he took care of, and his major-league-record fielding percentage of .976 in 1919 wasn't beaten until the Braves' Eddie Miller fielded .983 in 1942.

With the lively ball helping teams score runs almost at will, some managers began to see shortstop as a position where they could afford to put a defensive specialist. The 1930s saw such light-hitting shortstops as the Yankee's Frankie Crosetti

Five times a Gold Glove winner, Reds shortstop Dave Concepcion has an outstanding throwing arm, and the numbers to prove it. Twice he's gone over 500 assists in a season, and in 1977 his fielding percentage was .985—11 errors in 781 chances—the ninth best single season ever.

The Yankees' Phil Rizzuto (above, left, with Cleveland's sliding Dale Mitchell and Yankee second baseman Jerry Coleman) made life easy on managers like Bucky Harris. "I wouldn't trade Phil for any shortstop in baseball," Harris said in 1947. "He pulls a miracle out there every day."

and the Cardinals' Leo Durocher, who despite a lifetime .247 batting average was known as "the All-American Out." But the 1930s also featured some shortstops who were as dangerous at the plate as they were in the field—career .300 hitters like Joe Cronin of the Senators and the Red Sox, Arky Vaughan of the Pirates, and Luke Appling of the White Sox. Appling, known as "Old Aches and Pains," led American League shortstops seven times in assists, a record matched only by another great White Sox shortstop, Luis Aparicio.

The argument over designation of a golden age of shortstops comes down to two decades: the 1940s and the 1980s. In 1940 two great shortstops—St. Louis' Marty Marion and Brooklyn's Pee Wee Reese—made their major league debuts, while another—Cleveland's Lou Boudreau—played his first full season. Crosetti, Cronin, Appling, Vaughan and Miller were still playing, and the addition of the talented youngsters made shortstop the place to be. At 6' 2", with great range and a strong arm, Marion was known as "the Octopus," and led National League shortstops in fielding percentage four times. Reese was the captain and spark plug for the great Dodger teams of the late

1940s and early 1950s, while Boudreau was Cleveland's Mr. Everything—the team's top hitter, its manager, and a marvel at short, leading the league in fielding percentage eight times.

In the 1950s a barrage of Latin American defensive wizards hit the majors, led by Chico Carrasquel of the White Sox. Carrasquel, a native of Venezuela, then surrendered the Comiskey Park infield to Luis Aparicio, who played it like a violin. Winner of nine Gold Gloves, Aparicio is the majors' all-time leading shortstop in assists and double plays, and doubled as the American League's most efficient base stealer of the era. While Aparicio personified the flashy, pint-sized shortstop of the 1950s and 1960s, the Cubs' Ernie Banks showed that shortstops could hit the long ball and still excel in the field. Banks still holds the all-time record for home runs by a shortstop with 277, but in 1959 he set an National League record for fielding percentage, committing just 12 errors for a .985 mark.

Light-hitting shortstops were everywhere in the pitching-dominated 1960s. In 1967 Pittsburgh's Gene Alley and California's Jim Fregosi were the only regular shortstops in the majors to hit above .260, but the position was handled ably by

Baltimore's Mark Belanger played steady to Brooks Robinson's spectacular on the left side of the Oriole infield in the 1960s and 1970s. Belanger's .977 career fielding percentage is an American League record.

In 1988, his first full season in the majors, Mets shortstop Kevin Elster went Oakland's Walt Weiss one better. Weiss committed only one error after July 8; Elster committed no errors from July 19 until May 9 the following season—a record 88 straight errorless games.

such defenders as Dal Maxvill of the Cardinals, Hal Lanier of the Giants, Don Kessinger of the Cubs, and Bud Harrelson of the Mets in the National League, and Ray Oyler of the Tigers, Ron Hansen of the White Sox, Eddie Brinkman of the Senators, and Aparicio of the Orioles in the American League.

The 1970s and 1980s have seen great all-around players at short, like Baltimore's Cal Ripken, Jr., a cleanup hitter who led American League shortstops in assists four of his first six years in the majors; Detroit's Alan Trammell, a four-time Gold Glove winner who in 1987 hit 28 homers and drove in 105 runs; and Toronto's Tony Fernandez, a spectacular fielder with the best arm of any shortstop in baseball and a .322 average in 1987.

But few argue anymore over who is the best defensive shortstop of all time. St. Louis' Ozzie Smith has taken all the fun out of that debate. Smith has combined the agility of a gymnast, the reflexes of a hockey goalie, and the work ethic of a monk to redefine excellence at the position. Smith has the numbers, like the all-time record for assists in a season by a shortstop, but it's his flair for making plays that leave his teammates shaking their heads

that has earned him the nickname "the Wizard of Oz." And the one that first caught the baseball world's attention may have been the best. Smith was a rookie with San Diego on April 20, 1978, when Atlanta's Jeff Burroughs hit a grounder up the middle. Smith dived for it, but at the last second the ball took a bad hop behind him. Somehow he reached back, barehanded the ball, and threw Burroughs out at first.

And in 1987 Smith posted the most impressive number ever by a fielding specialist—a $2.34-million-a-year contract. A shortstop, who else?

When an outfielder patrols his territory,
baseball is no longer a team game. A
roughly defined parcel of land becomes
his exclusive responsibility. From 300
feet away he must instantly sense the
speed, distance and direction of a batted
ball, then go get it.

All-Time Fielding Leaders

All records are accurate through the 1988 baseball season.

PITCHERS

Fielding Percentage		Putouts		Putouts Per Game		Assists	
1. Don Mossi	.990	1. Phil Niekro	390	1. Dave Foutz	.79	1. Cy Young	2,027
2. Gary Nolan	.990	2. Ferguson Jenkins	363	2. Dan Petry	.79	2. Christy Mathewson	1,503
3. Lon Warneke	.988	3. Gaylord Perry	349	3. Nick Altrock	.78	3. Grover Alexander	1,413
4. Jim Wilson	.988	4. Don Sutton	329	4. Chick Fraser	.73	4. Pud Galvin	1,390
5. Woodie Fryman	.988	5. Tom Seaver	328	5. Jack Morris	.72	5. Walter Johnson	1,351
6. Rick Rhoden	.988	6. Tony Mullane	327	6. Carl Morton	.72	6. George Mullin	1,261
7. Larry Gura	.986	7. Pud Galvin	324	7. Ted Breitenstein	.70	7. Burleigh Grimes	1,252
8. Grover Alexander	.985	8. Rick Reuschel	319	8. Mel Stottlemyre	.68	8. Jack Quinn	1,243
9. General Crowder	.984	9. Robin Roberts	316	9. Larry Corcoran	.67	9. Ed Walsh	1,207
10. Bill Monbouquette	.984	10. Chick Fraser	315	10. Guy Hecker	.67	10. Eppa Rixey	1,195

Assists Per Game		Chances		Chances Per Game		Double Plays	
1. Addie Joss	2.96	1. Cy Young	2,388	1. Nick Altrock	3.72	1. Phil Niekro	80
2. Harry Howell	2.84	2. Pud Galvin	1,875	2. Harry Howell	3.61	– Warren Spahn	80
3. Ed Walsh	2.81	3. Christy Mathewson	1,836	3. Addie Joss	3.60	3. Freddie Fitzsimmons	79
4. Nick Altrock	2.81	4. Walter Johnson	1,679	4. Ed Walsh	3.48	4. Bob Lemon	78
5. Willie Sudhoff	2.76	5. Grover Alexander	1,633	5. Nixey Callahan	3.45	5. Bucky Walters	76
6. George Mullin	2.62	6. George Mullin	1,555	6. Willie Sudhoff	3.35	6. Burleigh Grimes	74
7. Nixey Callahan	2.58	7. Burleigh Grimes	1,548	7. George Mullin	3.23	7. Walter Johnson	72
8. Ed Willett	2.55	8. Tim Keefe	1,531	8. Barney Pelty	3.20	8. Tommy John	69
9. Barney Pelty	2.51	9. John Clarkson	1,526	9. Chick Fraser	3.12	9. Jim Kaat	65
10. Jack Taylor	2.49	10. Ed Walsh	1,499	10. Jack Taylor	3.03	10. Dizzy Trout	63

CATCHERS

Fielding Percentage		Putouts		Putouts Per Game		Assists	
1. Bill Freehan	.993	1. Gary Carter	10,360	1. Johnny Edwards	6.42	1. Deacon McGuire	1,859
2. Elston Howard	.993	2. Bob Boone	10,265	2. Johnny Roseboro	6.30	2. Ray Schalk	1,811
3. Jim Sundberg	.992	3. Bill Freehan	9,941	3. Bill Freehan	6.29	3. Steve O'Neill	1,698
4. Sherm Lollar	.992	4. Carlton Fisk	9,428	4. Jerry Grote	6.00	4. Red Dooin	1,590
5. Johnny Edwards	.992	5. Jim Sundberg	9,414	5. Tim McCarver	5.92	5. Chief Zimmer	1,580
6. Tom Haller	.992	6. Johnny Roseboro	9,291	6. Tom Haller	5.85	6. Johnny Kling	1,552
7. Gary Carter	.991	7. Johnny Bench	9,260	7. Tony Pena	5.85	7. Ivy Wingo	1,487
8. Jerry Grote	.991	8. Johnny Edwards	8,925	8. Gary Carter	5.84	8. Wilbert Robinson	1,454
9. Ernie Whitt	.991	9. Ted Simmons	8,906	9. Earl Battey	5.69	9. Bill Bergen	1,444
10. Rick Cerone	.991	10. Yogi Berra	8,729	10. Elston Howard	5.67	10. Duke Farrell	1,417

Assists Per Game		Chances		Chances Per Game		Double Plays	
1. Duke Farrell	1.42	1. Bob Boone	10,943	1. Johnny Edwards	6.92	1. Ray Schalk	226
2. Red Dooin	1.34	2. Bill Freehan	10,734	2. Johnny Roseboro	6.83	2. Steve O'Neill	175
3. Johnny Kling	1.33	3. Gary Carter	10,645	3. Bill Freehan	6.79	– Yogi Berra	175
4. Bill Killefer	1.32	4. Jim Sundberg	10,227	4. Tony Pena	6.54	4. Gabby Hartnett	163
5. Oscar Stanage	1.29	5. Johnny Bench	10,207	5. Jerry Grote	6.53	5. Jimmie Wilson	153
6. Chief Zimmer	1.28	6. Johnny Roseboro	10,073	6. Gary Carter	6.48	6. Wally Schang	149
7. Jack Warner	1.27	7. Carlton Fisk	10,056	7. Tim McCarver	6.41	7. Bob Boone	148
8. Ivy Wingo	1.21	8. Ted Simmons	9,936	8. Tom Haller	6.33	8. Deacon McGuire	142
9. Billy Sullivan	1.18	9. Johnny Edwards	9,710	9. Bill Killefer	6.27	– Jim Sundberg	142
10. George Gibson	1.17	10. Yogi Berra	9,619	10. Earl Battey	6.21	10. Rollie Hemsley	141
						– Ivy Wingo	141

FIRST BASEMEN

Fielding Percentage		Putouts		Putouts Per Game		Assists	
1. Steve Garvey	.996	1. Jake Beckley	23,709	1. Tom Jones	10.53	1. Keith Hernandez	1,631
2. Wes Parker	.996	2. Ed Konetchy	21,361	2. Candy LaChance	10.48	2. George Sisler	1,528
3. Dan Driessen	.995	3. Cap Anson	20,761	3. George Stovall	10.45	3. Mickey Vernon	1,448
4. Jim Spencer	.995	4. Charlie Grimm	20,711	4. George Kelly	10.37	4. Fred Tenney	1,363
5. Frank McCormick	.995	5. Stuffy McInnis	20,119	5. Wally Pipp	10.33	5. Chris Chambliss	1,351
6. Keith Hernandez	.994	6. Mickey Vernon	19,808	6. Ed Konetchy	10.31	6. Bill Buckner	1,332
7. Vic Power	.994	7. Jake Daubert	19,634	7. Bill Phillips	10.22	7. Norm Cash	1,317
8. Carl Yastrzemski	.994	8. Lou Gehrig	19,510	8. Walter Holke	10.20	8. Jake Beckley	1,315
9. Joe Adcock	.994	9. Joe Kuhel	19,386	9. Charlie Comiskey	10.15	9. Joe Judge	1,300
10. Mike Jorgensen	.994	10. Joe Judge	19,277	10. Long John Reilly	10.12	10. Ed Konetchy	1,292

Assists Per Game		Chances		Chances Per Game		Double Plays	
1. Bill Buckner	.88	1. Jake Beckley	25,505	1. Tom Jones	11.38	1. Mickey Vernon	2,044
2. Keith Hernandez	.86	2. Ed Konetchy	22,877	2. George Stovall	11.30	2. Joe Kuhel	1,769
3. Ferris Fain	.84	3. Cap Anson	22,299	3. George Kelly	11.09	3. Charlie Grimm	1,733
4. Vic Power	.83	4. Charlie Grimm	22,087	4. Candy LaChance	11.05	4. Chris Chambliss	1,687
5. Eddie Murray	.78	5. Stuffy McInnis	21,517	5. Wally Pipp	11.05	5. Gil Hodges	1,614
6. George Sisler	.78	6. Mickey Vernon	21,467	6. Ed Konetchy	11.04	6. Keith Hernandez	1,604
7. Rudy York	.77	7. Jake Daubert	20,943	7. George Burns	10.92	7. Lou Gehrig	1,574
8. Fred Tenney	.76	8. Lou Gehrig	20,790	8. Bill Terry	10.91	8. Jim Bottomley	1,560
9. Mike Hargrove	.75	9. Joe Kuhel	20,722	9. Cap Anson	10.84	9. Jimmie Foxx	1,528
10. Dick Stuart	.75	10. Joe Judge	20,719	10. Walter Holke	10.83	10. Joe Judge	1,500

SECOND BASEMEN

Fielding Percentage		Putouts		Putouts Per Game		Assists	
1. Tommy Herr	.988	1. Bid McPhee	6,545	1. Bid McPhee	3.09	1. Eddie Collins	7,630
2. Jim Gantner	.985	2. Eddie Collins	6,526	2. Fred Pfeffer	3.07	2. Charlie Gehringer	7,068
3. Frank White	.984	3. Nellie Fox	6,090	3. Cub Stricker	2.99	3. Joe Morgan	6,967
4. Bobby Grich	.984	4. Joe Morgan	5,742	4. Gerry Priddy	2.74	4. Bid McPhee	6,905
5. Jerry Lumpe	.984	5. Nap Lajoie	5,407	5. Bucky Harris	2.73	5. Bill Mazeroski	6,685
6. Cookie Rojas	.984	6. Charlie Gehringer	5,369	6. Nap Lajoie	2.71	6. Nellie Fox	6,373
7. Dave Cash	.984	7. Bill Mazeroski	4,974	7. Bobby Doerr	2.67	7. Nap Lajoie	6,259
8. Nellie Fox	.984	8. Bobby Doerr	4,928	8. Lou Bierbauer	2.66	8. Frankie Frisch	6,026
9. Tommy Helms	.983	9. Billy Herman	4,780	9. Cupid Childs	2.66	9. Bobby Doerr	5,710
10. Glenn Hubbard	.983	10. Fred Pfeffer	4,711	10. Nellie Fox	2.66	10. Billy Herman	5,681

Assists Per Game		Chances		Chances Per Game		Double Plays	
1. Hughie Critz	3.54	1. Eddie Collins	14,591	1. Fred Pfeffer	6.95	1. Bill Mazeroski	1,706
2. Frankie Frisch	3.42	2. Bid McPhee	14,241	2. Bid McPhee	6.71	2. Nellie Fox	1,619
3. Oscar Melillo	3.38	3. Joe Morgan	12,953	3. Cub Stricker	6.53	3. Bobby Doerr	1,507
4. Glenn Hubbard	3.36	4. Charlie Gehringer	12,746	4. Lou Bierbauer	6.42	4. Joe Morgan	1,505
5. Lou Bierbauer	3.34	5. Nellie Fox	12,672	5. Cupid Childs	6.32	5. Charlie Gehringer	1,444
6. Fred Pfeffer	3.33	6. Nap Lajoie	12,117	6. Oscar Melillo	6.16	6. Red Schoendienst	1,363
7. Rogers Hornsby	3.31	7. Bill Mazeroski	11,863	7. Hughie Critz	6.07	7. Bobby Grich	1,302
8. Bid McPhee	3.25	8. Bobby Doerr	10,852	8. Frankie Frisch	6.05	8. Frank White	1,267
9. Tony Cuccinello	3.23	9. Billy Herman	10,815	9. Bucky Harris	6.00	9. Willie Randolph	1,241
10. Cupid Childs	3.22	10. Fred Pfeffer	10,672	10. Nap Lajoie	6.00	10. Eddie Collins	1,215

THIRD BASEMEN

Fielding Percentage		Putouts		Putouts Per Game		Assists	
1. Brooks Robinson	.971	1. Brooks Robinson	2,697	1. Jerry Denny	1.60	1. Brooks Robinson	6,205
2. Ken Reitz	.970	2. Jimmy Collins	2,372	2. Denny Lyons	1.56	2. Graig Nettles	5,279
3. George Kell	.969	3. Eddie Yost	2,356	3. Billy Nash	1.53	3. Mike Schmidt	4,975
4. Don Money	.968	4. Lave Cross	2,304	4. Jimmy Austin	1.43	4. Buddy Bell	4,913
5. Don Wert	.968	5. Pie Traynor	2,289	5. Billy Shindle	1.43	5. Ron Santo	4,581
6. Willie Kamm	.967	6. Billy Nash	2,236	6. Jimmy Collins	1.41	6. Eddie Mathews	4,322
7. Heinie Groh	.967	7. Frank Baker	2,154	7. Frank Baker	1.40	7. Aurelio Rodriguez	4,150
8. Carney Lansford	.966	8. Willie Kamm	2,151	8. Hick Carpenter	1.37	8. Ron Cey	4,018
9. Clete Boyer	.965	9. Eddie Mathews	2,049	9. Lave Cross	1.34	9. Sal Bando	3,720
10. Gary Gaetti	.965	10. Willie Jones	2,045	10. Hans Lobert	1.30	10. Lave Cross	3,703

Assists Per Game		Chances		Chances Per Game		Double Plays	
1. Mike Schmidt	2.30	1. Brooks Robinson	9,165	1. Jerry Denny	4.20	1. Brooks Robinson	618
2. Buddy Bell	2.27	2. Graig Nettles	7,492	2. Bill Shindle	4.15	2. Graig Nettles	470
3. Bill Shindle	2.27	3. Buddy Bell	6,964	3. Billy Nash	4.08	3. Mike Schmidt	442
4. Arlie Latham	2.26	4. Ron Santo	6,853	4. Arlie Latham	4.04	4. Buddy Bell	430
5. Clete Boyer	2.24	5. Mike Schmidt	6,852	5. Denny Lyons	4.00	5. Aurelio Rodriguez	408
6. Jimmy Collins	2.20	6. Eddie Mathews	6,665	6. Jimmy Collins	3.89	6. Ron Santo	395
7. Graig Nettles	2.19	7. Jimmy Collins	6,539	7. Hick Carpenter	3.81	7. Eddie Mathews	369
8. George Brett	2.18	8. Lave Cross	6,401	8. Jimmy Austin	3.74	8. Ken Boyer	355
9. Darrell Evans	2.18	9. Arlie Latham	6,342	9. Lave Cross	3.73	9. Sal Bando	345
10. Brooks Robinson	2.17	10. Eddie Yost	6,285	10. Frank Baker	3.64	− Eddie Yost	345

All-Time Fielding Leaders

All records are accurate through the 1988 baseball season.

SHORTSTOPS

Fielding Percentage		Putouts		Putouts Per Game		Assists	
1. Larry Bowa	.980	1. Rabbit Maranville	5,139	1. Dave Bancroft	2.47	1. Luis Aparicio	8,016
2. Ozzie Smith	.978	2. Bill Dahlen	4,850	2. Honus Wagner	2.43	2. Bill Dahlen	7,500
3. Mark Belanger	.977	3. Dave Bancroft	4,623	3. Rabbit Maranville	2.39	3. Rabbit Maranville	7,354
4. Bucky Dent	.976	4. Honus Wagner	4,576	4. Monte Cross	2.37	4. Luke Appling	7,218
5. Alan Trammell	.976	5. Tommy Corcoran	4,550	5. George Davis	2.36	5. Tommy Corcoran	7,106
6. Roger Metzger	.976	6. Luis Aparicio	4,548	6. Herman Long	2.36	6. Larry Bowa	6,857
7. Tim Foli	.973	7. Luke Appling	4,398	7. Dick Bartell	2.31	7. Dave Concepcion	6,594
8. Dal Maxvill	.973	8. Herman Long	4,219	8. Bill Dahlen	2.28	8. Dave Bancroft	6,561
9. Lou Boudreau	.973	9. Bobby Wallace	4,142	9. Ivy Olson	2.27	9. Roger Peckinpaugh	6,334
10. Cal Ripken	.972	10. Pee Wee Reese	4,040	10. Bobby Wallace	2.27	10. Bobby Wallace	6,303

Assists Per Game		Chances		Chances Per Game		Double Plays	
1. Germany Smith	3.70	1. Bill Dahlen	13,325	1. Dave Bancroft	6.33	1. Luis Aparicio	1,553
2. Art Fletcher	3.56	2. Rabbit Maranville	13,124	2. Herman Long	6.32	2. Luke Appling	1,424
3. Bill Dahlen	3.52	3. Luis Aparicio	12,930	3. Bill Dahlen	6.26	3. Roy McMillan	1,304
4. Ozzie Smith	3.52	4. Tommy Corcoran	12,612	4. George Davis	6.22	4. Dave Concepcion	1,290
5. Dave Bancroft	3.51	5. Luke Appling	12,259	5. Bobby Wallace	6.10	5. Larry Bowa	1,265
6. Bones Ely	3.50	6. Dave Bancroft	11,844	6. Rabbit Maranville	6.10	6. Pee Wee Reese	1,246
7. Travis Jackson	3.50	7. Herman Long	11,419	7. Tommy Corcoran	6.09	7. Dick Groat	1,237
8. George Davis	3.49	8. Honus Wagner	11,292	8. Monte Cross	6.06	8. Phil Rizzuto	1,217
9. Jack Glasscock	3.46	9. Bobby Wallace	11,130	9. Bones Ely	6.06	9. Bert Campaneris	1,186
10. Bobby Wallace	3.46	10. Donie Bush	10,846	10. Honus Wagner	5.99	10. Rabbit Maranville	1,183

OUTFIELDERS

Fielding Percentage		Putouts		Putouts Per Game		Assists	
1. Terry Puhl	.993	1. Willie Mays	7,095	1. Taylor Douthit	3.01	1. Tris Speaker	448
2. Brett Butler	.992	2. Tris Speaker	6,787	2. Richie Ashburn	2.90	2. Ty Cobb	392
3. Pete Rose	.991	3. Max Carey	6,363	3. Dwayne Murphy	2.88	3. Jimmy Ryan	375
4. Amos Otis	.991	4. Ty Cobb	6,361	4. Dom DiMaggio	2.82	4. George Van Haltren	351
5. Joe Rudi	.991	5. Richie Ashburn	6,089	5. Mike Kreevich	2.81	5. Tom Brown	348
6. Mickey Stanley	.991	6. Hank Aaron	5,539	6. Sammy West	2.74	6. Harry Hooper	344
7. Jimmy Piersall	.990	7. Willie Davis	5,449	7. Sam Chapman	2.74	7. Max Carey	339
8. Jim Landis	.989	8. Doc Cramer	5,412	8. Fred Schulte	2.70	8. Jimmy Sheckard	307
9. Ken Berry	.989	9. Vada Pinson	5,097	9. Rickey Henderson	2.68	9. Clyde Milan	294
10. Tommy Holmes	.989	10. Al Kaline	5,035	10. Chet Lemon	2.68	10. King Kelly	290

Assists Per Game		Chances		Chances Per Game		Double Plays	
1. Tommy McCarthy	.23	1. Tris Speaker	7,461	1. Taylor Douthit	3.16	1. Tris Speaker	139
2. Chicken Wolf	.22	2. Willie Mays	7,431	2. Richie Ashburn	3.04	2. Ty Cobb	107
3. Pop Corkhill	.22	3. Ty Cobb	7,024	3. Dom DiMaggio	2.99	3. Max Carey	86
4. Sam Thompson	.21	4. Max Carey	6,937	4. Dwayne Murphy	2.98	4. Tom Brown	85
5. Tom Brown	.20	5. Richie Ashburn	6,377	5. Mike Kreevich	2.95	5. Harry Hooper	81
6. Curt Welch	.20	6. Hank Aaron	5,857	6. Sam Chapman	2.91	6. Jimmy Sheckard	80
7. Jimmy Ryan	.20	7. Willie Davis	5,719	7. Sammy West	2.88	7. Mike Griffin	75
8. George Van Haltren	.20	8. Doc Cramer	5,702	8. Max Carey	2.87	8. Dummy Hoy	72
9. George Gore	.19	9. Zack Wheat	5,411	9. Fred Schulte	2.84	8. Jimmy Ryan	72
10. Ed Delahanty	.19	10. Vada Pinson	5,370	10. Lloyd Waner	2.81	10. Fielder Jones	70

Position players must have played at least 1,000 games to qualify; pitchers must have pitched at least 1,500 innings. Sources: *Total Baseball,* edited by John Thorn and Pete Palmer, Warner Books; *The Baseball Encyclopedia,* seventh edition, edited by Joseph L. Reichler, MacMillan Publishing Company.

INDEX

Boldface indicates picture.

PICTURE CREDITS

Front Cover: Ozzie Smith by Anthony Neste

Back Cover: Pee Wee Reese, AP/ Wide World Photos

Front and Back Matter
4–5 John W. McDonough; 186 (sequence) Al Tielemans/Duomo.

Mr. Impossible
6 Tadder/Baltimore; 7 Ron Menchine Collection/Renée Comet Photography; 8 (left three) Herb Scharfman, *Sports Illustrated;* 8 (right) Neil Leifer; 10 Herb Scharfman/*Sports Illustrated;* 11 (top) Neil Leifer/*Sports Illustrated;* 11 (bottom) Ron Menchine Collection/ Renée Comet Photography; 12 (left) Ron Menchine Collection/Renée Comet Photography; 12 (right) AP/Wide World Photos; 13 (top left) Ronald C. Modra; 13 (top right) AP/Wide World Photos; 13 (bottom) AP/Wide World Photos; 14 (left) John Iacono/*Sports Illustrated;* 14 (right) Ronald C. Modra; 15 (top left) Ron Menchine Collection/Renée Comet Photography; 15 (bottom left) AP/Wide World Photos; 15 (right) AP/Wide World Photos.

In Defense of Fielding
16 David Walberg; 17 Ron Menchine Collection/Renée Comet Photography; 18 John W. McDonough; 19 (left) AP/Wide World Photos; 19 (right) AP/Wide World Photos; 20 (left) National Baseball Library, Cooperstown, New York; 20 (right) Al Tielemans/Duomo; 21 John W. McDonough; 22 Ron Menchine Collection/Renée Comet Photography; 23 UPI/Bettmann Newsphotos; 24 (left) National Baseball Library, Cooperstown, New York; 24 (right) AP/Wide World Photos; 25 National Baseball Library, Cooperstown, New York; 26 John W. McDonough; 27 John W. McDonough; 28 (left) AP/Wide World Photos; 28 (right) Ron Menchine Collection/Renée Comet Photography; 29 (left) National Baseball Library, Cooperstown, New York; 29 (right) Ron Vesely; 30 (left) National Baseball Library, Cooperstown, New York; 30 (right) Brown Brothers; 31 (left) AP/Wide World Photos; 31 (right) Bruce L. Schwartzman.

Bare Hands to Sure Hands
32 AP/Wide World Photos; 33 Ron Menchine Collection/Renée Comet Photography; 34 (left) AP/Wide World Photos; 34 (right) Mark Rucker; 35 National Baseball Library, Cooperstown, New York; 36 (left) Thomas Carwile Collection/Renée Comet Photography; 36 (right) Thomas Carwile Collection/Renée Comet Photography; 38 (left) National Baseball Library, Cooperstown, New York; 38 (right) Barry Halper Collection/Henry Groskinsky Photography; 39 (left) Mark Rucker; 39 (right) National Baseball Library, Cooperstown, New York; 40 Ron Menchine Collection; 41 (left) Lewis Portnoy/Spectra-Action, Inc.; 41 (right) Lewis Portnoy/Spectra-Action, Inc.; 42 (left) National Baseball Library, Cooperstown, New York; 42 (right) Dennis Goldstein Collection; 43 (left) Library of Congress; 43 (center) Library of Congress; 43 (right) Library of Congress; 44 (left) National Baseball Library, Cooperstown, New York; 44 (right) Hillerich & Bradsby Company Records, University of Louisville Archives, Louisville, Kentucky; 45 AP/Wide World Photos; 46 Ronald C. Modra; 47 AP/Wide World Photos; 48 (left) Ron Menchine Collection/Renée Comet Photography; 48 (right) AP/ Wide World Photos; 49 (left) John W. McDonough; 49 (top right) Malcom W. Emmons; 49 (bottom right) Culver Pictures; 50 AP/Wide World Photos; 51 (left) Mickey Pfleger; 51 (right) National Baseball Library, Cooperstown, New York.

Leather
52 Chuck Solomon/*Sports Illustrated;* 53 John W. McDonough; 54 (top) The Gifted Line, John Grossman, Inc., From the John Grossman Collection of Antique Images; 54 (bottom) AP/Wide World Photos; 55 The Bettmann Archive; 56 (left) National Baseball Library, Cooperstown, New York; 56 (right) National Baseball Library, Cooperstown, New York; 57 John W. McDonough; 58–59 (all) Bret Wills; 60 Bret Wills; 61 (all) Bret Wills; 62 (left) National Baseball Library, Cooperstown, New York; 62 (right) David Walberg; 63 (left) David Walberg; 63 (right) National Baseball Library, Cooperstown, New York; 64 John W. McDonough; 65 (left) John W. McDonough; 65 (right) National Baseball Library, Cooperstown, New York; 66 (left) Fred Kaplan; 66 (right) Jeffrey E. Blackman; 67 Bryan Yablonsky; 68 National Baseball Library, Cooperstown, New York; 69 (top) Cranston & Elkins/Photofest; 69 (bottom) AP/Wide World Photos; 70 Bruce L. Schwartzman; 71 (left) Jeffrey E. Blackman; 71 (right) Marvin E. Newman; 72 (left) National Baseball Library, Cooperstown, New York; 72 (right) National Baseball Library, Cooperstown, New York; 73 AP/Wide World Photos; 74 (left) Ron Menchine Collection/Renée Comet Photography; 74 (right) AP/Wide World Photography; 75 (left) Library of Congress; 75 (top right) AP/Wide World Photos; 75 (bottom right) Marvin E. Newman; 76 Jim McTaggart, Kansas City Star; 77 (left) National Baseball Library, Cooperstown, New York; 77 (right) Mitchell B. Reibel/Sportschrome East/West.

Skills Beyond Measure
78–79 John W. McDonough; 80 Nancy Hogue; 81 (left) Mitchell B. Reibel/ Sportschrome East/West; 81 (right) Manny Rubio; 82 (left) National Baseball Library, Cooperstown, New York; 82 (right) National Baseball Library, Cooperstown, New York; 83 Bruce L. Schwartzman; 84 National Baseball Library, Cooperstown, New York; 85 (left) Ron Menchine Collection/Renée Comet Photography; 85 (right) National Baseball Library, Cooperstown, New York; 87 (left) Mel Bailey; 87 (right) John W. McDonough; 88 (left) National Baseball Library, Cooperstown, New York; 88 (right) AP/Wide World Photos; 89 (left) AP/Wide World Photos; 89 (right) Al Tielemans/Duomo; 90 The Harry Naiman Collection; 91 (top) AP/Wide World Photos; 91 (bottom) AP/Wide World Photos; 92 (left) Lewis Portnoy/Spectra-Action, Inc.; 92 (right) *The Baltimore Sun;* 93 (left) John W. McDonough; 93 (right) Bruce L. Schwartzman; 94 AP/Wide World Photos; 95 Bruce L. Schwartzman; 96 (left) AP/Wide World Photos; 96 (right) Ron Menchine Collection/Renée Comet Photography; 97 (top) Walter Iooss, Jr./*Sports Illustrated;* 97 (bottom) Ron Menchine Collection/ Renée Comet Photography; 98 AP/ Wide World Photos; 99 (left) Fred Kaplan; 99 (right) Mickey Pfleger.

Off the Walls
100–101 Ronald C. Modra/*Sports Illustrated;* 102–103 National Baseball Library, Cooperstown, New York; 103 (right) Library of Congress; 104 National Baseball Library, Cooperstown, New York; 105 (top

left) Culver Pictures; 105 (bottom left) AP/Wide World Photos; 105 (right) National Baseball Library, Cooperstown, New York; 106 (left) National Baseball Library, Cooperstown, New York; 106 (right) National Baseball Library, Cooperstown, New York; 107 AP/Wide World Photos; 108 Marvin E. Newman; 109 (left) Ron Menchine Collection/Renée Comet Photography; 109 (right) National Baseball Library, Cooperstown, New York; 110 AP/Wide World Photos; 111 AP/Wide World Photos; 112 AP/Wide World Photos; 113 John W. McDonough; 114 (left) Bruce L. Schwartzman; 114 (right) John W. McDonough; 115 Jim McTaggart, Kansas City Star; 116 (left) Ron Menchine Collection/Renée Comet Photography; 116 (right) Lee Balterman; 117 (left) Mitchell B. Reibel/Sportschrome East/West; 117 (right) National Baseball Library, Cooperstown, New York; 118 AP/Wide World Photos; 119 (left) Mickey Pfleger; 119 (center) AP/Wide World Photos; 119 (right) AP/Wide World Photos.

How Hard Is Fielding?
120–121 David Walberg; 122 (left) Thomas Carwile Collection/Renée Comet Photography; 122 (right) Anthony Neste; 123 John W. McDonough; 124 (left) General Mills Inc.; 124 (right) Mickey Pfleger; 125 AP/Wide World Photos; 126 (left) National Baseball Library, Cooperstown, New York; 126 (right) John W. McDonough; 127 (left) John W. McDonough; 127 (right) Fred Kaplan; 128 Ron Menchine Collection/Renée Comet Photography; 129 (top) National Baseball Library, Cooperstown, New York; 129 (bottom) AP/Wide World Photos; 130 Jim McTaggart, Kansas City Star; 131 (top) Walter Iooss, Jr./*Sports Illustrated;* 131 (bottom) Anthony Neste; 132 (left) National Baseball Library, Cooperstown, New York; 132 (right) AP/Wide World Photos; 133 (left) Bruce L. Schwartzman; 133 (right) Bruce L. Schwartzman; 135 AP/Wide World Photos; 136 Jim McTaggart, Kansas City Star; 137 Nancy Hogue; 138 Heinz Kluetmeier/*Sports Illustrated;* 139 National Baseball Library, Cooperstown, New York; 140 (left) Ron Menchine Collection/Renée Comet Photography; 140 (right) National Baseball Library, Cooperstown, New York; 141 (top left) AP/Wide World Photos; 141 (top right) Fred Kaplan; 141 (bottom) UPI/Bettmann Newsphotos; 142

AP/Wide World Photos; 143 (left) Mickey Pfleger; 143 (right) Bryan Yablonsky.

Between the Lines
144 Jerry Wachter/*Sports Illustrated;* 145 Anthony Neste; 146 Chicago Historical Society; 147 Library of Congress; 148 (left) National Baseball Library, Cooperstown, New York; 148 (right) UPI/Bettmann Newsphotos; 149 Marvin E. Newman; 150 Ron Menchine Collection/Renée Comet Photography; 151 (top) AP/Wide World Photos; 151 (bottom) AP/Wide World Photos; 152 (left) National Baseball Library, Cooperstown, New York; 152–153 Tadder/Baltimore; 154 Jeffrey E. Blackman; 155 (left) Bryan Yablonsky; 155 (right) National Baseball Library, Cooperstown, New York; 156 Jerry Wachter; 157 Gary Quesada/B. Korab Ltd.; 158 (left) Library of Congress; 158 (right) Ron Menchine Collection/Renée Comet Photography; 159 (top left) Ron Vesely; 159 (top right) AP/Wide World Photos; 159 (bottom) John W. McDonough; 160 John Iacono/*Sports Illustrated;* 161 (left) National Baseball Library, Cooperstown, New York; 161 (right) Bruce L. Schwartzman.

Playing the Field
162 Ron Vesely; 163 Rawlings Sporting Goods, St. Louis, Missouri; 164 National Baseball Library, Cooperstown, New York; 165 (left) Mickey Pfleger; 165 (right) Ron Vesely; 166–167 (all) The Harry Naiman Collection; 168 (left) National Baseball Library, Cooperstown, New York; 168 (right) Ronald C. Modra; 169 AP/Wide World Photos; 170 (right) Bruce L. Schwartzman; 171 John C. McDonough; 172 Elmhurst Historical Museum, Elmhurst, Illinois; 173 National Baseball Library, Cooperstown, New York; 175 Ronald C. Modra/*Sports Illustrated;* 176 (left) Mickey Pfleger; 176 (right) C. Rydlewski/Sportschrome East/West; 177 (left) Mickey Pfleger; 177 (right) Bryan Yablonsky; 178 (left) Ron Menchine Collection/Renée Comet Photography; 178 (right) National Baseball Library, Cooperstown, New York; 179 (left) Klein & Elkins/Photofest; 179 (top right) National Baseball Library, Cooperstown, New York; 179 (bottom right) Mitchell B. Reibel/Sportschrome East/West; 180 AP/Wide World Photos; 181 (left) Anthony Neste; 181 (right) Bruce L. Schwartzman; 182–183 John W. McDonough.

ACKNOWLEDGMENTS

The author and editors wish to thank:

Peter P. Clark, Tom Heitz, Bill Deane, Patricia Kelly, Dan Bennett and the staffs of the National Baseball Hall of Fame and the National Baseball Library, Cooperstown, New York; Dennis Goldstein, Atlanta, Georgia; Nat Andriani, Wide World Photos, New York, New York; Reñee Comet Photography, Washington, D.C.; Thomas Carwile, Petersburg, Virginia; Joe Borras, Accokeek, Maryland; Kenneth E. Hancock, Annandale, Virginia; Dorothy A. Gergel, Springfield, Virginia; Dave Kelly, Library of Congress, Washington, D.C.; Robert F. Bluthardt, San Angelo, Texas; Mark Rucker, Saratoga Springs, New York; Julie Greenspoon, St. Louis, Missouri; Gail Prensky, Alexandria, Virginia.

FOR FURTHER READING

William Curran, *Mitts: A Celebration of the Art of Fielding,* William Morrow & Co., 1985.

Charles F. Faber, *Baseball Ratings: The All-Time Best Players At Each Position,* McFarland & Co., 1985.

Bill James, *The Historical Baseball Abstract,* Villard Books, 1988.

Jim Kaplan, *Playing the Field: Why Defense is the Most Fascinating Art in Major League Baseball,* Algonquin Books of Chapel Hill, 1987.

John A. Mercurio, *Chronology of Major League Baseball Records,* Harper & Row, 1989.

Daniel Okrent and Steve Wulf, *Baseball Anecdotes,* Oxford University Press, 1989.

John Thorn & Pete Palmer, *Total Baseball,* Warner Books, 1989

Rich Wescott, *Diamond Greats: Profiles and Interviews With 65 of Baseball's History Makers,* Meckler Books, 1988.

World of Baseball is produced and
published by Redefinition, Inc.

WORLD OF BASEBALL

Editor	Glen B. Ruh
Design Director	Robert Barkin
Production Director	Irv Garfield
Senior Writer	Jonathan Kronstadt
Text Editor	Sharon Cygan
Picture Research	Rebecca Hirsh
	Louis P. Plummer
	Catherine M. Chase
Design	Sue Pratt
	Collette Conconi
	Monique Strawderman
Copy Preparation	Anthony K. Pordes
	Ginette Gauldfeldt
Production Assistant	Kimberly Fornshill
Editorial Research	Janet Pooley
	Mark Lazen
Illustrations	Dale Glasgow
Index	Lynne Hobbs

REDEFINITION

Administration	Margaret M. Higgins
	June M. Nolan
Fulfillment Manager	Karen L. DeLisser
Marketing Director	Harry Sailer
Finance Director	Vaughn A. Meglan
PRESIDENT	Edward Brash

Library of Congress Cataloging-in-Publication Data
The fielders/Jim Kaplan.
    (World of Baseball)
    includes index.
    1. Fielding (Baseball)
    2. Baseball—United States—History.
I. Title. II. Series.
GV870.K37 1989 89–35943
796.357'24—dc20
ISBN 0–924588–04–7

Printed in the U.S.A.
10 9 8 7 6 5 4 3 2 1

CONTRIBUTORS

Jim Kaplan has written extensively for *Sports
Illustrated* and serves as editor of *Baseball
Research Journal* for the Society for American
Baseball Research. He has written other baseball
books, among them *Pine Tarred and Feathered: A
Year on the Baseball Beat* and *Playing the
Field*. As a tenth grader, he was a substitute
on the ninth-grade baseball team, then took up
golf and tennis.

Henry Staat is Series Consultant for World of
Baseball. A member of the Society for American
Baseball Research since 1982, he helped initiate
the concept for the series. He is an editor with
Wadsworth, Inc., a publisher of college textbooks.

Ron Menchine, an advisor and sports collector,
shared baseball materials he has been collecting for
40 years. A sportscaster and sports director for
numerous radio stations, he announced the last
three seasons played by the Washington Senators.

The editors also wish to thank the following
writers for their contributions to this book:
Robert Kiener, Washington, D.C.; Michael
Lecesse, Washington, D.C.; Leonard Hochberg,
Falls Church, VA; David Hoff, Washington, D.C.;
Eliot Cohen, Washington, D.C.; Andrew Keegan,
Alexandria, Virginia; Charlie Carr, Washington,
D.C.; Robert Mitchell, Alexandria, Virginia;
James Byrne, Takoma Park, Maryland.

This book is one of a series that celebrates
America's national pastime.

Redefinition also offers a World of Baseball Top
Ten Stat Finder.

For subscription information and prices please
write:
 Customer Service, Redefinition, Inc.,
 P.O. Box 25336,
 Alexandria, Virginia 22313

The text of this book is set in Century Old Style;
display type is Helvetica and Gill Sans. The paper
is 70 pound Warrenflo Gloss supplied by Stanford
Paper Company. Typesetting by Intergraphics,
Inc., Alexandria, Virginia. Color separation by
Colotone, Inc., North Branford, Connecticut.
Printed and bound by Ringier America, New
Berlin, Wisconsin.